NEWMAN'S WAY

THE ODYSSEY OF JOHN HENRY NEWMAN

by

SEAN O'FAOLAIN

ILLUSTRATED

NEW YORK

THE DEVIN-ADAIR COMPANY

1952

Manufactured in the United States of America

CONTENTS

CONTENTS

PUBLISHER'S NOTE

Newman's Way presents two fresh aspects of John Henry Newman: first, the almost perverse reactions on his part toward the numerous family with whom he grew up, and their equally perverse reaction to him; and, secondly, his lone, stark intellectual and spiritual struggle that culminated in conversion to the Roman Catholic Church.

Both aspects of this book reflect major new research. To those readers who might possibly be more concerned with one than with the other, it might be pointed out that the bulk of the first five chapters and of Chapter 8 is devoted to the growing Newman family, while the balance of the book considers more fully the specific pilgrimage of John Henry.

I think nothing more interesting, and it is strange to think how evanescent, how apparently barren and resultless, are the ten thousand little details and complications of daily life and family history. Is there any record of them preserved anywhere, any more than of the fall of the leaves in autumn? Or are they themselves some reflection, as in an earthly mirror, of some greater truths above? So I think of musical sounds and their combinations—they are momentary—but is it not some momentary opening and closing of the Veil which hangs between the worlds of spirit and sense.

J. H. N. to Miss Holmes,
November 4th, 1860.

What a veil and curtain this world of sense is! Beautiful, but still a veil.

J. H. N. to Jemima Newman,
May 10th, 1828.

ACKNOWLEDGMENTS

LIKE, I am sure, many others who have set out to write about
Newman in a spirit of high interest and eager admiration I
have discovered that the forest is deeper and the paths more
puzzling than I had anticipated when I began.   My original
conception was a sort of Conversation Piece, or family portrait.   It had not been done before; it would, I hoped, help
to humanize the whole Newman legend.   Before long I
found that J. H. N. was dominating the picture so much that
the title that began to form in my mind was "A Genius in
the Family," to which, on occasion, I irreverently added, as
a sub-title, "Or, a Blessed Nuisance."   Soon the book became a technical struggle to prevent him from so outshadow-
ing the rest of the family that further mention of their
fortunes would be felt as an intrusion, and I now greatly
doubt if I have succeeded in solving this problem smoothly.
It was almost a relief when his family dropped away from
him one by one, or he, in the proper egotism of a genius who
may have been a saint, gently pushed them from him, and
the end of the story, and the title, justifiably became his
alone.   So, the book and the title were not so much planned
as grew.   Still, if I were doing it all over again I do not think
I could, or would, plan it to go otherwise or end otherwise.

   After all, Newman had very little intimate life apart from
his family, very little at all, indeed, of what the world calls
"life."   For though his later path crossed and recrossed momentous events and the careers of many important people,
no lives were so closely woven with his as the small events
of the private lives of his father, mother and aunt, his
brothers and sisters.   Any writer would gladly devote the
labor of five, ten, or twenty years to Newman's forty-five in
the Catholic Church, to their hopes and heartbreaks, their

intrigues and betrayals, their immense problems, their panoply, their variegated personalities; yet these well-documented public years secrete what the earlier private years reveal, and only some dear intimate of the Oratory, such as Ambrose St. John—who, as Newman at one time hoped, might have written his Memoir—could have entered into his heart during that second life of broken peace and humble happiness, of trial, failure and triumph. None can hope to now.

I am indebted and grateful to several people. Like almost everybody who has written about Newman, I am indebted most of all to the kindness of the Fathers of the Birmingham Oratory for permission to make free use of their archives, and especially to Father Henry Tristram, probably the greatest living authority on Newman. Mr. John Mozley, of Haslemere, made my task easier by generously lending me his collection of letters. The Bodleian Library allowed me to work there on the James Mozley Collection. Those parcels from the London Library, which allow us to do so much of our work in the comfort of our own studies, were not so much a luxury as an indispensable facility. The preliminary research-work would have taken me far longer without the help of Miss Yseulte Parnell, and there must be many things I could never have found out without her experienced skill as a genealogist. Major Gerald Fox, of Tenby, searched the archives and memories of Tenby in the most thorough fashion for information about the last years of Charles Newman. I am very grateful to him. The Bank of England has kindly allowed me to quote from their records of Charles Newman's career as a bank-clerk. Mr. W. Hugh Curtis, of the Museum in Alton, helped me to trace the family's fortunes there, and the Secretary of Messrs. Courage & Co., Ltd., was also helpful. I am likewise obliged to Mr. Edward Cordrey of Oxford for help in identifying the Newman homes around Oxford. I am grateful to Professor Daniel Birchy for the stimulus of many interesting discussions and for kindly reading the

proofs.   Finally, as with a previous biography, I would like
to express a particular gratitude to my publishers for their
patience and their trust.

I must say one other thing.   Though there are plenty of
things in the story of the Newman family to invite irrever-
ence, I hope I have, at least, never been facetious.   As for
J. H. N., though he sometimes provokes an exasperated sigh
or an ironic chuckle, who can do other than revere that brave,
kind, solitary, gifted, tormented angel?

S. O'F.

Killiney, Dublin

SOURCES

FOR the early part of this narrative, as will be seen from the following notes, much use has been made of such sources as Parish Registers, Company records, contemporary Directories, Rate Books, Probates of Wills, the records of the Bankruptcy Courts and such like. Without these it would have been impossible to establish a number of interesting biographical facts which have hitherto not been the concern of Newman's biographers.

The main sources for later periods are the family letters. These are: (a) The collection preserved at the Oratory in Birmingham; (b) the James Mozley collection preserved in the Bodleian Library and hereafter described as JHMC.; and (c) the collection privately held by Mr. John Mozley of Haslemere, Surrey, hereafter described as JMC. I have used all of these, as well as the published collection of letters edited by Anne Mozley in *Letters and Correspondence of J. H. Newman*, two volumes, London, 1891, but I have referred to them in these notes only when it seemed necessary to support what might be considered a debatable point. Anne Mozley's collection I have described as AM.

Then come in point of importance the documents preserved at Birmingham, called by Newman "Autographic Remains," including various scraps, a Private Journal, Memoranda, and a day-to-day Diary. The "Memoranda" cover 1804–26. They illustrate the incompleteness of this group of source-material. It was first written in 1820–21, up to August, 1816; then faithfully transcribed in 1823, with additions; again transcribed in the Lent of 1840, with omissions; marked, in 1872, "now to be partially and finally transcribed with great omissions and put aside for good"; but again handled on May 15th, 1874, when he not only revised them but cut out with scissors or knife pages 7 to 22.

At Birmingham also there are shelves of other letters to
and from Newman's enormous body of correspondents.   Of
other MS. material I have used only the unpublished Autobiography of Maria Rosina Giberne.

I have read most if not all of the books usually read by
Newman students.   I list here only those to which I have
found it necessary to refer in the footnotes: others are referred to in the course of the narrative:—

TM.: *Reminiscences of the Oxford Movement,* by J. H.
Mozley, London, 1882.

WW.: *Life of John Henry Cardinal Newman,* by Wilfrid
Ward, London, 1913.

F.: *Contributions, chiefly to the Early History of Cardinal
Newman,* by Francis Newman, London, 1891.

PS. *Parochial and Plain Sermons,* by John Henry Newman, London, 1868–9.

VV.: *Verses on Various Occasions,* by John Henry Newman, London, 1883.

MW.: *The Young Mr. Newman,* by Maisie Ward, London,
1948.

Footnotes are reduced to the minimum since few general
readers will consult them and scholars will know already
where most of the information comes from.   But I give my
authorities for the results of original research.

THE NEWMAN FAMILY*

John Newman, 29 Oct.   Jemima Fourdrinier,
1767–1824   1799   1772–1836
25 Oct. 29 Sept.   19 Nov. 17 May

John Henry,
1801–1890
21 Feb. 11 Aug.

Charles Robert,
1802–1884
16 June 22 March

Harriett Elizabeth,
1803–1852
10 Dec. 12 July
m. Tom Mozley,
1836

Grace Mozley,
1840–
m. Wm. Langford

Francis Robert,
1805–1897
27 June 4 Oct.
m. Maria Kennaway,

Jemima,
1808–1879
19 May 28 Apr.,
m. John Mozley,
1836

Mary Sophia,
1809–1828
9 Nov. 5 Jan.

Herbert,
1838–
2 May

John Rickards,
1840–
7 May

Henry Williams,
1842–
22 Apr.

Jane Gertrude,
1844–
14 June

Francis Woodgate,
1846–
5 Apr.

Alfred Dean,
1848–
9 June

* For earlier generations of the Family see Appendix.

CHAPTER 1

A RISING YOUNG BANKER

THERE were three John Newmans. They were Grandfather John, whom we will call John I; his son, John II;
and his grandson, who is known to us all as John Henry
Newman. John I came from Cambridgeshire; from a place
called Swaffham Bulbeck. He was a very poor man.[1] When
—to go still further back—his grandfather William had died,
in 1742, he had left little to his heirs: a house, a common and
eleven acres of land. He left to John I's father: "All these
my three acres of arable land holden by Copy of Court Roll
of the Manor of Brughall to him and to his heirs for ever."
He left to his other four children the sum, each, of half-a-
crown. He left a token also to John I, his little grandson:
"All that Bed whereon I lye, with the Beadstead, Curtins,
and appurtenances belonging to the same, to him and his
heirs for ever."

Did this big tester-bed come swaying on a wagon from
Cambridgeshire into Holborn? For it is in Holborn that we
next come on John I, in 1763. He had been left orphaned
of his father when in his teens,[2] and as he was one of six
children, and as three acres of arable land are poor suste-
nance for a widow with six children, it was natural that he
should be sent off to London to seek his fortune. When we
come upon him in 1763[3] he is twenty-nine. We find him in
Holborn, behind the counter of a little shop in Leadenhall
Street, selling groceries. He describes himself as a coffee-
man.[4] He is married. His wife, Elizabeth Good—who will

1

duly be known to our family as Grandmamma—does not appear to have had any dowry. Grandfather John had to live modestly to the end of his days.

They had four children. The first, whom our family will speak of as Aunt Eliza, or Aunt Betsy, came in 1765. She lived—the Newmans were a long-lived clan—to be eighty-seven, and was a great plague to her dearly loved nephew J. H. N., who loved her dearly and whose religious notions must at times have been something of a small plague to her. The second child was John II, born in 1767. The third and fourth children, Mary, born 1770, and Thomas, born 1774, died when they were little: their small remains—Mary aged two, and Tom not quite four—now lie, Mary's in Saint George's, Hanover Square, and Tom's in St. Leonard's, Shoreditch.

Grocer Newman moved restlessly around London. Four years after we had first found him in Leadenhall Street we find him moved to fashionable Mayfair.[5] Not that he is living fashionably. He is living modestly on fashion. His house is in Brick Street, Piccadilly,[6] then called Portugal Row or Brick Lane; and even this modest house—it only cost £6 a year, little enough at the time—he may well have shared with his brother Roff, or Rolph, ten years his junior, who had also come up from Cambridgeshire to find employment.[7] Indeed a third brother, William, turned up too, for he was John II's godfather; and so did his sister, Elizabeth, who was godmother to the Mary who died so young.

Within five years John Newman had left Mayfair and gone back to the city. When his little boy, Tom, was buried there in Shoreditch, the funeral left from an inelegant address in Daggett's Court. Daggett's Court was outside the city's boundaries altogether, and must be counted a come-down even from Brick Lane. Those crowded courts were not sought after by well-off citizens.

As John II was now about eleven years old, and his sister

Elizabeth (Aunt Betsy) was thirteen, it is at this point that we should come on the explanation for the fact that these two children, with so highly unpromising a background, emerge in due course as a man and a woman of some education and culture. For, lo and behold, John II next appears as a full-fledged, prosperous banker, with an interest in music, writing letters in French—admittedly execrable French —and with his own armorial bookplate of the supposed Newman arms; and Aunt Betsy becomes mistress of a finishing school for young ladies at Strand-on-the-Green. How on earth did it happen? Unfortunately we have lost the trail in the dusk and smells of Daggett's Court, for after that the next and almost the last thing we know about John I is his death, twenty-one years later, in 1799, and his burial in Camberwell.[8]

How had John I fared in those twenty-one years between Daggett's Court and Camberwell? Was Camberwell a great rise or was it yet another fall? We must remember that London's suburbs under the Georges had social values different to ours. When Chelsea was shabby-genteel, Hackney decayed and Brompton laid out in market-gardens Camberwell was a residential quarter for the upper classes. Some pleasant old houses still remain there to show what a superior region it once was. This sounds as if John I may have become a success during those twenty-one years. But then, he had already lived poorly in a fashionable district when he sold groceries to Mayfair. He may have lived in Camberwell on similar terms; and a number of smaller terraces for humbler tenants also persist there from his period. We do know that he died intestate. When his widow took out Letters of Administration in 1801, the entry is marked "£5," followed by the word "Poor."

We naturally turn to his famous descendants for information about him. When we do we touch on so common a foible that we can hardly call it a Newman foible. His

children and grandchildren suppressed their low-born grandfather grocer as effectively as George Meredith, like Evan
Harrington, suppressed the low-born tailor. John I's grandchildren must have known about him. J. H. N., his father's
confidant, a most persistent inquirer into family history, certainly must have known about him. After all, *we* know.
Yet, although the father of our family was thirty-two when
the poor grocer died (and no father, as we know, has ever
been able wholly to resist childhood reminiscences), no word
about Grandpapa Newman is repeated in the voluminous
Newman papers. A banker, as John II became, with that
highly questionable coat of arms, a town house and a country house, who has married, as he did, into an old family with
a pedigree going back to a Norman viscount, may well have
preferred not to dwell on so humble an origin. A cardinal
could not. "(My) father," J. H. N. records, reticently, "was
a London banker, whose family came from Cambridgeshire." [9] The cardinal's sister, through her husband, Tom
Mozley, recorded genteelly that grandpapa had come of
"small landed proprietors." [10] But if the whole truth must
be told those few acres had originally come down from a
Newman who actually was a tailor.[11] Out of his needle and
thread, this obscure ancestor had bought six acres of land,
though he must have lived by his original trade. However,
nobody told a lie. Those descendants of the tailor who divided those poor few acres between them could be described
as "small landed proprietors from Cambridgeshire."

2

Grocer John died in July, 1799. That October John II
married. His wife was Jemima Fourdrinier, of Fourdrinier,
Bloxam & Walter, "At the Sign of the Globe," [12] 72, Lombard
Street. He was thirty-two; she was twenty-seven.

She was the only girl of her family. Her four brothers

thereby became the Uncles of our family—Uncle Henry, Uncle John Rawson, Uncle Sealey and Uncle Charles; so that her children, our young Newmans, would inherit a large number of cousins by this fortunate alliance. I count fifteen of them; and I do not count second cousins. As they included all our family's six names but one—John, Charles, Harriett, Jemima and Mary; the missing name is Francis— we will do well to be content to identify them vaguely as they come and go, much no doubt as their elders sometimes did in a pleasantly confused sensation of swarming young.

By coincidence,[13] this only daughter, Jemima, had lost her father in the same year as she found a husband who had just lost his father; and as her papa had been a man of means she was something of an heiress. The Fourdriniers were wealthy paper manufacturers—Jemima writes on the finest, lightest, gilt-edged 1794 Whatman—solid London merchants of the Thackeray type. They had their shop and town residence at 72, Lombard Street; business premises and warehouses across the street in Sherbourne Lane; a country residence at Stratford Grove, with eleven personal servants, gardener, coachman, chaise and horses, family paintings, a library, a wine-cellar, fine plate and glass. Her father, Henry Fourdrinier,[14] had been the sort of well-off business man who in his will could afford to bestow rings by the score to be worn by his friends in his memory; his Shakespeare lovingly to his sons; Macklin's eight-volume Bible bound in Russia leather to the Magdalene Hospital, of which he was a governor. Accordingly John II got a wife[15] with a tidy dowry of £5000; and we may remember that Elizabeth Bennett, as Jane Austen carefully records, had only £2000.

An interesting detail [16] about the marriage: the witnesses were her brother Henry and her aunt Elizabeth: no Newman connections, we observe. Papa has firmly cut away his past. Nor do we ever again hear mention of Roff, or William or Elizabeth from Cambridgeshire, though we do hear on one occasion of a Dorothy living with John Newman's mother; she may have been a Cambridgeshire relation. One other small example of this exclusion comes from the year in which the son married so well. It occurs in Holden's *London Directory* for 1799. All the tradesmen have listed their professions next to their names, while the gentry print the word "Private." John Newman, the grocer, is listed as "Private." Jemima's family could read the entry without a qualm.

The biographers of J. H. N. have accepted Jemima as a model wife and woman, and all we know of her encourages this admiration and sympathy, but she had one drawback as a wife. She was of a social class superior to her husband, so that if they lived rather better than his position or his prospects justified—as the event will show so lamentably—this was probably due to his ambition to live as well as his wife had lived before her marriage. But she, also, may have had high notions. That armorial bookplate, impaling the Newman arms on the Fourdriniers', makes us raise our eyebrows; it is matched by her insistence on having her cutlery engraved with a crest at a date, 1827, when she must have been hard put to have any cutlery at all. And as we shall have to observe, when John Newman was up to his neck in debt the allowance sent to his son John Henry at Oxford, either by the father's wish or by her wish, or by the wish of both, was approaching three times the young man's needs. Whether we are to blame Jemima's stolid and solid upbringing, or John's mushroom ambitions, her ignorance of the world of money, due to the fact that she was accustomed to lots of it, or his due to the fact that he was not accustomed to it at all, we cannot avoid observing a strain of rashness in the management of the young banker's household.

And here, at closer quarters now, we must again wonder how on earth papa Newman ever managed to become a banker. It was not the £5000 that did it, for Mrs. Newman's dowry duly descended to her children. Her daughter

Harriett told her husband Tom Mozley, who published it, that her papa had at first been chief clerk in a firm called Ramsbottom, Newman, Ramsbottom & Co., of 72, Lombard Street, and later a partner in the firm; which sounds a plausible enough approach to an august profession. But J. H. N. was greatly annoyed by Mozley's statement and denied that his father was ever a clerk in this firm. He said that his father had before this been a partner in a firm called Harrison, Prickett & Newman, of No. 1, Mansion House Street;[17] and that when this firm dissolved another was formed on a like basis; namely, the Ramsbottom bank. Which knew better, sister or brother? As usual, John is the more accurate, though without giving us the whole story, and Harriett gives the larger hint.

These are the facts, and one assumption following from them.[18] The original Harrison Brothers Bank had been set up in 1785, in Ironmonger Lane. By 1788 it was in Mansion House Street. By 1792 new partners had joined the firm, including one Bloxham, a name which links up suggestively with "Fourdrinier, Bloxham & Walter." (Did John meet Jemima—for we may also wonder how he did meet her—through these Bloxhams?) In 1794 John, aged twenty-seven, became, as his son said, a partner in this Harrison firm. In view of his origins, and Harriett's statement, it is difficult not to assume that he has been working in the firm, if not in some totally different one, on a salary basis, as chief clerk, before this date. In 1796 Paul Prickett joins the firm, which is still at No. 1, Mansion House Street. By 1799, the year in which John Newman married Jemima Fourdrinier, the firm is reduced to Harrison, Prickett & Newman. These three continued in partnership together, always at the same address, until at least 1807. Finally, the Ramsbottom, Newman & Ramsbottom bank was established in 1812, at 72, Lombard Street—the old Fourdrinier address. Harriett was therefore wrong in saying her papa had been a clerk in this firm. She may well have been confusing it with an earlier one.

If we are still left wondering how John II ever became a partner in any banking-firm it is well to remember that to be a banker then, or even now, is not necessarily the grand thing it may sound. There was nothing to stop anybody then, nor is there now, from opening a bank. A thrift society, or a building society, or anything of the kind that invites investments is, in effect, a bank. Two partners, with a capital of a couple of hundred pounds, without even as much as a second-hand safe, may start a bank. All that is required is a penny pencil, a sixpenny notebook, and the ability to re-invest profitably what the less enterprising cannot invest for themselves. Indeed for centuries many London merchants had carried on banking as a side line. This may explain a sentence in an early letter of Jemima's. She says she has been interrupted by the entrance of some friends whose visit has left her John "in high spirits in the possession of notes to the sum of £600." Naturally he is in high spirits. To be in possession of money is the first step in every banker's career.

Moreover, in those years between the American War of Independence and Waterloo, a peak period of Britain's industrial development, there was plenty of loose money about, as there always is in time of war. Thus, one of Henry Fourdrinier's bequests was to be paid out of "the Emperor's Loan," which reminds us that at the end of the century Britain was all Europe's banker; as Napoleon's futile paper-blockade of England in 1806, which did not prevent the French from marching to Eylau "clad in great-coats made in Leeds and shod with shoes made in Northampton," reminds us to what extent Britain was also Europe's shop. Under the last two Georges banks rose like mushrooms and went down like nine-pins.

There is, in fact, far less mystery about how John Newman started than about how he flourished.   For though a private bank may need no more than a good notebook to begin, it needs good connections to keep going.   How did he keep going?   We may recall Thackeray's *The Newcomes*.   Their private bank in Threadneedle Street had a double connection: Sir Brian Newcome, Bart., M.P., had the aristocratic and political West End connection, while his brother Hobson had the Dissenting connection; a happy blending of Park Lane and Bryanston Square, Tory and Whig, Parliament and Vestry, a Mayfair Church and a Marylebone Chapel, sermons in surplices and discourses in stuff gowns, or in no gown at all.   What useful connections could John Newman produce?   Surely the answer is that it was not he but the Ramsbottoms who had the money and the connections?

These were Richard Ramsbottom, senior, who was M.P. for Windsor in 1807, and his nephew John Ramsbottom who was M.P. for Windsor in 1810.   They successively represented Windsor up to 1832.   They were brewers and distillers as well as bankers, with premises in Windsor and in London: men of real substance.   The uncle resided on a famous Windsor estate, originally called Turret House, and later called Woodside, an impressive country seat in Gothic style, dating back to Queen Elizabeth, pleasantly secluded on one hundred and eighteen acres of land.   The nephew John resided in the West End, in George Street, Hanover Square.   (It must often have tickled John Newman to remember that he had been christened around the corner at St. George's when his father had been a coffee-man in Portugal Row.)   Ramsbottom senior was, as his behavior will show at the time of the bank-crash, a sleeping partner.   The two Johns did the work.   It is a fair presumption that the M.P. did the less active part of it, and that John's major, if not sole, investment would have been his industry and his brains. This is supported by his subsequent career. There is an over-sanguine flashiness about it, an excess of optimism, and at the end a touch of Wilkins Micawber.

The young banker's housekeeping was modest enough at the start. He set up his mother and sister in comfort in Peckham, then a high-class residential district. He set up his own house a stone's throw from the Bank of England, around the corner from the "Sign of the Globe," at No. 80, Old Broad Street.[19] For he and his wife were city folk, and in those years the City of London contained a compact society. Many of their acquaintances[20] lived within a few minutes' walk of the Bank of England, in Lombard Street, on Ludgate Hill, in Currier's Hall, Gracechurch Street, Austin Friars, and so on. For "little Jem"—John's pet-name for his young wife—all these neighbors would be potential callers, as she importantly wrote to her sister-in-law Elizabeth or Betsy Newman, a few weeks after her marriage. She had been out at Stratford Grove, in Upper Clapton, the previous evening, dining *en famille* with her brother Henry. When she came in, yawning and cold from the drive home at two in the morning, there was Betsy's very first letter awaiting her on the hall-table. She answered it with a formal stateliness:—

"I beg you to accept my thanks for all your polite attentions and the trouble you have had on my account, but particularly for your gratifying manner of expressing yourself pleased at my having become a member of your family. I flatter myself you will readily believe it will be the greatest happiness of my future life to merit and retain the good opinions of those who have honoured me with their approbation.

"Your brother's cold is much better. He as well as myself is rejoiced to hear his good mother is well. I entreat you to ensure a welcome to the united duty of her son and daughter.

"We expect Mr. and Mrs. McKay this evening. Poor I am almost a prisoner, you will say voluntarily so. The expectation of a call from several friends who have hinted their intention to visit Broad Street detains me at home lest my absence should be deemed impolite."

A few days later she is inviting her "dear mother and sister," with nice apologies for the unfamiliar, familiar title, to come over and spend the night. Likewise she and John would need to sleep at Peckham when returning these visits. They certainly did in January, 1801, for a reason delicately revealed in a letter of Jemima's when John had to take the pen from her weary hand and conclude: "Little Jem has not been able to finish this."

Three weeks later the baby was born. They called him John after his father's father, and Henry after his mother's father. That was February 21st, 1801.[21]

3

Mother and infant spent the summer in the agreeable Thames-side resort of Fulham, where Grandmamma and Aunt had now gone to reside in a pleasant house near the bridge.

This Fulham house was to become John III's most formative experience, one of his clearest and most happy memories. "I am what I am; and I am grown into what I am from that time at Fulham." Yet, he was less than one year old when he first surveyed it, and less than five when his grandmamma and aunt finally left it, and what he did remember of it is apparently trivial. If anything is trivial that childhood stores up for adult memory? If we cast our own memories back over our own childish records do we not find that the merest specks of existence dominate their farthest limits—a bent spoon, a hole in a table, a smell that can never be smelled again without whirling us like a leaf into babyhood? Dominations at once so trivial and so precious that we sometimes feel that they are far from unselective and may reflect some instinctive choice of soul? A curling wave can contain the moon: a bent spoon can contain all heaven.

We know what this infant's spoon contained.[22] The kitchen where Aunt Eliza one day superintended the making of apple-puffs. The room opening on the garden. It contained two card-racks with a lion on them, and pictures of the prodigal Son, and of somebody giving alms to the poor, and of the Unjust Steward, and another picture of somebody or other paying a number of people. They used to breakfast there, looking out on the sunny garden. He came downstairs one morning, step by step, on his short legs, and saw a wonderful vision: "the breakfast things looking bright and still." There was something even more wonderful than all these—a loft, with apples glowing on the floor, and a wonderful thing called a Mangle! Forty years after he could see it all, feel it all, his aunt fondling him, or showing him the pretty pictures in the Bible, while he pointed and cried, "That's like our Mister Owen." One would love to know what the aunt and the old grandmother looked like. Was the old lady very much "the grocer's wife?" Since Betsy opened a sort of school for young ladies she must have had some attainments, but her letters are those of a very simple, inexperienced woman.

This Fulham of 1801 was a pretty place. "Being so conveniently seated both for the passage to London and the pleasure of its walks," says an old guide-book, "it is filled during the summer season with an abundance of citizens and considerable persons, where, as at its neighbour Putney, and several villages on the Thames, they are handsomely accommodated with good lodgings, to their own satisfaction and the great advantage of the inhabitants." In 1801 it was a small place, not much over a thousand families, with old houses along the river, other pleasant little villages at hand, such as Parson's Green or Broom Houses; views from the river of the Bishop's Palace, and the two churches, and the green roll of the Surrey hills.   The child could see men fishing, for roach and dace and shad, and for rarer prizes like lampreys and sturgeon, which the Lord Mayor would sometimes claim for the king's table.   There are open spaces at hand, like Wormholt Common, sometimes called Wormholt Scrubs, near the road to Harrow.   The Life Guards exercised there.   The child could remember the wharf by the bridge. He could remember the malthouses.   He could recall the old almshouses, the pottery, the elegant terrace called Elysium Row.   He could remember . . .   Instead he remembered a Mangle; and a Lion on a card-rack; and Breakfast Things; and a family Bible.

In the autumn father, mother and baby were at Brighton, whence papa writes to Fulham that "the dear little fellow has had some bad nights but on the whole is well—entertaining to a degree and the admiration of all the cognoscenti in the infantile line."   Mamma corroborates.   "Our sweet child is as much admired as even grandmamma could wish.   It is universally agreed that Brighton cannot produce his equal, and this from *strangers*.   If this is the case Papa and Mamma may be allowed to think him unique.   He is just as he was at Fulham, charming all day, but does not sleep long together. I am in great hopes of bringing more *teeth* to town with us. One seems all but cut through . . .   Our days are a continued scene of health, happiness and pleasure."   Sometimes, nowadays, as when we read Thackeray or Dickens and find them sentimental, we cannot believe that so much continued happiness and pleasure ever existed in the world.

4

Just eight months after Brighton another baby was born. He came at twenty minutes before ten o'clock, to the tick, on the 16th of June, in the year of peace 1802.   "A fine little fellow he is," Papa gaily informs mother and sister. "Very like *his Brother* as he was *at his age.* I have the great pleasure to say that his dear mother is uncommonly well. It was over in thirty-five minutes. Though she was at times in great pain from four to six, but did not consider it then as labour was not until nine o'clock." They must not come to town to see her for a few days. She must be kept very quiet.

They called this baby Charles, a Fourdrinier name. "Sweet Charles is beautiful," she cries, overflowing with joy in her second baby: in recording which a biographer dimly understands the sigh with which God must witness the creation of some child whose sad future He alone perceives. This small head that Jemima dotes on was, to put it gently, a scatter-brain; to put it bluntly, "sweet Charles" was more or less off his head. He was to be the family plague for fifty years.

Charles was born, not at Broad Street, but at Number 17, Southampton Street, now Southampton Place, the Newmans having by this date left the city and risen as high as Bloomsbury. They never pierced as far west as what Sidney Smith would presently call the parallelogram, the fashionable Georgian center bounded by Regent Street and Park Lane, Oxford Street and Piccadilly. But they climbed high enough. Perhaps too high? Number 17, as one can see still, was an imposing town-house; the district, near Bloomsbury Square, was fashionable; the house must have needed a staff of servants; and though we are not among the wits and politicians of Holland House, life in No. 17, Southampton Street, is not without its own modest elegance. In the winter Mrs. Newman's pianoforte arrived. John Newman, also, had a warm love for music.

The Mrs. McKay who had been one of Mrs. Newman's first callers at Broad Street wrote to her, many years after John II died, to say that she had heard one of his grandchildren, Grace Mozley, singing. "I could not help thinking as I looked at her how delighted her Grandpapa Newman would have been to have heard her sweet tunes, remembering so well as I do his enthusiastic delight in all that pertains to this science." His son Francis also testifies to his love of music; and we know that he encouraged his son John to master the violin. We may be permitted the pretty picture: the mother playing, the father and children by her side. As one looks up at what must have been the nursery windows and thinks of the children who were beginning to fill it, one feels it appropriate that the plaque which has since been placed there should be decorated with cupids.

We hear the names of a few new friends. Mr. Mullins, a blind clergyman, and Mr. Levy, a Stock Exchange broker who lived in Russell Square. Two very loyal friends were a Mr. Capel and a Mr. Ellis, the first a founder-member of the Stock Exchange, both connected with the Bank of England. They were to stand firmly by John Newman in his thin days, and they were all good friends to poor Charles.

A third child, the first girl, Harriett was born in 1803.

5

John Newman's fortunes went on climbing. In the next year[23] he decided that a banker should have a country house as well as a town-house. He chose a delightful house in a delightful place, Grey's Court, or Grey Court House, set deep in the country beyond Richmond, at Ham. To get there they must have driven in their chaise across Richmond Park, thence down to river level, and so by a long, soft, yellow lane called Sandy Lane almost to the brink of the Thames. Then they would come suddenly on the tall, square-set Georgian house, with its lawn, shrubbery and kitchen-gardens bordering the unfrequented lane on the right-hand side, its façade fronting a road which leads between old, red-brick walls down to the river. It was an old house,[24] already nicely mellow, when Jem and her two children stuck candles in all the windows on the night of Trafalgar. John never forgot how he stared at them, lying in his bed, watching their gleam melting circles of mist on the frosty glass.

It must have been a heavenly place for children. Its fine trees included a great plane whose massive branches sustained a swing; a dozen acacia-trees, tall as the tall plane; a Spanish chestnut; a delicate larch. A large Magnolia flowered up to the house in June. The children in their cots, in the front room at the top, would waken to hear the soft swish of the gardener's scythe as he artfully mowed the lawn. What other sounds? Footsteps downstairs crossing the central hall, with its single pillar like a tree-trunk. Old Lady Parker's macaw squawking from the garden next door. A far-off "Gee-up" from the bargees on the river. The rooks cawing. What to do? Across the fields the children could see the three formal terraces that still conduct foot and eye down to the majestic double row of elms along Lord Dysart's walk. There, on the second and third terraces, intersected by grass paths, they could see their vegetable and fruit gardens, whose cauliflowers were colossal and whose apricots were bigger than apples. How hard it was to leave off eating gooseberries if one managed to creep among the bushes of an idle morning. Haymaking. Fun on the river. Playing a game of being Ulysses and Argus. There are islands on the river for Ithaca or Same. What mild-eyed cow was called Io, and what tune did Hermes play? Gathering wild flowers in the fields about. "Marster John," a servant writes when the child is just four, "desires his deuty and wishes me to send you some wild violets." In the evenings the boys will play billiards—precocious children, six and seven—in the poorish billiard-room over the old greenhouse in the garden. Another happiness: Gum-Ma came to live here when she and Betsy left Fulham, and before they went on to the little farm at Norwood known in family language as "Fairfield." At night mother and aunt read "The Lay of the Last Minstrel" aloud. John Henry used to sit between them, drinking it in eagerly.

Ham is another astonishing domination of place. Years and years after,[25] when John Henry Newman was sailing past the island of Ithaca, he thought less of Homer than of Ham. The rock that looms before his ravished eyes is in the shape of Ithaca, but it could as easily be Eel Pie Island. He writes: "I thought of all the various glimpses which memory barely retains of that earliest time of life when one seems almost to realise the remnants of a pre-existent state." In Naples,[26] in a nightmare, he dreamed that he was escaping to the bower and shrubberies of Grey Court House. When he was a boy lonely at school and dreamed of heaven, why Heaven was Ham. And when he writes, "The night is dark and I am far from home . . ." this home is not only Heaven but Ham, or home, where he will see again

those angel faces smile
Which I have loved long since and lost awhile.

And yet, he saw it, after he was six, only once (in 1808), and once more, five years later (in 1813) for a few hours, and he was there only in the summer time: four summers in all. Papa and Mamma saw even less of it. They would shuttle to and from Southampton Street. Parties would be in town.

A fourth child was born in Southampton Street in the June before Trafalgar. They christened him Francis.

6

On that autumn morning of 1807 when the children were being driven away in the chaise to winter in town John must have looked back fondly, thinking, "I will be with you again next summer." So he was, briefly, in June, and sent a broom-flower by his papa to his mamma, then occupied with her fifth baby, to be called Jemmy, after her mother's mother. He came there that June (1808) from Ealing school, where they had sent him in May. It was an odd time of the year to begin, but he could not stay in Bloomsbury with the baby coming, and there must have been nobody in Ham to look after him at the time. Probably Grandmamma had by then joined her daughter Betsy at Vine Cottage, Norwood,[27] the third of John Newman's country homes.

Really, these Newman children had the happiest of childhoods. This at least their papa lavished on them. Vine Cottage was a little farm which you got to by driving down to Dulwich village, there asking the way to Norwood, there asking the way to Knight's Hill Green, and there asking for Vine Cottage, which would suddenly appear as a tiny house with a vine creeping all over it, "so small that it could almost be handled, and so large that it could hold as many friends who chose to come." Somebody who visited it and stayed in it though it was already full was driven to suggest that the walls were of India rubber. It stood alone on a heath, a *terra incognita* (as John called it), "the wild beautiful haunt of gypsies"; so remote, so lost in the unspoiled country that if one of the Shetland ponies escaped over a hedge he might not be found for a week; and no wonder, with the great whispering North Wood on its flank, three miles long, and all those vast thicketed commons scattered about it, Streatham and Croydon and Penge and Westwood, crossed by mere footpaths, and the whole region sparsely speckled by a farm here and a farm there, or *The Horns* inn, or the windmill creaking over Bree Hill. In the Newmans' day the gypsies were already being slowly edged back into the woods, though Byron, who went to school at Dr. Glennie's on Lordship Lane, could still visit them clandestinely. Since then London has marched all over the place, and nothing remains of the wilderness but some of the old names, like Julian's Farm Road, and Gypsy Road, and Lordship Lane. A few green remnants from the golf-course down to the Crystal Palace show where a wilderness once sheltered the last of the Romanies. For our six children from Southampton Row—the last child, Mary Sophia, was born in November, 1809—this secluded Norwood Cottage renewed its novelty every summer for about six years. They came there when the leaves budded out; they left it sadly when the leaves began to fall. They would stay on there as late as October, facing back unwillingly to dark and dull Southampton Street where Ann the maid would have acted as caretaker all through the summer. One year they were, for some reason, unable to spend the summer at Vine Cottage and it became a black-letter date in their lives, with nothing much to lighten its bleakness but an excursion to Fairlop Oak in Epping, the giant oak around which that eccentric man Thomas Day, of *Sandford and Merton,* used annually to haul the block that was to be his coffin, in a wheeled boat. ("He was odd, my dear boy," said papa. "And *worse* than odd!") Of that dark year Harriett wrote that the children sighed at being separated from "the freshness and freedom of their beloved Fairfield." [28]

Norwood was, evidently, the one place wherein the six children saw themselves as a group and free. It was their den, parliament, cabal, Liberty Hall. There they were reunited after the scholastic separations of the year to plot, to confide, to observe one another and all grown-ups. There they exchanged mamma and papa for Gum-Ma and Aunty. And how delightful that sort of exchange always is! Aunts and uncles are essential for childish content: governors but not despots, allies as well as kin, bonds but not chains, courts of appeal, bestowers of largesse, great illusionists who give us the satisfying sense of being free of the nest without any of the pains of actual freedom.   If we were fixing the Newman children in place, like the Brontës at Haworth, or the Barretts in Wimpole Street, we would speak most aptly of the Newmans of Norwood.

CHAPTER 2

AN EVANGELICAL HOUSEHOLD

1

SCHOOLDAYS and holidays now became, from 1808 on, the natural rhythm of the boys' lives. It does not appear that the three girls ever went to school, although their mamma had, in her time, been to a Mrs. Magnollay's boarding-school in Camberwell. She had been a lone girl and now enjoyed educating her own three girls at home.

The boarding-school to which Papa Newman sent off his three boys, so very young, surely much too young—John went when seven—was a private school in Great Ealing village called Great Ealing School.[1] The building was an old rectory, at least as old as Edward VI, but it was not an old school: its headmaster, the Revd. George Nicholas, of Wadham College, had only come into it through his marriage with a Miss Shury, whose father had come into it in the same way by marrying the daughter of the founder, a Revd. Mr. Pierce. It was, that is, a modern private school. Why Mr. Newman selected it for his children is to seek unless it was because it was not far from Ham. It was far enough from London; for Ealing was then a rural village, reached only by a lumbering coach whose sloth made the journey the equivalent of about forty or fifty miles today. Mr. Newman cannot have chosen it because Dr. Nicholas had a reputation as a good classicist, for when J. H. N. went up to Oxford he impressed his tutor chiefly by his mathematics, and Bishop

21

Copleston judged him "not a good classical scholar," and
he later envied his brother-in-law Tom Mozley his classical
training at a public school.   Still, there was the makings of a
tradition in Ealing School, and Nicholas must have been a
personality.   His school became well known to a later generation when the list of famous men who had passed through
it included the Newmans, Sir Henry Lawrence, Thomas
Huxley, whose father had taught mathematics there in the
Newmans' time, Captain Marryat, the Gilbert of the oper-
ettas and *"Bab Ballads,"* Thackeray, Hicks Pasha.   Not that
the Newman boys could have met any of these, one or two of
whom had passed out of the school before their time, like
Marryat, already fourteen-year-old midshipman in 1806, and
most of whom came much later, like Thackeray.   They may
have seen one famous man who taught there occasionally,
Louis Philippe, King of the French, who used to come over
from Twickenham to give lessons in geography and mathematics, or to take a hand at whist with Dr. Nicholas in the
drawing-room.   In their time the associations of the school
were all strictly contemporary.

It was as overcrowded as a tenement.[2]   It dined, in the
Newmans' time, some three hundred boys in the red-tiled
dining-hall that ultimately became a furniture repository.
Architecturally it was a complete jumble.   Nicholas had
built on to it bit by bit to house his growing population.   He
filled up an old moat; made dormitories out of an old brewery and a former wash-house; erected new buildings in the
yards; used five cottages down the road as "studies."   It
cannot have been very healthy.   One year Charlie got ringworm there.   John was sick there too and he had squalid
memories of its sick-room.   Years after he was reminded of
it when miserable in an inn in Sicily: "the most forlorn place
I ever was in," one window, no glass, brick floor in pieces,
filthy walls, three doors with gaping planks.   "I lay down
on my so-called bed and thought of the sick-room at Ealing,

and my mind felt very dry, and I thought 'What if I should lose my reason?'" The whole place had to be pulled down in the end because of pervasive dry-rot. The best part of the school was the outside of it, in fine weather, for Nicholas had managed to enclose some twelve acres for playground, cricket-field, fives court and tennis courts, with space for rounders on a sloping meadow, or for football, or a game called Long Rope—Frank Newman loved this game—or for Prisoner's Base. In a contemporary drawing we can see boys playing hoops, leap-frog and marbles in the gravelled yard that went up to the wooden stockade behind the jumbled school-buildings. They are dressed in knee-breeches, top-hats, pantaloons, hessians, tail-coats and cravats. We must imagine the three little Newmans costumed so.

A later pupil, George Macfarren—he became Sir George Macfarren and Principal of the Royal Academy of Music—spoke of his life there as "the very hardest ship that sails the ocean of existence"; and his biographer[3] speaks of the "roughness and discipline" of Ealing Great School. We know that the tiny John Newman wept there, teased by the other boys. ("O, Sir," he wept to his headmaster, "they will say such things! I can't help crying . . . O, Sir, but they will! They will say all sorts of things!")[4] But he was a solitary whose schoolfellows never, or scarcely ever, saw him taking part in any game. He preferred to read, and even write, during a good part of his daily playtime. He composed such verses as:

> While some at Fives attack the patient wall
> And others glory in the bat and ball,
> Be our employ in philosophic ease
> Calmly to eat the scanty bread and cheese
> Which black-eyed Johnson of the untidy cap
> Cuts off for twopence to each hungry chap . . .

The footnotes to such lines occur in his pocket-diary. "Sum ire domum in minore tempore quam hebdomada. Huzza!"

adding that he wishes it were tomorrow. He kept a little
stick with the schooldays notched. The notches disappeared all too slowly.

We have no portrait of the child.   If we may believe that
the softness and delicacy of childhood returns to an old face,
that the gentle years before passion buds are renewed in the
years of passion spent, we may deduce from the portraits of
the old cardinal the features of a boy with dreaming eyes,
big, tender lips, a noble forehead, sad, lifted, doggy eyebrows, an exquisite modelling of bone from brow into cheek,
though in childhood the chubbiness of his age would make
everything soft and unwritten. His two brothers were
handsome as youths and as men. One who knew Frank
said he was the most beautiful young man he had ever seen.
Another who saw Charles in his old age found in him a mix-
ture of Mephistopheles and Jupiter Olympus. As a child
John must have had a tender attractiveness. As a youth he
must have had something of the quality of Donatello's young
John the Baptist.

Over-imaginative, not over-strong, thrown among hundreds of older boys who were to become the burly heroes of
Empire, the extroverts of bench or church, so timid that at
one time he used to bless himself before going out into the
dark, his mind running on "unknown influences, on magical
powers and talismans," [5] he must have endured at least as
much as Macfarren did.   The child's happiest refuge was in
his own mind: reading, Scott especially, *Waverley* and *Guy
Mannering* in the early morning—that would be when he
was fourteen or fifteen; writing poetry *On the Death of a
Beggar,* or *Lines on Nelson;* or composing moral axioms; or
day-dreaming: "I wished the Arabian Nights were true."
His sense of physical reality became weak. This tendency
developed to an abnormal degree. He seems to have become what some psychologists would call alienated or dis-
sociated. At times the world hardly existed for him. "I

thought life might be a dream, or I an angel, and all this world a deception; my fellow-angels by a playful devise concealing themselves from me, deceiving me with the semblance of a material world." [6]

Happily he gradually became attached to his headmaster, and so acclimatized to the school that when his parents thought of changing him to Winchester he begged to be left where he was.[7] Frank was quite happy there. One wonders what thoughts went through the wandering weak head of their younger brother, Charlie.

2

The annals of all young families are largely medical, of intense interest to all concerned, of no interest to anybody else—one of the many things that novelists and biographers skip. "A fig for such trivial truth!" they say, and dismiss one half of a mother's life. Unless the summer of 1810 was an abnormal one for sickness our family was a very vulnerable one. Harriett was ill in July; so was Frank; John was sick both at home and at school; he came home again twice before the end of September; and the summer had begun badly with Charlie coming home from school with that dirty ringworm. When we think of the six children in a row, all steps and stairs, John aged nine, Charlie eight, Harriett seven, Frank five, Jem two and Mary in the cradle, we see that family cares have begun for John and Jemima Newman.

That summer they all, except the baby, went trundling off to the seaside.[8] John went first with his hearty father, bowling down to Hastings in the gig; a two-days run in nice June weather. Mother and her second three children came slowly after in a post-chaise. Jemmy came after them all in another post-chaise with a servant and the luggage. They paused for a couple of weeks at Hastings and went on to Worthing. This journey had its special perturbations for

Jemima, as young John Henry remembered thirty-five years after when he wrote to tell Jemmy how distressed his mamma had been that day so long ago. She missed her husband somehow at Brighton and had to go on without him, all of a flurry, to Worthing. It was meeting the Charles Fourdriniers in Brighton that confused her. But John Henry always remembered things as sensitively as he endured or enjoyed them. Sometimes his memory was a torture. "There is something mysterious to me that I cannot communicate in early scenes, nor pleasurable, I cannot tell why. When the Bowdens in 1836 took me to Ham my pain was most piercing. I had no pleasure. Yet, I am drawn to them. I cannot understand it."

They had a great adventure while they paused at Hastings. One day at Saint Leonard's the mother, Charlie and John got up a cliff and could barely get down again. In later years John was drawn back to this spot, too; and Harriett wrote a little tale about it, called *The Sheep Walk*. It is so suggestive of the characters of the two older brothers, and, like the litany of family illness, so much the stuff of actual childhood, that we must pause at it if we want to know how these people really lived. Harriett's account begins:[9]

"'Now, mamma,' said Charles, one day, 'it is a beautiful morning. You said the first fine day you were at leisure, you would take us to see how those high hills look when one is upon them.'

"John echoed his brother's wish; and on their mamma's assent, with many exclamations of joy, the little boys flew for their caps and were ready for their walk before their mamma could be ready for them.

"'I am sure,' cried Charles, after waiting, as he thought, very long and very patiently, some half-minute, 'I am sure I wish ladies wore hats and hung them on a peg like men. What a trouble it is to go upstairs and dress always!'

" 'And I am sure, Charles,' returned his brother, who was always full of thought and never at a loss for an answer, 'I am sure that neither you nor I should like to see mamma go about in a frightful hat like a man.'

" 'Why, they wear them on horseback,' said Charles. 'Why not walking?'

"John was a little bit perplexed for an instant, but, after scarcely a pause, replied, 'Well, if mamma had to dress every time she goes out as ladies do for riding, she would be ten times as long as she is now.'

" 'Well, I am glad I am not a lady,' said Charles, with the grand air young gentlemen assume when they make such speeches. 'So much dressing and tidiness, and thought about whether one's fit to be seen or not!'

"J. H. N. chides him sharply and turns the combat by inspecting his dusty jacket. 'And no gloves!'

" 'It is not respectable, Charles! Indeed it is not respectable!' "

Mamma arrives, observes the "no gloves" and packs Charles off to tidy himself. A quarter of an hour later Charlie is duly discovered with one leg on a trunk, lost in a book, just as he had stood fifteen minutes before while his nurse brushed his back.

" 'Ah, Charlie!' says John, 'I wish you had a little more stability. You are too much for the whim of the moment! Now, is he not mamma? I could hardly get him away from his book.'

" 'But,' mamma smiles, 'you also sometimes like a book?'

" 'In moderation,' John replies. 'Always in moderation!' "

Off they go, Charlie now lost in thought, with the broad expanse of sea and land extending every moment beneath them as they advance up the hill under the brilliant sun and clear sky, until at last they come to a beautiful, clear little path—"Just made for us," cries John—which they take up the cliff-face. They discuss philosophically as they go Char-

lie's solemn ruminations about the appurtenances of greatness, such as crowns, scepters and so forth: all, apparently,
apropos of having to wear gloves on a broiling July day.

As they climb, John now in front, the path gets narrower
and narrower, until, on turning to look whence they have
come, Mrs. Newman becomes quite frightened. "That path
by which they had ascended presented a most fearful aspect
from behind. The very narrowest thread, winding in and
out, on the very outer edge of vast precipices, over-hanging
an unknown depth below which the sea washed the foot of
the cliff!" They manage a few more steps upward to where
the path ends in impassable crags, and she at last realizes, in
terror, that they are caught upon a sheep-walk!

"John perceived his mamma's disturbance, but was not
aware of its cause; he supposed a sheep-walk was some terrible place, about which he knew nothing; but he kept silence,
as he was a little boy who had every great respect for the
feelings of elders, and especially of his parents, and he feared
distressing his mamma at that moment."

They turn back, Charlie is now leading, and ("a not unusual transition," remarks Harriett) he suddenly becomes
bold and spirited, skipping and pirouetting back and forth,
to the terror of his mother which she dares not show, knowing the child's volatile nature and how readily he could, on
the turn of the wrist, lose all control of himself. Indeed she
has much to do to quieten "the beaming excitement visible in
his eye" as the implications of being on a sheep-walk, never
before trodden by human feet, gradually spreads in his fragile mind. Step by step they make the perilous descent.
Charles becomes subdued. John is silent. At last, safe on
the sands again, Jemima faints upon her knees, returning
thanks to their Father in Heaven, while the two children
cling around their dear mamma's neck and share her feelings
of joy and thankfulness "in so far as was consistent with their
years and their characters."

What impresses us most about those simple annals is the shrewd characterization. Close-knit families like this, nicely graded, eight years between the eldest and youngest of six, sharpen themselves on one another by mutual observation. From these tales we also get an intimate family-picture of Southampton Street in this same Autumn of 1810.[10] It occurs in a "Family Adventure" called *The Netting-Box*. Here we gather that on coming home from Ealing in the summer John Henry had seen his mother making a veil, and decided to buy her a nice work-box, or netting-box, though indeed he did not rightly know then what a netting-box was. Taking a pencil and a scrap of paper he counted his money. He had frugally brought home a few shillings from school; a kind Fourdrinier uncle had made him a present on his return; his mother had kept a small hoard of old coins for him, including a five-shilling piece, which he thought he might reasonably spend since it was not an ancient coin; and he would get his allowance from his papa before returning to Ealing. All told he was quite surprised how much he could claim to possess, if only he could secretly lay hands on it. He took Aunt Betsy into his confidence, and she kindly offered to advance him enough money to buy the box, and to assist him in choosing it. So off they both went hand in hand one morning into Bloomsbury's streets, aunt and nephew, and after much searching, and with the help of a most patient shopkeeper, John lit at last on a box which he thought entirely delightful.

"Its form was rather oblong, and it was sloped off at the top. It was made of the root of the yew tree, and seemed spangled all over with polished shaded stars, covered, as they were, with fibres of the most delicate pencilling. It stood upon four balls—not four ugly feet, as John said of some of the others he saw, nor four common-looking gold balls—but four softly shining, smooth, enduring balls of ivory, the purest white. It was lined with bright red, with red velvet cushions, one of which was heavily weighted, and in one of the well-contrived compartments within, lay in tempting readiness, the brightest of keys." We are left to imagine his mother's pleasure on receiving this token of affection; as well as John's in offering it to her.

It was after this that they went to the sea, and after the seaside to their beloved Norwood; and then, late one autumn evening they returned to London to hear a strange tale of a visitor whom Ann the maid had been obliged to allow into the library that very morning to write a note to Mrs. Newman. This person—"Not a gentleman, ma'am, I think"— had sat down and scribbled and scribbled under Ann's watchful eye, for she had left the door open in order to observe him, and come in and gone out under various pretexts, such as to get the coal-scuttle, or to make up the fire, or to brush the hearth, or to straighten the curtains. But the strange man wrote on, and on—"Scratch, scratch!" moaned Ann. "Scribble, scribble!"—until at last the baker jangled the door-bell. Still she would not go; and still the man wrote on and on; and again the baker pulled fiercely on the wires until Ann had to leave the room lest her employers should find an empty bread-bin on their return.

Mrs. Newman, much puzzled at this story, slowly opened the stranger's letter. She gazed at it. Slowly she lifted it up for Ann to see. The girl went as pale as ashes. "The letter was written in no language under the sun, except it might be in that of the nation who walk upon their heads; for the lines were upside-down and topsy-turvy, and the letters inside-out, and the hind part before. . . ." Of course, the netting-box was gone, its weight having misled the thief into thinking it contained valuables, and they never recovered it, or the unfinished veil, or Mrs. Newman's pretty Salisbury scissors, nor did they hear any more about it, except from a pawnbroker who had refused to buy it from the thief. John Henry scraped up enough money to buy his mother another box for Christmas, but the second could never, to be sure, replace the first; it was the tiniest bit bigger; it had no shaded stars; it was of tulipwood; and it had only gold balls for feet. "Nevertheless," says Harriett, "it was still the kind gift of a kind son; and it came into the house more in the character of a hero than the other. It was always a pleasant sight, and will always continue to be, to those who know its history and who love those who had to do with it."

These simple, persuasive tales make one feel that the New-man children were a self-sufficient family. Their father says so expressly, and disapprovingly, on one of the few occasions when he, rather than their mother, takes the center of the stage in Harriett's tales. In discussing with his children a party of other children who have just left Fairfield, rather unpleasant children as it happened, he says:

" 'They possess one quality, and one essential quality, in a better and higher degree than you. They are more social as a family than you are.' "

To this Harriett protests that her brothers and sisters are very fond of being together.

" 'Yes, my dear, your own selves together,' replied her papa, 'and I do not wish you ever to cease to esteem your own family as your choicest society; but in order to secure its being worthy this esteem, you should be willing at the same time, to mix, in a simple, good-humoured manner, with any you may happen to fall in with.'

" 'It is a great bore,' remarked John Henry.

" 'Dreadful!' responded Charles."

3

One begins to wonder how much pleasure this busy, hearty, and at times harassed man got out of his children.

That day, certainly, one could imagine him turning away
with a sigh from his eldest son on hearing him reply scornfully to somebody's remark that Frank was sociable enough:
"He likes *everybody!"* One feels that sociable Frank was
much nearer to his father's ideal Englishman. Not that John
Newman bore any other resemblance to Frank, or indeed to
any of the family. John Newman was, in fact, the least
typical Newman of all the Newmans. He was an outsider
in his own home. When we look from his sons' fine-drawn,
classical intellectual features to his we can hardly keep from
a burst of laughter at the dark round bull's eyes goitering
out of the round Cambridgeshire peasant's face, with the soft
round lips of the born talker protruding good-humoredly between the cleft under the round nose and the cleft in the
round chin. Nothing could be less aristocratic, less troubled, less intellectual than this genial extrovert's face. It
may sum him up quickly for a lover of life and of his fellow-
men to say that he was a member of the Beefsteak Club,[11]
where one likes to visualize the solid father of so ethereal a
pair of sons enthusiastically devouring the good stuff that
had, in the opinion of the Beefsteakers, made Englishmen
the splendid fellows they were, and won them so many wars.
It was a highly sociable club whose aim was to combine
feasting and patriotism in the one jovial act; whose thoroughly English oath of loyalty ended solemnly with the
words, "So Beef and Liberty be my Reward"; and whose
duties were two and only two, that each man should wear
a ring engraved with the words, "Beef and Liberty," and
meet his fellow-members at regular intervals to preserve the
Liberty and devour the Beef. The dinners were held at the
Bedford Coffee House, or in the old Lyceum, and were both
generous and simple: vast beefsteaks sizzling on pewter
plates, garnished with baked potatoes, Spanish onions, beet-
root and eschalots, followed by a single course of toasted

cheese, washed down with porter in pewter tankards, whisky toddy or punch. The entrance fee was £26 5s. Each dinner cost another five shillings. John and Charlie Newman would have fled from such orgies in horror. But then, they were not bankers, though fate would for a time make Charlie a bank-clerk, and it was a good club for a banker to belong to. The Prince of Wales was a member. Various members of the peerage belonged to it. So did several lawyers, M.P.'s, professional men and other big-wigs. Mr. Newman belonged to another sociable club: he was a Freemason of high standing.

Clearly John II was not the type of man likely to be of much help to his sons. He was too bluff, too unimaginative; and he was not, in their sense of the word, a religious man. He was deeply shocked, for example, by Psalm 109 wherein David complains of his enemies and curses them roundly:

"Let his days be few, and let another take his office! Let his children be fatherless, and his wife a widow! Let his children be continually vagabonds, and beg! Let them seek their bread also out of their desolate places! Let there be none to extend mercy to him . . ." [12]

And so on, down to the highly illogical "As he loved cursing so let it come unto him!" A Freemason, full of fraternal love, would not relish so fierce a religion. Mr. Newman would probably be a Rotarian or a Buchmanite in our day. Though, to be fair to him, such savage anathemas must have sounded very odd in the refined accents of Oxford's Anglicanism: they need, surely, the vigorous brogue of an Irish parish priest? He was also pained by the famous sentence in Romans 12:

"Vengeance is mine: I will repay, saith the Lord."

But was he not rather unsubtle in this, since the following
verse annotates the Lord's "vengeance" with an almost
kindly irony?

"If thine enemy hunger, feed him; if he thirst, give him drink;
for in so doing thou shalt heap coals of fire on his head."

He used to say to his family, with a shrug, "Well, I am a
man of the world"; or, "I don't pretend to be a religious
man." We feel that he must have wilted sometimes under
the religious intensities of his children. When he would
cry, "Oh! give the devil his due!" in his easy, hearty way,
they probably raised pained eyebrows. Or, he would say,
with more than a touch of impatience, when religious history
was being discussed: "I wonder how it is that clever men
don't see that it is impossible to get back to any certainty,
when they are *so* confident!" The fact is he was much less
interested in religious notions than in good music, in good
beefsteaks, in his ideas of enriching England by planting its
waste-spaces with trees, in Benjamin Franklin, in Thomas
Jefferson. "We hold these truths to be self-evident, that
all men are created equal, that they are endowed by their
Creator with certain inalienable Rights, that among these
are Life, Liberty and the pursuit of Happiness." He was
the sort of Englishman who takes his morality from Shakespeare rather than from the Bible.

To us, weak, all-tolerating Liberals of the twentieth century, there may seem nothing surprising in all this. Mr.
Newman's aversion to the uncompromising Hebraism of the
Psalms, and of Saint Paul, is likely to strike us as the natural
aversion of a humane and civilized man. Yet, his boys were
deeply shocked by him. Frank once confessed that he went
around wondering in Evangelical whispers if his papa was a
Christian at all! It is an awestruck admission which opens
up for us one of the most fascinating sides of life under the

Hanoverians, an influence that filled a great part of the lives of our family and had a profound influence on its most famous member—Evangelicalism.

4

Today Evangelicalism is not much more than a word to most of us, and at that a rather dreary word, suggestive of tracts in the letter-box, a windy harmonium on the pier on Saturday afternoon, a small group in somber blue-and-red uniforms singing Toplady's "Rock of Ages." If we imagine that Evangelicalism meant no more than this to the 18th and 19th century we have forgotten a great deal. To put it at its lowest—and such men as Wilberforce, in their fight against slavery, should remind us that it often soared nobly —Evangelicalism was once fired by an excitement and an enthusiasm that nothing can match today, except possibly Communism. To put it lower still, though on consideration we may seem to be putting it higher, England has lost a very great pleasure by concentrating on problems more imminent than eternity, and by developing a deplorably cool attitude towards such questions as Predestination, Final Perseverance, Election, Imputation, Salvation or Grace.

And yet, up to as recently in some places as fifty years ago or even less, Englishmen cultivated this domestic art of religious dialectic with a passionate devotion, as, indeed, one would only expect of a race that had been cultivating it ever since Wyclif and Langland. The generation of Arnold Bennett (one thinks of *Anna of the Five Towns*) must often have witnessed the dialecticians of this religious Reformation practicing this now lost art at a white heat of fervor never experienced by the dialecticians of the social Reformation that was already replacing them. No brethren of the Socialist Sunday School, chanting the gospel according to William Morris, can have enjoyed such intensities of exalta-

tion as the Plymouth Brethren of whom we read in Gosse's
Father and Son roaring out "For ever with the Lord" or "Just
as I am without one plea!" or knitting their brows over the
fierce dialectic of the Epistle to the Hebrews; or glowing
over the application of Revelation to the Harlot of Rome; or
rejoicing at the blow struck for Christ if a papal customs
officer was hit on the head in Sassari, or if some dotty tried
to murder a Grand Duke in Tuscany.

Young John drank deep of the heady stuff when he was at
school. His delicate imagination remained colored by the
experience for thirty and more years of his life; perhaps to his
last day. Frank drank not so much deeply as widely: his
taste, if not his creed, was catholic. Charlie dabbled airily,
though frightening his family more when he said he was
orthodox than when he said he was an unbeliever, and in
any case he preferred in the main that other incoming Socialist creed which was finally to swallow up the Evangelicals. Aunt Betsy and Grandmamma can only be described
as addicts. Mamma and the girls were very serious, though
comparatively moderate in their views. Papa alone was im-
mune. The boys did not, however, get their extravagant
ideas at home, nor when we think of their tolerant and civilized father and mother, and of what Evangelicalism at its
best could mean, was it likely that they should.

5

What did Evangelicalism mean? What did the Evangelicals believe? To define a creed is impossible where there
is no homogeneous body of faith. The core of Evangelicalism was, and is, individualism in religion. Its main emphasis was on the message which the gospels—or evangels—
carry to each man; a message often interpreted in opposition
to the traditional teaching of the Church or disseminated to
the neglect of doctrine as traditionally established. In-

dividual interpretation led to individual experience. Conversion was personal and carried a personal and private assurance of reconciliation with God in this world, and of ultimate salvation in the next. So much individualism inevitably shattered every attempt at organization.

The substantive, organized, antique church had little interest for the Evangelicals. They disrupted it blithely, as their methods show. It was one of the sanest groups of Evangelicals, those called the Clapham sect—their leader, William Wilberforce the abolitionist—that went roving Britain buying up the rights of livings, or advowsons, so that one is reminded of *Dead Souls* when the Revd. Charles Simeon says: "Bath will sell for at least £5000, having five churches under it . . . Got to the length of my tether as you will readily imagine with twenty-one livings in my possession . . . Strongly urged to purchase Bridlington with six thousand souls." [13] The extreme form of this saintly investment was the private chapel set up by hopeful preachers, as nowadays a cruder speculator might set up a night-club, to rake in 10 per cent on pew fees and offerings where the Funds might only offer four. In 1824 there were as many as fifty-nine private evangelists' chapels in London alone. All Evangelicals are born schismatics. Frank Newman once said, "I am anti-Everything."

Behind it all, one feels there lay, and perhaps there still lies the old familiar, admirable, deplorable, vitalizing Puritan strain that never really abandons the English religious character, which is always oscillating dangerously towards Calvinism, always shying away pragmatically from its too-cold logic, yet is always drawn back again and again by its burning magnet. One sees this plainly, as Dowden brilliantly pointed out in his essay on "Bunyan and Herbert," in the persistent contrast in English letters between the lone Puritan and the sociable Anglican. On the one side there is the Bunyan-type, living an incandescent inward life, inside a small community whose common pulse he feels as if it were his own, for whom religion is not an organization or a tradition, but a unique personal experience, whose whole religious life is a drama in which God and the Devil pull for his soul. On the other side is the Anglican, Herbert, a member of a large, old, widespread community. He is buttressed round by all sorts of forms, ceremonies, rites, rituals, conventions and emblems. His life follows well-appointed paths. His religion is as placid as habit. To the lone sheep, hearing the wolves growl at night about him, his whole life a form of darkness lit only by the eyes of his Enemy and his Friend, these Anglican intermediaries are useless. For him nature and the supernatural are a total dualism. Life is an absolute conflict, unmediated. "God have mercy on me!" he cries, tearing at his bosom in his drab conventicle. Meanwhile his more sanguine fellow-Christian prays quietly and securely for God's assistance, while reflectively pulling his ear in his cathedral pew.

The core of the Evangelical creed is summed up clearly by a typical Evangelical, who was far from simple-minded, John Bird Sumner, Archbishop of Canterbury, and we are grateful for the rare, clear statement.[14] How, His Grace asks, is man to be restored from his fallen state? He replies that deliverance "*is not dependent on what man has done or is to do; but is already wrought, and is to be received, not gained; it is freely conferred, not wrought out by repentance and obedience.*" If this does not take us the whole journey to Luther's famous advice to Melancthon, "Sin and sin boldly, but the more firmly believe," it goes dangerously near to it. It leads us at least to the rim of the cow-eyed crowds singing under the churchyard yews:

> Nothing either great or small,
> Nothing, sinners, no;

Jesus did it, did it all
  Long, long ago.
Weary, weary, burdened one,
  Wherefore toil you so?
Cease your doing; all was done
  Long, long ago.

We have, evidently, come a long way from Beefsteak and Liberty. Have we come too far? Let us return to John Newman's sons.

6

The gropings of the young, their extravagant enthusiasms, their sophomoric glooms, their fitful happiness, their frightening gallantry, their unfounded fears, their adolescent certainties and their apparently incurable despairs are part and parcel of the joy and heartache of parenthood. In the summer of 1816, when he had much else to cope with, John Newman had to watch his eldest son cleave suddenly to the most narrow brand of Calvinistic Evangelicalism. In due course, Frank followed in his brother's footsteps. Charlie was to develop ideas even more exasperating to his despairing papa.

In later life John Henry would never have it that he had experienced the prescribed and passionate form of Evangelical "conversion." It is true that he never travelled the formal sequence of conviction of sin, terror, despair, the sudden glorious news of the free and full salvation which the apprehension of Christ offered to all men, with its lovely, soothing sense of pardon and its assurance of salvation, culminating in a great sign of joy and peace at the certainty that the converted will now persevere to the end. Yet his cool account of the matter is a bit too cool.[15] It is that his conversion was simply an assent of the same kind that we all give to all general propositions whenever we swallow sound and unsound ideas in one sweeping act of the mind, or hold with certitude that something is true in general which contains particular untruths: as when a man says "I am a Liberal," yet disagrees with, perhaps, a dozen tenets of the Liberal Party. So, after calmly examining the variety of doctrines that he henceforth accepted, as it were *en masse*, he agrees that what he did at the time of his "conversion" was to transfer his utter conviction as to certain of these doctrines to a general "state of mind relatively to Luther's tenet of justification by faith only."

The analysis is characteristic of the way in which, as a grown man, he will always blend a meticulous intellectual accuracy with a delicate perception of the subtleties of the mind—a blending which makes the reading of his dialectic, as of his personal memories, such a delightfully refining experience—while omitting totally to record the simultaneous war of the emotions. This gift of analysis has to be constantly and carefully guarded against for this very reason. All Newman's biographers have taken him too admiringly at his word in these post-mortems, failing to realize that in analyzing his own inward crises he always transformed emotion into intellect, and that once the experience passed into the refinery of his mind it was, in a sense, falsified. This is what happened, he says, in terms of belief, of opinion, of intermediate or final conclusions; and it is so. But is it *how* it happened? Is it *all* that happened?

Nobody knew better than he by what random and urgent leaps the mind flashes from one distant point to another towards its conclusion, like a man leaping dangerously from floe to floe over a half-frozen but moving river. One also feels that nobody knew less than he what the heart, the emotions and even the senses were doing in between point and point, or even what flashes of hot desire can urge the mind

beforehand to leap this way rather than that. Newman
understood the complex machinery of his mind as a master
understands his violin. He knew very little about that dark
palpitating throb which so often governed his mind. He
knew next to nothing about men and women. He often
paid very dearly for it. He was a Shelley of the intellect.
So, his final summary of what he calls the "reality" of his experience is pure intellectualism. "The reality of conversion:
as cutting at the root of doubt, providing a chain between
God and the soul (i.e., with every link complete). I know I
am right. How do I know it? I know I know. How? I
know I know I know, etc., etc." And we are referred to *The
Grammar of Assent*, pp. 195–7.

On his conversion, then, we may fully accept his analysis
as to the conclusion to which the adventure swept him,
while insisting that in that sweeping act of the mind what
interests us first of all is the impulse. That impulse was both
long anterior to and coterminous with the act of conversion.
"No! No!" Newman would have demurred. "Assent is a
decisive act of the will." Doubtless, ultimately. But in his
day men did not know much about the pre-conscious assent,
that first, secret, unconscious unacknowledged refusal or
surrender. It is pointless for him to talk of "a general state
of mind." Is he, or any man, in such powerful emotional
crises no more than a state of "mind"? His conversion is
better described, by himself, as the effect of having received,
in his own words, "deep religious impressions" which—at
once passing over from impression to definition—he describes as "Calvinistic in character."

We may prefer to see his conversion as the more or less
normal burst of light and inward rush of faith, however afterwards he may intellectualize it. Most of Newman's intel-
lectualizations are autopsies or post-cogitations. They are
quite untrustworthy as complete accounts of what happened.
Indeed, were it not so, and so often so, one might sometimes

think it a great wonder that the light of Faith ever managed to break through an intellect so finely webbed. On this occasion it broke through as a flash of lightning that struck the boy when he was fifteen. He could not, on looking back, perceive any premonitions. But in religion, as in love, we can have no certain premonitions of our fate; the *coup de foudre* that strikes us in an instant generates in a storm that may have to cross seven oceans for its delicate appointment with our hearts.

But what can we know of his heart? We know only a very little; but I feel that we may, without impertinence, think we know more than he did. He has told us more than he thought in a manuscript volume, as yet unpublished, called *Memoranda*, marked "Personal and Most Private." Let us look over it. It covers the years 1804 to 1826. He obviously thought it important, for he mauled it over a great deal, tore out many pages, scrawled over many sentences so as to make them indecipherable. He first wrote it in 1820–21; transcribed it in 1823, with additions; in 1840, with omissions; in 1872 he marked it "to be partially and finally transcribed with great omissions and put aside for good"; but in 1874 he went at it again and cut out fifteen precious pages at the beginning. Its purpose was to have given his dear friend of later life, Ambrose St. John, an "idea of his mind," in case Ambrose should write a memoir about him. The chief, perhaps the only sure thing—but it is much—that we gather from this introspective book-keeping is that the child was sealed very early by the thumb of God to the Unknown. He was no child, certainly, of this earthly earth. He is, to begin with, a very serious boy indeed who at fifteen confides to his journal:

"Paucis diebus mihi domum ibitur. Tunc Satanas me novis, quamvis notis illicobris (*illecebris?*) assiliet. Tu mihi vires suppedita, ut mundum, ut carnem, ut Diabolum supinem. Imprimis, serva me ne cedam mundi illicobris; ne catibus, (*cantibus?*) choreis, oblectationibus nimiis attractus, ea Deo meo preferam; ne tui obliviscam (*obliviscar?*). Serva me obsecro . . . Heu! Miser ego! Peccavi. Aeternam damnationem mereor propter portentosa facinora mea. Et quoque nimia luxuria (gluttony) me serva. Fac me temperatum, sobrium, castum."

("In a few days I must go home. Then Satan will leap upon me with new though familiar enticements. Give me strength that I may defeat the world, the flesh and the devil. Especially watch over me that I may not yield to the enticements of the world; lest drawn too much by its songs, dances and allurements I prefer these things to my God. Guard me, I beseech Thee . . . Alas! Wretch that I am! I have sinned! I deserve eternal damnation for my monstrous crimes! . . . Guard me, too, from too much gluttony. Make me temperate, sober and chaste.")

He also gave his explicit opinions about dancing. "Ea condemno!" In support he quoted Saint Paul's and Saint John's commands to avoid the desires of the flesh and the eye. "Procul a me sit illud!"

A persistent element in his character produced one strange, even frightening, entry: it shows him when he was eleven standing outside himself, or inside himself, looking at himself convolutedly, or as what we would say nowadays in a highly introverted manner. He wrote: "*John Newman wrote this just before he was going up to Greek on Tuesday, June 10, 1812, when it only wanted three days to his going home, thinking of the time (at home) when, looking at this, he shall recollect when he did it.*" It is an entry that one reads many times. "I am thinking this, thinking what I shall think when I read it again and think what I was thinking when I was thinking it."

He may have been already converted when he wrote an equally frightening school essay on Worldly Fame. He has marked it "Written by me in 1816-17"; that is when he was fifteen or sixteen. He piously preserved this strange essay all his life; he preached several times on the same theme; he published three sermons on it; and he referred to it in the *Apologia*. It is the thought of a boy for whom physical reality is no more than a dream. His unboyish view of the world's famous men, so early conceived, so persistently held, is, to quote from his sermon on "The Immortality of the Soul," that "this outward scene, its pleasures and pursuits, its honours and cares, its contrivances, its personages, its kingdoms, its multitudes of busy slaves, what are they to us? Nothing—no more than a show." Famous men have thereby, in all their fame, no more reality than characters in a fiction. It is, I have found, deeply impressive to hear this essay read aloud by a boy's earnest voice, full of youthful certainty and idealism. I give its central portion, slightly abridged, and mark the boyish emphasis:

"The fame I intend to discuss is the knowledge your contemporaries have of you while living, and posterity when dead. On this I advance an assertion which has often struck me very forcibly. And that is that there is NO such thing as a *person* being famed. Let it not be thought a quibble when I say that it is *his name* that is celebrated *and not he himself*. For instance, the name of Addison is everywhere known and flourishes with undiminished glory. But *he* is not famed! For his name does not more belong to him than to the tailor who made his coat or to the barber who shaved him. So that if it were possible for Addison, his tailor and his barber to rise from the dead, and each claim the name of Addison to himself . . . as to their appearance one could not be believed more than another! *The name of Addison does not point out any individual!*

"Therefore, the foundation of fame is unstable. The connection between the name and the possessor of the name is dissolved with death, and consequently all the superstructures fall with the foundations on which they rely; like the Indian notion of the earth, which is supported by a tortoise, and that by some other animal, and that animal by nothing.

One would dearly like to have been present when his teacher handed back this essay to him, and some such conversation as the following ensued:

Teacher: Young Newman! What on earth are you trying to say in this extraordinary production? Tell me this. If I say the name of Julius Caesar to you, doesn't that bring a real man before your eyes?

Boy: Oh, no, sir! For if it did I should ask you to point him out to me.

Teacher: Naturally I can't do that. Julius Caesar is dead.

Boy: That is my point, sir. All that remains now of Julius Caesar is his name.

Teacher: But, good gracious, he can be recreated for you: his face, his feelings, his ideas, his achievements, his very thoughts in his very own words.

Boy: (Sadly.) Shadows, sir! Mere shadows!

No public personality would ever be of the least importance to this boy, least of all, perhaps, his own public personality. For him the only real personality is the private personality, the anonymous secret, known inadequately even to ourselves, a mind working on a mind, known fully only to the Infinite of which it is a part. So another Saint Mary's sermon will insist:

"Survey some populous town. Crowds are pouring through the streets; some on foot, some in carriages; while the shops are full, and the houses, too, could we but see into them. Every part of it is full of life. Hence we gain a general idea of splendour, magnificence, opulence and energy. But what is the truth? Why, that every being in that great concourse is his own centre, and all things about him are but shades, but a 'vain shadow,' in which 'he walketh and disquieteth himself in vain.' Each has his own hopes and fears, desires, judgements and aims. He is everything to himself; and no one else is really anything. No one outside of him can really touch him, can touch his soul, his immortality.

He must live with himself forever. He has within him a depth unfathomable, an infinite abyss of existence; and the scene in which he bears part for a moment is but like a gleam of sunshine on the surface."

Against this it is to be said that his boyish diaries are far more often those of a natural, normal lad. "Dancing lessons. . . . Party. . . . Party. . . . Play. . . . Great wind. . . . Walked in sleep. . . . Home. . . . Dancing. . . . Haymaking. . . . Bathing. . . . Boating. . . . Rehearsal in dresses. . . . Rehearsal before boys. . . . Grand night. . . ." He recalled, too, after the great change, that though he did desire before it to be a virtuous boy, he had not only no desire to be religious, but actually disliked the idea, so that when the Calvinistic clergyman at school who converted him, a Reverend Mr. Mayers, contended against the *Essay on Man*, the boy humanistically defended Pope's position that "virtue alone is happiness below."

It was to this highly sensitive child that Mayers had been lending Calvinistic books, on this tremulous conscience that he had been working for some time when chance put the boy suddenly at the complete mercy of his mentor. In March, 1816, Mr. Newman ran into financial trouble, almost a bankruptcy, as a result of which the boy was left at school throughout the summer vacation. "It was a time of reflection and when the influence of Mr. Mayers would have room to act upon me. Also I was terrified at the heavy hand of God which came down upon me." He has dated the experience precisely: "the first and last days of my conversion: August 1st and December 21st, 1816."

The experience must have been searing. Thirty-five years after that long and lonely summer in an empty school he still spoke of it in awe: "I know perfectly well and thankfully confess to Thee, O my God, that Thy wonderful Grace turned me right round when I was more like a devil than a wicked boy, at the age of fifteen." It is the genuine, exaggerated vocabulary of Evangelicalism. It is also the language of something far deeper and higher in aim; for it is to be accepted as a picture of reality only as one accepts the words of all men who strive after sainthood; to be rejected and scoffed at, every word of it, by any lesser or more common measure.

And this is what he called "a state of mind." Surely, rather, sheer agony of soul? Forty-eight years afterwards he described his release from that agony, in the *Apologia*, as an instantaneous "inward conversion" whereby "I was elected to eternal glory." Searing is the only word for that experience of being bound, burned, branded, half-consumed, . . . "isolating me from the objects which surrounded me, confirming me in my mistrust of the reality of material phenomena, and making me rest in the thought of two and two only absolute and luminously self-evident beings, myself and my Creator." One is inexpressibly relieved when it is all over, and the boy has at last surrendered to the joys of Heaven and the gyves of Geneva.

CHAPTER 3

HARD TIMES

1

THAT year John Henry saw French prisoners marched
through London, and people in the dense crowds solemnly lifting their overcoats to see if they really had tails
like apes. Mr. Newman, with his usual optimism, saw 1815
only as a great year of promise, and at Christmas wrote some
sanguine verses on this theme for the play that his young-
sters were, as usual, performing at Southampton Street. We
may see him, back to the fire, expanding happily to his
theme:—

> When Europe's sons disarm nor longer wage
> Destructive wars, the peaceful mimic stage
> Still keeps remembrance of their martial facts
> And registers each deed through five long acts . . .
> Now universal peace has cheered the world
> And thrifty commerce has her sails unfurled . . .
> Oh, may all wars from henceforth be confined
> To mimic pictures and the scenes behind!

It was a fair but fatal wish. As so often happens after
wars, money began to contract. People who formerly had
money to entrust to banks now began to draw it out faster
than the banks could withdraw it from where they had invested it. In that winter after Waterloo more banks disappeared than have ever been recorded. Presently it was the

49

turn of Ramsbottom, Newman & Ramsbottom. They closed
their doors on March 8th, 1816.

Panic at once set in at Southampton Street. Dickens
would have done the scene beautifully. Mrs. Newman's
first thought was economy. They must get out from under
the expense of their big town-house, paste up a "To Let"
bill in the windows, retire to their beloved cottage at Norwood to take stock. The girls were accordingly packed off
with Aunt Betsy and Grandmamma to "Fairfield," where
they would be sheltered from such mortifications as clamant
creditors and, if it were to come to that, hard-faced bailiffs.
Not, as Jemima forewarned her sister-in-law, that even the
"peaceful Cot" was safe. Vine Cottage might have to go
too. "As soon as I can get away from this house I shall. I
tremble at the unavoidable *daily* expenses; of course at present we can form no plan, but my idea is if your brother (she
means John) can possibly manage to come to the Cottage for
two months while we collect our poor scattered senses—and
then it will begin to be in beauty to part with." That is,
in May it will look its best and fetch a better price. And
after May? She still had her jointure under her father's
will, £5000 invested in the Funds. (The returns began to
drop presently, but she held on to her money and, in the end,
shared it out among her children.) If the worst came to
the worst surely John's friends would find him a post somewhere? He was only forty-nine. Perhaps he could work in
"the brewery"? By this she means the brewery in Thames
Street, Windsor, where the Ramsbottoms had an outlying
office called Ramsbottom & Co., cozily snoozing in the odor
of malt.[1]

For three weeks John struggled alike with his creditors
and his colleagues. It never once occurred either to him or
to Jemima that they could do anything but pay to the last
penny. Their one ardent wish was to make up things
quietly, so that no one might be injured and they might re-

tain their name unsullied.   In their misfortune husband and
wife came nearer to one another than they had ever done in
their days of prosperity.   "John and I," she wrote to her
sister-in-law, "love each other with increased affection.   We
begin to see the bottom of each other's heart."   They also
plumbed the hearts of others.   The senior Ramsbottom
proved a weakling; he locked himself up in his house and
only came to the office after they had sent for him three
times; and then he seemed absolutely determined not to
lend a hand to prop the falling fabric.   But they had good
friends, too.   The junior Ramsbottom stood firm, so that "the
two Johns" were two-thirds of the battle, and worked well
together.   Mr. Capel, the banker, stood solidly by them.
Dr. Nicholas of Ealing School loyally told the parents to
leave the boys at his school.   The Fourdriniers stood by.   It
was a godsend to have Aunt Betsy to watch over the girls.
As friends gathered and the first awful few days passed it
seemed as if the humiliation of the *Gazette*—that is, a public
announcement of bankruptcy—could after all be avoided.
It was, though they were to endure that humiliation, too, in
due course.

Never once did Jemima whine or falter.   Her husband
stood his ground, went to the office to see and be seen by
everybody, and finally paid to the last penny.   Jemima's
thoughts were all on two subjects: their honor and their
"dear dear Creatures" whom she kept away from her, the
boys at school, the girls at the cottage, only because she
could not bear seeing them "with firmness."   She visits the
girls at Norwood ("our Dears . . . our three Loves"), bringing food and a maid with her, hastening back in the winter
dark to the threatened home.   It is most moving of all when
she calls young John down from school, to discuss the whole
matter with him, now aged fifteen.   "I am anxious to know
how the dear fellow feels and I trust to be able to soften any
keen feeling he may have."   We are left to ride back with

him in the coach, guessing his solemn thoughts, all compounded of love for his mother, worry for his father, speculation on the grave ideas he is imbibing from Mr. Mayer's
Calvinistic books, and, we hope, naturally boyish enough to
sigh that there will be no summer holidays this year.   Before
April 2nd Mr. Newman had cleared up the mess.   Every
creditor was paid, but the Norwood cottage went, Southampton Street was stripped of its grandeur, and Mr. Newman's
career as a banker was over.   He did become a brewer after
all, though not in London or Windsor, but in Alton in Hampshire, whither he went to work as manager of a brewery
owned by a man named Hawkins.[2]   It was the best the
Ramsbottoms could, or the most they would do for him now.

2

So, one morning in that October, the girls woke and looked
out, not at Southampton Street but on the High Street of
Alton.   They found it a quiet, pleasant old town, with beautiful walks and rides through hop-gardens, over rich, rolling
wooded country.   They must have known that it was White
of Selborne's country.   They did know that Miss Austen
had already sent out her first novels about it from Chawton
down the Winchester Road.   When they read *Emma* it
evoked Alton.   Their new home—it is at the far end of the
High Street, No. 59, now called "Swarthmore"—rose directly
from a narrow pavement behind a low hedge, its mellow
brick covered over with ivy, its tall, deeply-recessed door
indrawn behind three steps.   It is a fine two-story house,
topped by wide attics and dormer windows.   It looks its
best when the slanting evening sun reveals its graceful
Georgian proportions.   Behind it the girls found a crumpled,
elongated, old-fashioned garden, with a winding path that
led to the rear gate, to the stables and the brewery's chimneys.   There were flower-beds and a seat bowered in trees.

It was a dignified house, a house of standing, a roomy, comfortable, spacious house, and they really had no fault at all to find with it, except that it was not Vine Cottage.[3]

Harriett had already given tongue about this, even before she said goodbye to Vine Cottage and the wild heaths about it. She thereby earned a chilling reproof from John Henry, so characteristic of the insensibilities to which sensitive natures are prone that it must be given in full; though one should, perhaps, be indulgent to him on this occasion because it is an aunty letter, and because he meant well, and because he never could resist intellectualizing about his own or other people's feelings, and because he was very young.

"Oct. 30th, 1816. My dear Aunt . . . Why should Harriett be sorry at leaving Norwood? I will not say it is not natural, but if she would give me leave to hint to her some few considerations I hope I shall hear of her stoical front disdaining to feel any affection for the place in which she has delighted these last eight years.

1. Let her reflect that her brothers are in a worse situation than she is at leaving Norwood; I shall begin with his case which is the easiest of the three, with his who saw Norwood later than the other two, with his who is writing; when he left Norwood on one Monday morning he must have been conscious to himself he would never see it (as his home) again; let her ask herself whether he was in the least unwilling to leave it, tho' he liked it, perhaps as much as she did—No, he thought that there was no reason why he should not be as happy as he had been before, whether his home was at Alton or Norwood, Ealing or Ham, Southampton Street or anywhere else where he may in future be. If Harriett is with the same persons as before (of course I include the chickens) why may she not like Alton as much as Norwood? I have done this extremely *mathematically*.

2. Now for the other two; they left Norwood with no expectation of not seeing it again; they consoled themselves with the hope of living there again, of mending the walk towards the pigs, of bettering their garden, of improving the place etc., etc., and

yet they will not see it again.   Let Harriett ruminate this in her
brain and digest it well. . . ."

A solemn youth.

"Next Monday there is a ball, I shall not go to it if I can possibly
avoid it. . . .   Did you ever read Bishop Newton on the Prophecies?"

His mother replied: " 'Thou reasonest well.' "   Then she
went on to tell him of her difficulties: how "poor little Mary"
was ill again—she was always frail—and how she had hired
a cook; and how their things had been delayed on the road;
and how she was looking forward to seeing all her children
around her soon; and how she knew well that his assistance
in educating the girls would be valuable, though he was
likely to find them relaxed in their studies if they did not
soon get into train again.   She was, no doubt, grateful for
his serious interest, though she did presently begin to wonder if he was not taking gravity too far.

Yet, John was right, if seemingly cold and insensitive;
right, at any rate, as for John Henry Newman.   This power
he had of cutting his losses rationally was of a piece with his
non-rational doubts about the world's reality.   It is easy to
dismiss what so barely exists.   His philosophy should have
given him, simultaneously, the power of enjoying equally
whatever came his way, since no one thing or place can have
pre-eminence over another in a world so insubstantial as this,
"whether Alton or Norwood, Ealing or Ham, Southampton
Street or anywhere else where he may in future be."   An old
Oratorian father, now gone to his rest, once said: "Newman's
secret was simply that he didn't give a damn about this
world."   This may be true, but he could also have said with
Bernanos: "When I am dead say to this gentle realm of earth
that when I lived I loved it more than I ever dared to say."

Up to a point he had it both ways. His weakness was that
he would always love most passionately when all was gone,
always speak his love too late.

What must chiefly strike us about John Henry in those
years is that he ought to have been the happiest of the whole
family, being the most sheltered. He was up at Oxford that
winter, entered Trinity College at the immature age of under
sixteen, called into residence the June after. He only spent
his vacations at Alton, and after the Long Vacation of 1819
stayed up entirely, thereby escaping much of Alton's atmosphere of worry, and all its final debacle. And he probably
was happy in his own grave way, although his capacity for
happiness was always limited, as he seems to realize when he
writes to Frank: "Here at Oxford I am most comfortable.
. . . For the calm happiness I enjoy I cannot feel thankful
as I ought. How in my future life, if I do live, shall I look
back with a sad smile at these days!" [4] Alton produced from
him little beyond three pastoral poems, written, as the dates
show, out of some pleasant holiday hours—he published
them characteristically as "Memorials of the Past"; some sol-
emn-cheerful letters to his mother—"The long prospect is
before me. I anticipate that soothing, quiet, unostentatious
pleasure which only an equable, unvarying time of living can
give"—and a typical entry in his notebook, philosophically
pensive, euphuistically balanced, schizophrenically third-
person: "And now at Alton where he never expected to be,
being lately come from the Vacation at Oxford where he
dared not hope to be. How quick time passes, and how ignorant are we of futurity!" The youth seems in those years
to link two equally peaceful lagoons: this old town where
they can all enjoy a blessed calm after a brief storm, and his
cloistered refuge where in the long summer he will have the
college gardens to himself, with their gleaming lawns and
their snapdragons glowing in the sun, and where, when twi-
light falls, he will write down his solitary's content to hear

the bells toll over the High: "The Sunday evening bells are pealing. Oh! the pleasure of hearing them. It leads my mind to a longing after something, I know not what. It does not bring past years to remembrance; it does not bring anything. What do they do to me? I have a kind of longing after something dear to me, and well known to me, very soothing. Such is my feeling at this minute as I hear the evening bells of Oxford."

Yet, when he revisited Alton fifteen years after they had all left it he found the experience painful; as he always did in his melancholy researches of things past. Too many strong feelings were awakened in him. He warmed only when he remembered the first evening of his return from Oxford, in the summer of 1818, after winning a scholarship at Trinity, and his father coming forward with the joyful cry of, "What a happy meeting this!" Otherwise it was like seeing the ghosts of old friends. "As we came near, and I saw Monk's Wood, and the church, and the hollow on the other side of the town, it was as fearful as if I were standing by the grave of somebody I knew, and saw him gradually recover life and rise again."

He never guessed how bitter his mother's memories of that town were. The bank-crash had shaken her sense of security badly. Things were still so far from improving that she confessed afterwards that she lived those three years at Alton in a state of fearful anxiety, and in constant dread of worse trials that she could already see approaching. For John Newman was not making a success of things, and he would never make a success of anything ever again. In fact he was borrowing heavily to recoup; which reveals that he was not a salaried manager, but in some sort a lessee of the brewery.[5] In December, 1818, when he was two years in Alton, we find him mortgaging his personal assets—shares in the Southwark Bridge Co., and his Life Insurance policy—for a loan of £1000 from the Richard Capel who had already been so loyal at the time of the bank-trouble. It was a small Insurance Policy, only £250. For a one-time banker it was a small loan but he was never able to repay it. This is the kind of cruel detail that lifts the window-curtains on all apparently sedate and solid homes, like No. 59, High Street, Alton, leading us to wonder what life was really like behind that cozily ivied façade, what conversations went on when the children were abed, and Aunt Betsy and Grandmamma out of the way, and husband and wife could be themselves without concealment. Did the rest of Alton, one wonders, ever guess that all was not well in No. 59? Or are the domestic interiors of all small towns sealed chambers to the rest of its inhabitants; not to speak of to us, strangers living a century after? We shall never know what was said there, or left unsaid, thought and felt, apart from Jemima's general admission as to the constant anxiety and dread. We shall never know why Jemima said to John Henry, in answering that letter about his return visit to Alton: "Your recollection of your dear father's greeting cheers me greatly. I have always a nervous dread lest you all recall him only in pain and sorrow."

Those last five words are disturbing. What did she mean by saying that they might only remember their father "in pain and sorrow?" It cannot have been merely because he was a failure that, as she went on, the boys should be "borne down by injustice and a too sensitive concern for one's disappointed hopes"? After all, John and Frank went through Oxford, and though it is true than John had to slave to help Frank through college, he could also note that during eighteen months, from December, 1816, to the Long Vacation in 1818, when he got a scholarship worth £60, valid for nine years at Trinity, his father sent him about £320. (The loan mentioned, we will note, is dated *December*, 1818.) Surely this £320 was a generous allowance. Writing to his mother in May, 1827, he says: "The yearly College expenses with us

do not amount to £80. This includes board, lodging, service, dues, tuitions, coals, washing and hair-cutting. I believe other colleges are about the same. The great expenses
of a college residence are in the private extravagances of a
young man." John Newman was generous to his son.
Charles, it is true, had ultimately to take a job in the Bank
of England; but then Charles was no student, and was more
than odd. It is such a terrible thing for a mother to fear
lest her children should think of their father "only in pain
and sorrow" that we are left speculating wildly as to what
drove so gentle a woman to say so harsh a thing. Had her
husband foolish or extravagant tastes? Why exactly did he
fail this second time? There are unfortunately no records
from the brewery to show what happened to John Newman
in Alton.

We will sympathize with the stay-at-home sisters—fourteen, fifteen, sixteen—especially with Harriett, the eldest
girl, who would have had keen ears and eyes for mamma's
absent-minded sighs and troubled looks. We will be especially indulgent to Harriett. If, in later life, she should ever
be a trifle shrewish with her eldest brother we will remember
that even the most delicate-minded of men can, when they
live too much in the mind, be mightily obtuse about other
people's feelings in their preoccupation with their own.
Yet, guarded allowances have to be made here, too. She
and John and all of them feel more than they say, are softer
and more emotional than, in the typical English way, they
pretend. The Newmans were a tight-lipped family. It is
not the parents only who muffle their own nerves. They all
preserve the silence of courage. So, not a murmur of com-
plaint comes from one of them when, by November, 1819,
they have to uproot themselves again, and leave the town,
bag and baggage, as they had entered it only three years
before, except that there were no animals this time, because
there was no Norwood to receive them.

Back in London John Newman began to lead a life that hangs midway between Père Goriot and Wilkins Micawber: a double life behind the respectable family façade. No single word has crept into their letters or memoirs about his secret. There can be no certainty that any of them knew about it. Did he keep it dark even from his wife and his eldest son? John Newman had become a tavern-keeper. His business house at 18, Saint James's Walk, Clerkenwell, is described in his bankruptcy papers as a "brewhouse." [6] The rentals tell us that the house had passed from hand to hand every ten years or so. Since 1766 it had been Walford's, Sellon's, Thorpe's, Newman's and Ellis's.[7] John Newman gave £100 a year for it. Ellis only gave £50. But this is because he shared the rent with a man named Gardner who, we find, gave £10 a year for the cellar "under the Tavern." It was at most a modest brew-house, with a pub attached. It may have been a pub with its brew-house attached.

3

One small incident about this time, the summer of 1820, shows us that there is a sense in which the whole story of the Newmans is a comedy of incongruities and incompatibilities between theories of life that were too neat, too rigid, too moral, and the protean nature of this world that refused to squat in pigeon-holes. John Henry was in this the biggest sinner of the family, being also its most moral and most idealistic member. He nourished, from the womb, a great many tightly-wound, inborn ideas which, since he was not the sort of man who easily or ever discards ideas—an obstinate, deeply-grooved mind—he would spend many years and much spiritual sweat in unwinding; basic ideas that he would expand like an elastic net in order to contain that larger and more humane concept of life which experience

teaches us all to be necessary, unless we propose to live and
die in a perpetual series of futile and ridiculous stumbles and
bumps against the nature of common reality. One of his
ideas was an inordinate respect for authority—the fixed system so beloved by all men of firm character—almost as if,
his brother Frank once sourly remarked, he thought authority something sacred for its own sake.

The royal proceedings against Queen Caroline, in 1820,
brought out this tendency in full blast, though in justice to
him the whole of England had been disputing about the
Queen's morals ever since George IV had made Lord Liverpool propose a Bill in July to deprive his consort of her
queenly prerogatives on the old, and as it proved, had indeed
already been proved, baseless ground of sexual misconduct.
A public trial of a Queen of England for committing fornica-
tion with an Italian servant one night in Naples under a
ship's awning could not fail to flood the pubs and clubs with
angry arguments and foul obscenities; the more so since anybody who knew anything at all about the court and politics
knew well that the King's private life had been far from
virginal, and suspected, correctly, that he had been for years
married secretly to Mrs. Fitzherbert.

But if it was not surprising that even such quiet homes as
the Newmans' were shaken by this sordid dispute, it annotates the mental rigidity, the innocence and the remoteness
from life of young John Henry that he came out so strongly
for the King. There was a nasty clash about it in Southampton Street. John Newman, old Beefsteaker, naturally
knew far too much about George IV's reputation, and was
much too humane and too broad-minded to turn against the
unfortunate if foolish Queen. He was astonished and pained
to find his son pitilessly against her. He became so angry
as to mistake moral fanaticism for self-seeking, and finally
burst out at his son one day, in furious sarcasm—he must
have been living on his nerves all that year:—

"Well, John! I suppose I ought to praise you for knowing how to rise in the world. Go on! Go on! Persevere!
Always stand up for men in power! And in time you will
get your promotion!"

Frank Newman ought to have been on his brother's side
in this dispute, for he also had meanwhile come under the
Calvinistic influence of the Revd. Mr. Mayers. He was so
distressed at John Henry's inflexibility that he now felt that
his father was the only Christian among them.

It is a small incident, but we might revert to it later when
John Henry is struggling with other forms of authority: for
it is alike symptomatic of his rigid nature and his lack of
experience, and a forewarning of how far he will need to expand in order to work with men, or fight successfully against
them. Yet, in a sense, he never would change. As he was
born he would die. He would merely adapt theory to experience with greater and greater intellectual subtlety, or
more and more infusions of imagination and poetry: his suc-
cessful substitute—the best substitute of all intellectuals—
for the humanity, geniality and tolerance of more easy-going
men, like his warm-hearted father. It would be his salvation from the dreadful danger that always threatened him,
and at which for all his self-excoriations he never guessed—
the danger of being an intellectual snob.

4

While his father labored to keep the little business in
Clerkenwell afloat John was cramming ferociously for the
Schools, sometimes working as much as fifteen hours a day.
He was happy—"I am more happy here than I suppose I
ever was yet" [8]—but his happiness did not last. He over-
strained himself. He worked himself into a failure. To
everybody's surprise he came out "under the line" with a
second. That was in November, 1820. It was a bad blow

for his father, who must have been hoping that his son's
success would balance his own lack of it. For himself it was
more than a humiliation, the worse for being undeserved.
It was a disaster in the inmost core of his being, and he was
unbalanced for weeks after it.[9]

It is easy to see why this first failure of his life shattered
him so utterly. Oxford was fast becoming his home. He
was beginning to realize that here was his real happiness,
where he had taken the snapdragons rooted in the Trinity
wall as his emblem of security and content. He seems in
these years most himself when he is musing gravely on religious matters in Oxford or playing in his lodgings on the
Cremona his father bought him: Haydn or Mozart—duets by
Viotti, pieces by Vaccari or Spagnoletti; reading with equal
pleasure the realistic Crabbe and the romantic *Ivanhoe*,[10]
which shows that nobody can judge young men by their
reading, they rove so thirstily. It is true that even when his
religious gravity was most pronounced a burst of secular
ambition for a brilliant career at the Bar could calm him
with its worldly distraction;[11] but the distraction was ephem-
eral and when he had been most keyed up by the challenge
of the Schools the quiet and stillness of Oxford could always
lull him to rest again.[12] The truth is that since childhood
he had been marked out for the cloister and the academy.
He was not made for the hurly-burly; hardly even for communion with men. His father had already commented on
that. Everything, school, religious influence, family mis-
fortunes combined to cut him off from the market-place.
He would always see this great, busy, important world as a
tiny ball whirling through space. All its histories would
at one and the same time be as timeless as Creation and as
brief as a wink. His interest in such things would never be
much more than that of the poet, the philosopher, or the
priest. Is it any wonder then that his failure in the Schools
temporarily unseated his reason? Far more than a mere ex-

amination had been at stake. Oxford was, of this world, the
one place blessedly nearest to not being of this world. To
fail in that Eden was a disaster at Heaven's gate. He was
made for Oxford, as he would finally be marked "made in
Oxford."

The stars were not wholly cruel. He still had his Trinity
Scholarship—five more years of it to run—and since a second-class B.A. was not, apparently, likely to make a first-class
lawyer, and his sense of a religious vocation had become insistent, he easily persuaded his father to allow him to opt for
the cloister. He would live, for ever, among those golden
stones and gleaming lawns, that student's life of which
Edward Thomas once said that its great joy is that it really
seems to be for ever. Still, Oxford did not fall into his lap.
He had to slave for it. This youth for whom the world was
a shadow had a character of iron. If money from home
was no longer forthcoming he would take private pupils.[13]
Frank must at all costs be got through the university. A
hundred pounds a year from a pupil or two would be a
godsend. When he returned to Oxford in February, '21,
he wrote sadly in his Diary, thinking of his earlier ambitions:
"And now at Oxford, but with far different feelings; let the
date speak." But he was not repining. He was sturdily
preparing for a life of penury. In '21, when he had Frank
up to stay with him in Seale's Coffee House[14] to grind for
his matriculation, he wrote, "God is feeding me by the
ravens."

The prospect of having Frank in Oxford delighted him.
The actuality was not a success. The brothers did not pull
well together. His younger brother, if we may judge by his
later life, strikes one as being clever, cocky, shallow, good-
hearted and devoid of subtlety. He could easily have been
exasperatingly self-assured. Frank was generous about it
all. Seventy years afterwards he still gratefully remembered
the "inestimable benefits I received in my rising manhood

from my eldest brother. . . . I was able to repay his money but that could not cancel my debt, for he supplied me not out of his abundance but when he knew not whence weekly and daily funds were to come." On the other hand, John cannot have been an easy young man to live with either. He was positive and inflexible. He had a devilish temper, passions so ungovernable as to unman him, and a tongue that could clip a hedge. We must accept his own word for this in his confession to his mother: "While with Frank at Oxford I have felt a spirit of desperate ill-temper, and sullen anger rush on me. . . . So violent has this sometimes proved that I have quite trembled from head to foot and thought I should fall down under excess of agitation." [15] Again (in his own private Memoranda): "I am horribly vain of my attainments, abilities and performances. And as to pride it is leading me every minute into ill-nature, anger, lying and uncharitableness." He scourges himself for this over and over again. "Hot and violent. Want of meekness and gentleness. To Frank very violent, ill-tempered and perverse." When he heard, in January, '22, that Frank might not come up to Oxford at all he saw it as "a just rebuke and punishment for the wicked ill-nature and moroseness with which I treated him last term." Again: "Not a day passes without disturbance." Again: "Not so cruel to Frank." Again: "Constantly impatient with Frank."

We will naturally minimize all this. Few men can have had so self-exacting a code, striven so earnestly, as Mauriac puts it, to "purify the source." "Pound me, O Lord, into small bits. Grind me down. Anything for a meek spirit." When he had been going for the scholarship in '18 he had cried, "O Lord God of Hosts, grant it not to me if it is likely to be a snare to me." Two and a half years later he writes: "I have just read the above. Lord, I tremble. Could I thus so earnestly pray . . . and in a few short weeks become so vain, so puffed up, so proud, so quarrelsome, so very wicked? . . . So trifling a good fortune and it must stop my prayers, lull my watchfulness, blind me, lead me back to wallow in the mire!" Still, these wild cries did not come out of nothing. He must have had—who has not?—his devils to contend with; and so, in living with him daily, must Frank.

It is pleasant to find him doing something quite relaxed, human and silly. A friend from his Ealing school-days got into debt at Oxford, and hit on the brilliant notion that if he could only get a play accepted by Drury Lane all his difficulties would vanish. He put it up to Newman and to another friend at Christ Church, named Owen, and they agreed to approach Harley, the actor-manager of Drury Lane, well known to London audiences as a comic singer affectionately called Fat Jack.[16] John sat down and wrote a couple of songs for Fat Jack. We are disappointed, if not surprised, to find that nothing came of it and Drury Lane has, alas, not preserved the ditties.

CHAPTER 4

HARDER TIMES

1

BEFORE Alton John and Jemima had never shared a home with Aunt Betsy and Grandmamma. After Alton they decided to put the two of them into one of those small, pretty-looking houses at Strand-on-the-Green, hard by Kew Bridge, which get all there is of summer sun and winter damp. Little floodwalls to keep out the tides have since been built across the doorways with steps up from the pavement and steps down to the door. Even then, in some houses the entrance was lifted to the first floor, making a pleasing, if ominous, outside staircase. Here Aunt Betsy opened her shabby-genteel Finishing School for Young Ladies, to be described in her Advertisements as follows:—

A Lady of the Established Church who takes only a limited number of young Ladies will have some vacancies at Easter. The most unremitting attention paid to health and morals. The most approved masters attend. The situation healthy and a short distance from London. The most respectable references can be given.[1]

She was now fifty-five, and despite vicissitudes and annoyances she held on until she was over sixty. She only barely held on, and was constantly approaching a new crisis. Once we see her scribbling her simple profit and loss account on a comforting letter from one of her nephews, the

67

dotty Charles. The left-hand column looks uncommonly like income from six guests; the right, uncomfortably like expenses:—

£'s	(?)		£'s	(?)	
1	50		4	80	
1	42		3	90	
1	28		Wg	20	
1	35		Coa	20	(Coal?)
1	30		Wgs	10	(Wages?)
1	6		R&T	50	(Rate & Taxes)
	191			270	
				191	
				79	

Whether profit or loss the answer to her sum cannot have given much joy to the poor lady, or to her relations. Generally she was up to her ears in debt, with the Kew shopkeepers clamoring to be paid and nothing but the generosity of her relatives to keep the bailiffs from her door.

Strand, as the Newmans called it, was in 1820 a remote waterside hamlet.[2] Its great charm was that it was uncluttered and unhemmed. Even today there is everywhere a generous sense of space and light. The broad river has laid down wide flat terraces of silt in its loops. On lively, windy days when the houses shimmer across the brightly ruffled water their long flickerings make it seem wider still, and on calm days when the reflections briefly edge the shore the vast sky inflates the vacancy of the river that repeats it. In their time there was an even greater sense of spaciousness and light, for there was, then, nothing between Strand and Chiswick but long country lanes, and level open market-gardens lay all about it, and the Duke's Meadows filled the great bend of the river. The little hamlet itself was a Dutch exterior, with a windmill turning by Kew Bridge, and a line of willows swaying along the quay, and alms-houses and an old red-brick malt-house snuggling low on the river bank, and their Kew Bridge was not our Kew Bridge but an antiquated high-backed one that the carters cursed for its steep slopes. The girls strolling there would have seen the blue flash of the king-fisher, the white swirl of gulls, heard the swish of herons' wings. Sunrise was distant light. Sunset lasted long—an iridescent slow-coming dusk. The girls would have had no urban sensation. After dark London's glow would be dim, a banked fire. It was utterly silent at night, when the only sound they would hear from their bedrooms would be the water muttering, and the mud whispering, and if they peeped out they might see a star in the water. By day their Strand was more busy than ours. It had its boat-builders and bargees, scullers and ferry-boats. Sails were often folded when the rivermen drew in beside its several inns. One found them clustered around "The Indian Queen," or "The Bell and Crown," with their signposts extending out over the water and their wooden steps touching the beach. Rivers were roads then.

The first of Miss Newman's Young Ladies were, naturally, little Jemima Newman, now aged twelve, and her sister Mary, now aged eleven. A letter to Jem from our Père Goriot in London mentions another resident:

"J'ai le plus grande plaisir en vous ecrivant. J'espere que vous avez tous les charmes de la leisure en enjoyant les beautes de la Nature sur les grande Riviere de la Thames. Envoyez mes regards particulaire de votre digne Grandam et Tante n'oublierant ma chere Fille votre soeur Mary. J'ai le desire grande vous voir tout sur le pont de Kew. Regardez votre Livre, approchez quand vous somme appelè et fermez la Porte apres vous. (*This was a regular family joke.*) N'oublions pas de presenter mes meilleurs regards à la Dame Magnollay. Je suis ma chere Fille, Votre Pere, J. N., Bloomsbury, Rue de Southampton, 3rd Sept., 1820. Mdlle. Jem Newman."

Mamma had been a pupil thirty-six years before at this Mrs. Magnollay's boarding school in Camberwell. She was now well on in her sixties.

This adds up to three unprofitable ladies and two unprofitable children. From time to time we hear of others who presumably paid fees. There is a child named Eliza Dodds —"*excessively* good natured" Jem exclaims—who insists on wearing her hair up and her petticoats long, so that although only thirteen she looks quite fifteen. The Fourdriniers also patronized the school. We hear of Anna Maria, who would have been the daughter of Uncle Charles Fourdrinier, and a cousin to the Newman children on their mother's side. Other young ladies who reside from time to time in this band-box of a house include a Miss Legh, whose name reminds us that the Ramsbottoms and Leghs were partners in the Windsor Brewery; cousin Louisa, the daughter of Uncle Sealey of Cannon Street; a Miss Platt, a Miss Vine, a flirtatious Miss Bode, a Miss Ann Johnson, and a Miss Boxall. The only "masters" or teachers we hear of are a Mr. and Mrs. Byrne, a pair who, Harriett tells us, distinguished themselves by giving their first lesson on a June 6th, and their last lesson on a June 22nd, with a prim comment thereon from the same Young Lady that hints more than it says about Aunt Betsy's competence: "I hope Aunt will have their place supplied in a more suitable manner." Likewise the only references to servants are a grumble from Miss Mary about one Filby who will keep on bothering her for sugar, and a comment on a Penelope who has been, she says, "*congedié*" for ill-behavior.

In this tiny world everything is Lilliputian and important; everyone palpitating about bonnets, bobbins, patterns, pens, pen-knives (when pocket-knives really were *pen*-knives), ink-glasses, chilblains, styes, colds, with lots of nicknames, and secret passwords, and occasional high-doings; happy, girlish intimacies whose course is never interrupted by the much less happy doings of the monster humming and smoking self-importantly down three loops of the river.

Life oscillated here between the sedate and the breathless. *Sedate:*—"On Sunday afternoon," Jem writes, "we went to Kew chapel which is very small indeed, its exterior promised something much larger." (We note, in passing, this word "chapel," even if Aunt Eliza does advertise herself as of the Established *Church*.) "After chapel we continued our walk as far as Thomson's house at Richmond." This was James Thomson, the poet, who lay buried in Richmond Church. We must see them in the heavy elaborate Walking Dress of the times, garbed like Eskimos. Nothing but a toe is visible. So costumed an athletic young woman of today would be perspiring at the end of a mile: it is nothing to them to walk five miles to Mortlake and four to Little Ealing in one day. "Last Friday along the towing path towards Richmond." This Jem describes as a most beautiful walk "which was increased by the beauty of the day. The sky was streaked beautifully with Red and Purple, which was reflected with all the beautiful mimicry of water on the serene and waveless bosom of the Thames, which at that point meanders so much out of a straight line as to be opposite our window. Indeed we can see Richmond Hill there." She would not see it now when ten thousand roofs have turned all these once rural parts into a crowded suburbia.

Breathless:—Harriett, from town, tells Jem to bring a snowy camese out of her drawer, and three loose roses, and buds out of her table-bag, and her purple spenser out of the bottom drawer, and Oh! "the sarsanet is 4s. 3d. a yard . . ." Instructions and news and parcels pursue the Thames' tides, "by Guiseley's boat"—or parcels are left to be called for at "The Waggon and Horses" at Kew—mamma's ear-rings, the white net from mamma's long bottom drawer. "Aunt has just discovered your silver pencil-case in a drawer in the kitchen." We can hear them crying, "Oh! Bagwag! I must have left that at Strand!" or, "Oh! Bag and a half! That's up in town!" "What did you send me your pink hat for? Little plague!" Mary! Take care Mary's hair is neat and her ringlets disposed hübschly. Jemima! Curl yours! Francis! Take care of your sisters and do not be late!" Jokes fly. A stye in the eye may turn into a pigstye. Horseness gives nightmares.

There were high jinks the day brazen Mr. Pote called on the flirtatious Miss Bode and Aunt Betsy kindly put them into the "sallon" and sent in tea, and Mrs. Bode arrived storming like a mother in a melodrama with, "Where is my daughter?" And on being told where she was: "Miss Newman, you must have lost your *senses!* How *could* you do such a thing when you knew I wouldn't even *see* this man? Tell him to leave *at once!*" But this was something dear, ineffectual Aunt Betsy could not, or would not do, and an hour later the two doves were still murmuring in the "sallon," with Mrs. Bode fluttering up and down the stairs, until in the end she fell down the stairs altogether and had to be put to bed. So it goes from day to day. The maid is dismissed. Miss Platt has been *impertinente*. The escritoires have come, but all the Young Ladies said, "How ugly!" "Whereat I," says Mary, "cried out, 'There's thanks!'" So they all said of course that they were much obliged. "Miss Boxall got a cake, *and* wine, *and* a letter!"

One presumes that the sedate hours were the more numerous, the breathless ones an effort to compensate. Mary gives us the extraordinary time-table at Strand, "our *Gothic* hours," she calls them. She says she is alone from six to eight—and she presumably breakfasted at eight o'clock, for the first bell goes at seven; she is alone again from nine to twelve. She may have done a little study then. At twelve she goes for a walk until two. She then lunched, presumably with the boarders, until three. She was then alone again until half-past five, when there was tea: dinner would follow at seven. During the vacant hours, she says: "I have written *millions* of letters to my correspondents . . . I am sure I have written *pages* of French." After dinner there was communal reading. That evening they were at *Charles XII*, probably Voltaire's "Life": she mentions that they find it more attractive in English than in French. But tonight she has dodged *Charles XII*. She is writing in the dining-room, at eleven o'clock, glancing out at the moon over Richmond Hill. "Il faut me retirer. Adieu."

Their Strand may remind us of other villages of our own youth that were both a mere hour from London and hundreds of years removed from it until things like radio, television, the penny post, the telephone, electric railways and the daily paper suddenly telescoped time and space. They might have been living in Haworth, or Connemara, or some little German duchy, or some Italian mountain village for all they knew of the world of men and affairs.

During that summer of the Coronation (1821) the young people were all packed into Strand-on-the-Green. Harriett and John went up from there to London to see the state procession, rising before dawn, getting the coach at four, arriving at the stand after six, waiting five solid hours to see the procession go and come from the Abbey, arriving home exhausted at six in the evening. "The king looked very pale going, but much better going back." Did they, as they waited for the return of His Majesty, hear how the Queen had been turned away from the Abbey door? That night they would have had a lot with which to entertain the old grandmother in the parlor at Kew, with the window open to catch a cool breeze from the river and the hiss of oars from a homing skiff. The ugly duckling Charles was there too. The old people loved him. His aunt found him a great comfort, and he could always knock a laugh out of his grandmother.[3]

2

The month after the Coronation procession of the King
their mamma saw the funeral procession of the Queen, and
she was downcast enough already. She had not seen her
children for "an age," and when she wrote to them sending
newspaper reports about the royal funeral she confessed that
she did not know when next she should have the joy of seeing
them.[4] Was their health good? She enclosed 2s. 6d. as
pocket-money for Jem, also exercises sent on by John for
Jem and Harriett—Jem to shackle Milton to rhyme and Harriett to put a passage of Voltaire's *Henriade* to verse. A
mild Evangelical, one thinks, who recommends Voltaire to
his sister. She did not speak of business matters to her
young. She let them be happy while they might.
    One Friday, a month later, September 28th, John Henry
was summoned from Oxford. He may have guessed why if
he remembered how he had been summoned from Ealing
five years before at the time of the bank-crash. That Saturday they discussed the latest family crisis, conjoined by danger into love and understanding. On Sunday it was all
spoiled by a painful scene.[5] Their father asked Frank to
make a fair copy of a business letter for him. Letters were
probably flying hither and thither in those final weeks, and
the poor man's wrist, sick of clutching the pen, or shaking
with fear. Frank replied that he could not do what his father asked. Had his father forgotten that it was the Sabbath? His father flew into a rage, John Henry was called
downstairs to mediate, and backed up Frank. We may guess
what the half-demented father said next by what, a little
later, he said when he heard that John Henry was attending
the Low Church services and vociferous sermons of one
Revd. John Grant, a fiercely anti-Romanist preacher and
voluminous writer, then rector at Kentish Town Chapel.[6]

"Take care!" he bade his son, when on reproving him he had found himself drowned with scriptural quotations. "Take care! It is very proper to quote scripture. But you *pour* out these texts like bushels of malt! Have a guard! You are encouraging a nervous morbid sensibility and irritability of mind! I know what it is! I know it perfectly well! It is a disease of the mind!" Then he had remembered suddenly that his son had done worse: he had begun to write for a sheet called "The Christian Observer." "And let me tell you my opinion of 'The Christian Observer.' It is this, it is *humbug!* That last thing you wrote for it was more like the composition of an old man than a youth entering life with energy and aspiration."

It would be the same this Sunday afternoon. J. H. N.'s face would button up, Frank would frown, Charles would stare, the girls shrink at the loud voices, and Jemima's pale face would come between them.

"Oh! Very well!" John would shout. "*Very* well! Our affairs are on the brink of ruin. But for all these boys care. . . . I'll copy my letter myself! I will slave myself to the bone. . . . I'll. . . ."

One hears the banging door.

They were reconciled the next morning. John, with frank manliness, paid tribute to his father's candor, forbearance and generosity, the more remarkable, he admitted, considering his load of worldly cares. Before he went back that Summer his father advised him that the ship was sinking and that he had better take back with him to Oxford any little treasures he especially cherished. He did not and was sorry afterwards. One wonders, indeed, if the young man grasped the situation at all? Two weeks later he was writing to his mother, from the secluded calm of an Oxford Sunday, a philosophical letter which she doubtless accepted in the spirit of its good intentions, as she had done with his "mathe-

matical" letter explaining why Harriett need feel no regrets
at leaving Norwood for Alton:—

". . . of course," he wrote, "whatever you say concerning (my
father) and his anxieties must interest me very much. There
is no one who is on any side without cause of sorrow; and, this
being the case, it is a most happy thing to feel one's particular
distress comes from without. When I look around I see few
families but what are disturbed from within. . . . We have not
had to weep over the death of those we love. We are not dis-
quieted by internal variance. We are not parted from each
other by circumstances we cannot control. . . ." (This was not
so, as Jemima knew only too well.) "And then as to the very trial
itself," he went on, "there is nothing in any way to fear! 'All
things work together for good to those who love God.' I am
firmly and rootedly persuaded of this. Everything that happens
to them is most certainly the very best, in every light, that could
by any possibility have happened. . . ."

Even while she was reading this comforting letter Jemima
knew that all was up. The printers of *The Gazette* were
setting up the words that all London would be reading in the
following Saturday's issue that John Newman had failed for
the third time:—

"*November 1st, 1821:—Whereas a Commission of Bankrupt
is awarded against John Newman of Clerkenwell, Middlesex,
Brewer, Dealer and Chapman, and he being decided a Bankrupt, is required to surrender himself to the Commissioners
. . . on the 10th and 20th days of November . . . at one of the
Clock in the afternoon at Guildhall, London, and make full Discovery and Disclosure of his Estate and Effects. Creditors are
to come and prove their debts, and choose assignees. At the
last sitting they are to decide if he is to be allowed a Certificate.
All debtors to give notice to Mr. Ellis, Solicitor, 14, Southampton Buildings, Chancery Lane.*"

She and John were already compiling a list of their Estate and Effects, including, with their usual absolute honesty, her own smallest trinkets,[7] thankful that the aunt and grand-mother were safe in Strand-on-the-Green, that the children were protected from the humiliations of their fall, that there was a roof to shelter them in Kew. What a Christmas it must have been!

In January their life in Southampton Street was put up for public auction. One sees the numbers stuck on the furniture, the tabbed bundles of knives and forks, the leaning pictures. Alien feet wander over the house. Comments turn possessions into objects. Memories are impersonalized, devitalized. Among the things the family tried to save was John Henry's collection of music.[8] They bid too low and lost it. Jemima wept bitterly that night at dinner. Her husband tried to comfort her by saying cheerfully that he would buy it all back from the purchaser. Fifty years later a friend of the family, a Mrs. Fox, rummaging in an auc-tioneer's rooms came on the old worn, musty volume, bearing the inscription *John Henry Newman*, 1817, showing his faint pencil marks for the shifts over the more difficult passages. Mrs. Fox was curious to know how it had come to be lost, and sent it on to John Henry with a puzzled query. John knew well enough how it had been "lost," but he had to shuffle. He could not bear to tell the whole truth. He said, "How can I answer for a boy's negligences fifty years ago?" After that auction none of them would, for years to come, have had any household gods. They were homeless.

The bankruptcy proceedings dragged on for almost a year. One pathetic entry in the public *Gazette* tells us that in May, 1822, the creditors were asked to meet the Court of Com-mission in Basinghall Street to assent or dissent to the assignees' kindly proposal that they should restore her brooches, bangles, ear-rings and so forth to Mrs. Newman.

One hopes they agreed. John did not get his final Certificate until the Autumn. Meanwhile he went to live with his wife, Harriett and Charles, in No. 3, Kentish Town Terrace, presumably in lodgings. It is still there, now called Grove Terrace, a pleasant row of old houses standing back from Highgate Road, with sloping lawns in front, rich with lilac and laburnum. They did not stay there for long; they probably could not afford it. In the heat of June they were down in East Street,⁹ now Dombey Street, which is one of the meaner streets off Lamb's Conduit Street, in Holborn.

From there John, aged fifty, tried to make his fourth start in life. He applied from that address to be admitted to the Musicians' Company, that is to the same livery company of which his father the grocer had been a member, and without which he could not go into trade, though what trade he was now hopefully proposing for himself is unknown. Grocery? He gave his profession as "Gentlemen" and his address as "East Street, Red Lion Square." In fact the solid, residential Red Lion Square is a considerable distance away. This East St. house is still there, with a narrow hall and dark-panelled stairs. But even this was more than they could afford.

Presently they moved out of Holborn into York Street Covent Garden. They would have lodged there very modestly, though not, at least, in today's rank odor of cabbage-stumps. Inigo Jones' great piazza, arcaded on the north and east, was still open to the sky. The Earl of Bedford could still survey from his extended terrace along the south side the strong pillars of Saint Paul's lit by the rising sun that would fall freely across the open green. Saint Paul's is now buried among back-streets, only fleetingly visited by the sun, and much by the soot and by office-folk lunching as sparsely as the sparrows. By the time the markets had come to clutter it all up John Newman had abandoned the struggle, and Dickens was revelling in the smells and grime about Drury

Lane. Yet if York Street really does, as some Dickensians
believe, cover the site of the old burying-ground of St. Mary-
le-Strand, the pestiferous and obscene patch where Lady
Dedlock's lover was buried, to which Joe the crossing-
sweeper led her, and where at last she was found by her
daughter, lying cold and dead, it cannot even in John's time
have been too pleasant. They had one famous neighbor.
Thomas De Quincey[10] lodged close beside the Newmans;
perhaps next door. Did John and he ever meet, ever talk
over a dram about their dreams?

3

The disaster shook young John out of his dreams. Since
his failure in the Schools, in the winter of 1820, he had been
delving into all sorts of unrelated studies. He had taken up
geology, mineralogy and astronomy, he had thought of
studying Arabic and Persian—the typical voracious student
reaching out for the world's knowledge. Then, in the autumn of '21, a daring design began to bud in him. A telling
passage in his novel *Loss and Gain* records the birth of this
great idea. He describes how his hero, that is one may believe himself, climbed one night to the top of one of Oxford's
towers to make observations of the stars, and how, deflected
from the speckled brightness above to the darkness below, the earthly-minded youth began to wonder, as he
looked down into the gas-flecked, dark-shadowed quadrangle, whether he might ever become a Fellow of this college
or that college, each of which he singled out one by one from
the roofs and towers spread below. In the light of this
inextinguishable flame of ambition we cannot be much impressed when he confesses that, on February 21st, 1822, the
day on which he came of age, he shed bitter tears because he
was no longer a boy; nor when he tells his mother, in a fit of
Wertherish gloom, that he is not sorry so great a part of life

is gone, crying, "Would that *all* were over!"   His mother
told him, by return of post, to drink more wine and to take
more air and exercise.   The essential fact is that against the
advice of all his Trinity friends, and without having, in the
cooler moments, the least hope of immediate success, he
dared to study for an Oriel Fellowship.   It was a wild ambition, and his friends shook their heads at so much presumption.   A man who had won only a second-class B.A. degree?
Daring to claim equality with a giant like Keble who at
eighteen had won two firsts?   But John Newman had more
than a prominent nose: he had also a prognathous jaw.   He
buried himself away from the world for six months and
sweated for that Fellowship.

On the Friday morning of Easter week as he sat playing
the violin in his lodgings on Broad Street he heard a knock
on his door.   It was the Oriel butler.   The butler, after re-
covering from a slight surprise at finding so scholarly a gentleman playing the fiddle at such an hour, made the usual
formal speech.   "I have, sir, I fear, disagreeable news to announce.   Mr. Newman is elected Fellow of Oriel and his
immediate presence is required there."   The new Fellow, in
his ignorance of Oxford ways, thought the butler's speech
not so much formal as over-familiar and coldly answered,
"Very well," and went on playing.   The butler, what between the fiddle and the coldness—was he accustomed to
receive a guinea on such occasions?—asked if he had mistaken the rooms.   The new Fellow said, "No!," it was quite
all right, and went on fiddling.   But no sooner was the butler out of sight than he dashed the violin on the sofa and was
off long-leggedly down the High for Magpie Lane, at so
extraordinary a pace—a bus would shriek at him on the High
today—that the tradesmen along the way rightly interpreted
the bells ringing out from three towers to announce the election of a new Fellow ("I had to pay for them") and bowed

in admiration at his success and smiled in anticipation of his future favors.

His heart should have hammered with pride. He had not only wiped out the humiliation of the Schools, but raised himself at a blow from obscurity and need to competency and reputation. Instead he was overcome with shyness and modesty: he nearly sank through the floor when Keble shook hands with him. He wrote in awe to his delighted father that they addressed him as "Newman," and that he was so abashed that he could hardly bring himself to address them, in turn, as "Tyler," or "Hawkins" or "Keble." That evening he took his seat in chapel and afterwards dined with a large party in the Common Room. The date, April, 1822, may be taken as his true coming-of-age.

The ultimate effects on his mind and life were decisive. He wrote later that it "opened upon him a theological career, placing him upon the high and broad platform of University society and intelligence, bringing him across those various influences, personal and intellectual, and the teaching of those various schools of ecclesiastical thought, whereby the religious sentiment in his mind, which had been his blessing from the time he left school, was gradually developed and formed and brought on to its legitimate issues." We shall see presently what this typically cool post-cogitation meant in more human and emotional terms. The immediate effects were gratifying in another way. He could do much more, now, than write philosophically consoling letters to his parents; he could help them with money; he could help Frank, who had matriculated under his tutelage and was ready for Worcester. He wrote to his father masterfully, "Everything will—I see it will—be very right if only you will let me manage." His mother delightedly replied: "I fully accord with you when you say, Let me alone. I shall do it all well: if you will let me manage, all will be right. This is just the

text I have preached whenever your Father and I have discussed the subject. For many months I always begin and
end by saying, 'I have no fear, John will manage.' "

He did manage. How he "managed" is summed up easily.
He slaved harder than ever before. For the greater part of
that Long Vacation of 1822 he took only four hours' sleep.
Frank alone cost him, from 1821 to 1827, nearly £600. He
had four pupils at the start of 1823. He was considering
applications from two more. It was a year of such laborious
study from its beginning to its close that when he retired he
often found himself trembling with exhaustion in the bed.
He was writing learned articles. He was watching over his
sisters' education, telling Harriett to perfect her translation
of Tasso, or to work at her "Andante minor"; praising Jem,
at Strand, for her correct illustration of the generation of
asymptotic curves; asking small Mary, aged fourteen, to fill
in the words omitted in such elliptical phrases as, "The Duke,
brave as he was, shuddered," or "You are as odd a girl as ever
I saw." He felt the days and months flying past him. "And
I seem as if I would cling hold of them and hinder them from
escaping. There they lie entombed in the grave of Time,
buried with faults and failings and deeds of all sorts, never to
appear till the sounding of the last trump. . . . Keep me
from squandering Time! It is irrevocable!" When he was
ordained Deacon in June, '24, he began duties in a parish of
two thousand souls; preaching, holding services at Saint
Clement's, visiting from house to house. One day after
finishing with his pupils in the evening, he sat down to
an article on Cicero for the *Encyclopedia Metropolitana*,
worked on it until four in the morning, and then walked in
the dawn eighteen miles from Oxford to Worton to take over
the pupils of his friend Mayers who had left them in his care
while on holidays.

His father was now fading. One day in the summer of
'24 when he was walking by the river with his wife he said

to her, "I shall never see another summer." On Sunday, September 26th, 1824, his son was, for the third time, called home suddenly. The dying man recognized him, tried feebly to put out his hand, and managed to say "God bless you." The next afternoon he spoke for the last time. He could then only barely articulate, "God bless you," and "Thank my God!" His final words were "My dear . . ." On Wednesday the doctor threw in the towel. That evening all his family joined in prayer, commending his soul to God. John read out his epitaph: the 53rd Chapter of Isaiah. "A man of sorrows and acquainted with grief. . . . He was despised and we esteemed him not. . . ." They buried him in Saint Paul's graveyard, Covent Garden.[11]

It was a dim October morning, with the leaves whispering down over the greening slabs and sooty grass of the churchyard as the family returned to their York Street lodgings to take stock. There was not much stock to take. Their poverty simplified their problems. John and Frank would live in Oxford. The mother and the three girls must, somehow or other, cram into the little house at Strand-on-the-Green. When they turned to Charles they found that he was already cogitating plans of his own.

CHAPTER 5

MOTHER AND CHILDREN

1

SEVERAL years before he died John Newman had abandoned all hope for his second son. He gloomily gave it out to the family as his distinct opinion that Charlie would never make his way in the world. Soon afterwards Charlie, not without some reason in the circumstances, apparently gave up all hope of his father, and decided that the only hope for himself and for the world at large was Socialism. To his heartriven family he might just as well have declared himself an atheist, an anarchist, an abortionist, or a Roman Catholic. We will bear in mind that this was the year 1823, not 1923, when young people were mad about anarchists and abortionists, and when it was becoming smart to be a Roman Catholic, especially a wicked one. He had, in fact, gone over neck and crop to the atheistical socialism of the Welsh reformer, Robert Owen of Lanark, though he was later to break away from Owenism and, so little do things change, invent a New Moral World of his own.

What Charlie's N.M.W. revealed to this old and immoral world is now mostly lost to us. All we know of it is that his brothers considered it neither likable nor moral, and there is no record to show that it ever had many, if any, followers. He also, in later years, formed a friendship with George Jacob Holyoake, whom students of the century will recall, according to their political opinions, either as "the" agitator,

or as "an" agitator.[1] Holyoake edited a periodical trucu-
lently entitled *The Reasoner*[2] and Charles wrote for it the
sort of unintelligible articles one would expect from its title.
This alone measures the immensity of the chasm between
him and his family, especially if we remember that Holyoake
once stood in the dock in what was known as "The Last Trial
for Atheism," and was put into Gloucester Jail for public
blasphemy.

Charles was a particularly odd rationalist. When sending
Holyoake his papers on "Causation in the Universe" the poor
fellow would at times say: "My mind is leaving me and when
it returns a few months hence I will send a further paper";
like Charles Lamb's sister Mary who used to put her strait
waistcoat in her basket and go herself to the asylum when
she felt the days of her aberration approaching. Holyoake
considered him a "Naturist" and nothing more, or what
would nowadays be called an Agnostic; a mild Naturist one
feels, never so passionate as a certain, pantheistic Cornish-
man of whom Holyoake records that he could never dig a
deep well lest he should kill the heart of the world. But
these articles in *The Reasoner* do not tell us what he believed
as a young man. They are late in date, 1860 onwards.
They were mostly reprinted seven years after his death under the title *Essays in Rationalism* with a preface by Holyoake and a sympathetic little memoir by J. M. Wheeler;
which indicates that he was held in affection by his own set.

On one tenet of Owenism Charles was always crystal
clear: namely, that since character is made by circumstances
no man is responsible for his actions and should, therefore,
not be punished for them. He never lost hold of this idea.
It was his prime defense and it became his last ditch. In
the end he declared that he had been born under such dis-
advantages that he might as well give up all attempt to support himself, and informed his family that he had as much
claim in justice on them to support him as if he were bed-

ridden or a cripple. They would have saved themselves and him many years of fruitless worry and greater expense if they could have accepted this attractive, and now widely accepted, socialist principle at the outset of what he miscalled his career, and paid him a dole.

Charles was the first to break up the family circle. Immediately his father died, and the hand of authority was removed, he declared that he could not stand so religious a family a moment longer. He moved to separate lodgings and, apart from brief returns to the fold when ill, or unemployed, or feeling lonely, he lived the rest of his life away from them. We find him at 8, Charterhouse Street, opposite the old, dirty Smithfield Markets, with their smelly, open pens; at 9, Church Row, Islington; and at 53, Surrey Row, Blackfriars Road, all while he is clerking in the Bank of England. We find him teaching or studying in various parts of England, France and Germany. We constantly lose his trail. Once we pick him up again in 7, Hope Place, Bird Street, West Square (Newington-Lambeth) with a woman, lying in his shirt on a heap of straw. We find him in Boulogne and Bristol.[3]

There are times when Charles seems the most appealing of all the Newmans. Everybody agreed that he was an amusing companion when he was not an exasperating one. His old grandmother loved to have him come to Strand for a gossip. He could keep his mother and sisters in peals of laughter for a whole night. He was generous, with that old attractive Newman open-handedness which made Frank say that John scattered money like a prince; and we remember their father's lavishness. Charles once squandered nearly £1000 in a couple of months, and not on morality. All John's words about him are—his period of exhaustion and total exasperation aside—warm and generous. He says that he was sensitive, affectionate, upright; that he attached complete strangers to himself, and not briefly but over years; and that he could often argue with great fairness, moderation and clearness of intellect. Even his minor failings are appealing, such as a childlike greediness for seed-cake. And it was hard on him to have been born into that evangelical, conventional, commonsensical household. He must have been at the end of his disgust with them when he cried out in exasperation that of all the mad families in this mad country of England the maddest of the lot was his own, that the maddest person with whom he was acquainted was his brother Frank, later to be a Fellow of Worcester and Professor in University College, London, that after him he rated in point of lunacy his brother John—whom he was at that moment addressing—or if not John, then he himself; and if not himself then that great man, his revered teacher, Robert Owen of Lanark. John records this with the weariness of one who has gone far beyond saying, "We'll all be telling this as a good story in a year's time." He merely says that at times Charles did actually seem to his friends to be mad, and that at times he himself called himself so. The family twice took medical judgment on him, presumably with the idea of having him locked up.

Charles was not mad. His views, in so far as they agreed with Robert Owen's teachings, may have seemed extreme to the 1820's; but they were, at least, no more eccentric or unconventional than some of those with which Frank was to load the second-hand barrows of London—volumes on Women's Suffrage; on *Married Morality; The Errors of Jesus;* anti-vaccination tracts; *The Crimes of the House of Hapsburg; An Essay towards Reproducing the Ancient Numidian Languages out of Modern Tongues; Essays on Diet; A Collection of Poetry for the Practice of Elocution;* Kossuth translated into English, Hiawatha into Latin, and Tom Moore into Greek; on through a list which fills four jumbled pages of the British Museum catalogue. Charles' trouble lay, not in the unbalance of his brain, but in the unbalance of his

temperament.   His trouble was that he was at once sensitive
and ineffectual, which is one of the worst possible dishar-
monies in any man.   All would have been well had he been
ineffectual and insensitive about it; or, like his brother John,
sensitive but effective.   As it was, he developed a colossally
preposterous pride, which was patently no more than a hopeless kind of self-compensation.

What enormous differences can be produced within a family of identical background and like temperament by the
slightest alteration of emphasis!   It is a thought which often
occurs to one when listening-in to the Newmans.   The
brothers were all egocentric to a high degree.   John was the
most egocentric of the three, deeply introspective, constantly
self-concerned, tirelessly self-recording.   The next world re-
volved round him; but that it was the next and not this was
his salvation, since his doubts about his soul's future induced
humility in his body's present, a check which he fully
needed, since he had an abundance of self-conceit.   Charles
was without this check of humility.   He had nothing to be
humble about.   He merely had enough to be foolishly conceited about.   It was this dropsical conceit that stimulated
him to insult everybody who dared to wish him well, or was
so unwise as to try to save him from his favorite delusion
that he was everyman's equal.   John was fully aware of the
danger to Charles of this sad delusion, which he unsmilingly
called "a vivid notion."   He suffered many an insult from
Charles in the effort to save him from it.   One gets the impression that John loved him more than he loved Frank, and
he appears to have loved him to the end.   After all, each of
them was in his own way unfitted for "this pragmatical pig
of a world."

For the moment we may install him as clerk in the Bank
of England.   There John, through his friend Bowden, whose
father was a director, managed to secure him a post in
December, 1825, "humiliating himself" to ask for it, accord-

ing to Frank. The Bank's records[4] give his religion as "Church of England." The directors little knew the awful truth! He said he had kept his father's books at Alton, the father being listed as a brewer, but not as a bankrupt. He diplomatically mentioned that he was weak from a recent fever, but now much recovered. He was single, free from debt, belonging to no club, with a fair handwriting and ready at accounts. He began at a salary of £60 a year, and was happy enough for about a year and a half, when we shall find him in serious trouble for the first but far from the last time in his exceedingly troubled life. It hardly needs mentioning that he is then assailing one of his best benefactors. But what was that to Charles? Somewhat later on he will be found assailing the entire Bank of England.

2

Harriett, now twenty-one, pink-cheeked, blue-eyed, hair in long curls, was the prettiest, much the most intelligent, and by far the most independent minded of the Newman girls. Perhaps it was because she was so independent that she never became quite as intimate with John as her more gentle sister Jemima. She stood up to him. They sparred with one another. They sometimes hurt one another. She called him, in half-joke whole-earnest, Mr. Worldly Wiseman, implying that he was a Mr. Know All, to which he might well have replied with a *tu quoque*. He did call her a Miss Minx, and a Miss Spitfire, affectionately. Once he said, less affectionately, that she was full of perversions but could not really help it. Once she told him he was lacking in respect. Harriett probably quizzed him more than he liked. Frank said of her that "she was not like Jemima, charming to everybody; to some she could speak disagreeable truths plainly," and he surmised painful collisions between her and John; he suggests, too, that she may have pained him by sharper words than we might guess.   In both surmises he was correct.

Did John ever realize sufficiently how much their poverty and the limitations of duty cost his sisters?   Harry was twenty-one in the December of her father's death, but to be twenty-one did not mean emancipation for a young woman in the age of George IV.   She would fill most dutifully for the next twelve years the ordained role of the eldest daughter of a widowed mother.   Her rests would be her respites, though she will not feel them as respites because she is a dutiful child of her times and she has a zestful interest in all types of people, and life has taught her how to entertain herself.   Anyway, who ever notices that youth is going until youth is gone?   Immediately her mother dies she will wake up with a bang, find herself thirty-three and seize her liberty so avidly that John will be shocked at her incontinence, and speak of her weak sense of duty.

There was a barrier between them: her warm temperament, the thing given, the act of God that ground her so hard and clear, like a lens.   Or is it merely that there is in every woman a man-frustrated dream: the womb's tithe, the midwife's toll?   Perhaps she was one of these pre-emancipation women who in a more liberal society would have lived actively and bored everybody.   And Harriett was more lucky than most!   She produced her little books; she ultimately married; she became a mother.   While she waited for these things she saw too clearly, spoke too sharply.   Her letters are by far the most graphic of all the Newman letters, and the most human.   They alone give us hard, bright thumbnails of days and people.   She had a Gallic streak.   She and John would inevitably knock sparks off each other, and sooner or later sheer apart.

When brothers and sisters diverge they diverge utterly. So much that is shared in childhood cries out against so little

that is shared after it.   The stay-at-home thinks, "We have
everything in common.   I understand you better than anybody else."   The wanderer, whose glass is always filling and
refilling, knows that this "everything" is constantly dwin-
dling.   Once again it is the divergences between John and
his family, not the correspondence, that fascinate us.   It is
his search for meekness that chiefly distinguishes him from
Harriett.

Harriett scorned humility.   She once spoke about one
George Shuttleworth, a friend of Aunt Pownall at Totten-
ham, as "full of bad *ethos.*"   This word, by the way, she
borrowed from John, who introduced it into the English
language.   She added that Mr. Shuttleworth's bad *ethos*
lacked even "the amicable excuse of pride."   The world was
important to Harriett.   She was the most earthy of the Newmans.   From this arose her insistence that people should
come clean.   She loathed evasive silences.   She proudly refers several times to her success in drawing some shy man out
of himself; though she might then, in a characteristic phrase
of her own, "give him a good trimming."   At a party she
could always, again her own phrase, "hold the balance of
power."   Her constant technique was to challenge.   She
still does.   One is eager to come to grips with her.   Her danger was that, in her unguarded conceit, she might squeeze
her orange dry and lose the juice.   Once she reduced Hurrell Froude to silence and was pleased as punch with herself.
Who else would not have preferred to hear Froude talk?

She could be more than cool about her kindest and best
friends.   After enjoying the hospitality of John's friends the
Rickards, at Ulcombe, she feels arrogantly that Lucy Rickards is daring to write too often.   "I begin to be quite tired
of the sights of Lucy's 'Miss Newman, (c/o) Mr. Giberne
Esq.'"   When Lucy refers to her husband as Samuel she
makes the name absurd by putting it in inverted commas

like the wrinkles of a smile. She quotes Lucy that "Samuel" will persuade John to stay with them "by *wise* talk." Her underlining is a shrug. When Lucy promises to introduce her to some dear friends she cries, "What plagues these Rickards are!" (However, when Mary told John that Sam Rickards was planning to learn the piano even John gave a "malicious" laugh, and this is gentle Mary's adjective. Another time he laughed "queerly" at Samuel.) When another Rickards friend, "poor old Cobi," became engaged Harriett says, dryly, "He is in the highest spirits, and her father, and his father are all pleased and I suppose it will all go on as smoothly as romance could possibly desire; that is to say, after a score of years waiting for a living, the young and blooming couple will be transformed into the fat rector and his worthy wife."

From this visit to the Rickards at Ulcombe she sent home a good-humored quiz of John which shows them at their happiest. Having characteristically trimmed one of John's friends, Bowden—she says he has put off John's visit because he must go to Italy; "to study Law I suppose," she sniffs prettily—she goes on: "By the bye John is at times so very troublesome that I am obliged to say, 'Master John! Do be quiet! I never saw anything like you. If you are so obstreperous I must tell your mamma, sir!' He is always singing *Lucy Dear*. I am quite alarmed and make him give an account of where he has been and whom he has been talking with whenever he leaves me . . ." And then she tells how he and she and Lucy Rickards were all set off laughing for a full five minutes because John wanted to bury a couple who would have preferred to get married; and then tried to marry the wrong couple, who would thereby have been twice married; and then tried to marry the right couple in the wrong name. One wishes that they could often have been as merry as this.

3

I think the two younger girls, Jemima and Mary, were at first in closer confidence with one another than with Harriett, and all three closer to one another than with John.   Jem and Mary probably kept little things secreted from Harry, though it was probably very difficult to deceive that eagle, elderly eye.   ("To show H. that I *can* keep a secret from her," Mary writes, "I will tell *you* one.   I am writing some verses.") This little conspiracy of intimacy would be natural.   There was only a year between Jem and Mary; and Mary was six years younger than Harriett.   But I think, too, that this changed after their papa died.   Before this Harriett is still valiantly sealing her letters with a little lantern and the hopeful motto, "Brighter Hours Will Come."   When he is gone, the little lantern is blown out, and her seal becomes a plain black oval bearing the one word, "Harriett."   The three girls seem to come closer together, as if for comfort.   In the May following they are huddled closer still by another loss: Grandmamma died at Strand, aged ninety-one.   Harriett now ends her letters to Jem, "Believe me my dear little Cat (Jemima Catherine), your affectionate Bird."   She calls Mary her "woodcock" and her "woodrose."   Mary calls Jem, "Mum, dear mum."   They are like three small girls holding hands in the dark.

4

Frank (now a student in Worcester College; paid for by John) had for some time been gravely perturbed for his brother's eternal salvation.

Francis had already observed the danger-signs before he inherited the low arcades, the crescent pool, and wide fields of Worcester, at that time on the outskirts of Oxford.   They

were then in lodgings off the High, at Palmer's in Merton
Lane, that alley-way from the High to Merton which all the
efforts of the Oxford authorities have never prevented from
being better known to all Oxonians as Magpie Lane, after a
dear-departed but unforgotten Oxford whore. In these
dusty lodgings—convenient to Oriel, where Frank dined at
the Buttery—there lived also an interesting character, Blanco
White, a former Catholic priest, escaped alike from Spain
and Rome. John played violin duets with Blanco, and
when they tired of music the two elders would sit down to
long theological discussions. The seventeen-year-old Frank
gradually began to give ear to these arguments, and soon
noted, in dismay, that they had a way of ending up with the
sharp warning from Blanco to John: "Beware, Newman! If
you follow that clue it will draw you into Catholic error!"
By this he meant, or, so Frank understood him, self-flagella-
tion and the maceration of the body for sinful thoughts and
the like. Once more what a narrow line, one thinks, can
divide the most antagonistic beliefs! Calvinism can apparently slip over into Catholicism by a mere shift of emphasis!
It can also happen the other way round, as such heresies as
Jansenism show.

Frank's suspicions presently received a shocking proof.
One day, in the autumn of '24, as he was busily arranging
his furniture in his new rooms he saw, to his horror, an en-
graving of the Blessed Virgin hanging on the wall. This
picture now hangs in the Cardinal's bedroom in the Oratory
at Birmingham: it is Correggio's "La Madonna col Divoto."
It is not a straight-forward picture of the Virgin, who is only
a part of the picture, appearing, after the Italian convention,
in a *nuovole* or cloud of glory, high above a group of men-
dicants in the foreground. But Frank saw nothing except
the idol. He went off hot-foot to remonstrate with the print-
shop. There the shopman explained that Mr. John Henry
Newman had ordered the picture. Hot-foot Frank went

back to John, and the fatal collision occurred. John mildly
quoted, "Blessed art thou amongst women." Frank retorted
that Christ had said to like words from another woman, "Yea,
rather, blessed are they who hear the word of God and keep
it." He insisted that our Lord thereby disapproved of hon-
ors being paid to His mother.

"And, in any event, my dear John," he cried rationally, as
if one could be rational about such matters, "what is the
use of invoking a being who cannot hear you? The Virgin
is not omnipresent!"

We may imagine John's delicate reply. When Frank gave
a Low Church snort at this "whimsicality," John could only
indicate that the meaning of the New Testament is not complete without the gloss of subsequent tradition. He then
quietly removed his gift, and kept it all his life. Many years
after when Frank recorded the incident he still felt the
breach poignantly. It became unhealable when John was
ordained in the following May. "The Church was now
everything to him," Frank sighed. "To me it was nothing!"
And, he goes on to say that henceforth they "seemed never to
have an interest or a wish in common."

Was Frank being willfully obtuse? Or, again, merely being aridly rational? Surely, to be ordained a priest—how
could his imagination so fail him as not to realize it?—must
be a searing, even a frightening experience for any man.
When we think of the long preparation, the many doubts,
the growing awareness of the extent of the human sacrifice
demanded, the tug-of-war between the flesh and the spirit,
the frightening sense of finality, absolute as death, surrounding the ultimate decision, and think, then, of the immense
spiritual responsibilities to others that a young man of
twenty-five feels himself called on to assume, we may well
believe that anybody so vibratingly, so exquisitely, so self-
tormentingly sensitive as John Newman, so aware by his
nature of the thinness of this mortal veil, must have felt the

ordeal as terrifying as if, like Lazarus, he must die to the world only to come back and suffer it again.

He said as much, speaking of his "terror" at the finality and obligation of his vow. He had written then in his Private Journal: "It is over! At first when the hands were laid on me my heart shuddered within me. The words 'For ever' are so terrible." He was still trembling the next day: "For Ever! Words never to be recalled. I have the responsibility of souls on me to the day of my death." If we do not sensitively understand this we will, like Frank, understand nothing of his utterly devoted, self-sacrificing life; we will, like Frank, dig a chasm between us and the tremulous movements, the immovable motives of his soul.

If, in thus looking back to the middle twenties, Frank implies that he and John henceforth formed a truce of non-cooperation and tactful silence his memory is also astray. He was still helping John in his parochial duties four or five years later. Indeed, so little aware was John that there had been any "collision" at all that when Frank came of age, in June, '26, he wrote him a birthday offering of some characteristically sincere, and characteristically ingenuous verses calling on him to take Holy Orders forthwith in grateful memory of their dear grandmother:—

> In her affection all had share,
>   All six, she loved them all;
> Yet on her early-chosen Pair
>   Did her full favour fall . . .
>
> So it is left for us to prove
>   Her prayers were not in vain:
> And that God's grace-according love
>   Has fall'n as gentle rain . . .
>
> Dear Frank, we both are summon'd now
>   As champions of the Lord;—

Enroll'd am I, and shortly thou
Must buckle on the Sword;

A high employ not lightly given,
To serve as messengers of heaven!

Frank rejected the embarrassing invitation, as he well
might since he presently came to the point of rejecting the
whole basis of the Church of England, the Thirty-Nine Articles. He had subscribed to them in order to be admitted to
the University, he had admitted their "classical and spiritual
beauty," but he soon saw that very few academicians believed in them. "I felt," he says, with his usual downright-
ness, "that the system of compulsory subscription was hollow, false and wholly evil."

This decision nicely illustrates the essential difference between the two brothers. John would also come up against
the Articles. He would walk cautiously all around them,
take them one by one in his delicate fingers, fray them apart
with subtle care, and write a pamphlet, to be known for ever
as "Tract 90," whose burthen was that the earliest Fathers of
the Church could have accepted almost any of the articles
since they were all subject to interpretation in the light of the
tempers, times and intentions of their authors, who were, he
considered it hardly deniable, bred, born and dyed in the old
Catholic tradition. Not that the result for both was not
much the same. Frank abandoned the Church of England
because he could not accept the Articles. John's proof of
the acceptability and Catholicism of the first reformers astonished the entire Church of England so much that it went
far to astonish John himself out of it.

5

There were other clashes between the two brothers.
Frank told all about it later in a book called *Phases of Faith,*

which was his *Apologia Pro Vita Sua.* (This writing of *Apologias* was a fashion of the 19th century; some of them, like those of Augustus William and Julius Charles Hare, uncles of that tireless traveller A. J. C. Hare, had a considerable popularity.) One clash that he describes here had to do with the episcopacy, and his account is very revealing both of himself and of John:—

"I had," Frank recalls, "on one occasion dropt something disrespectful about bishops or a bishop. . . . My brother checked and reproved me—as I thought very uninstructively—for 'wanting reverence towards Bishops.' I knew not then, and I know not now, why Bishops, *as such*, should be more reverenced than common clergymen; or clergymen, *as such*, more than common men. In the world I expected pomp, and vain show, and formality and counterfeits: but of the Church, as Christ's own kingdom, I demanded reality and could not digest legal fictions. I saw round me what sort of young men were preparing to be clergymen: I knew the attractions of family livings, and of a respectable position and undefinable hopes of preferment. I knew further, that when youths had become clergymen through a great variety of mixed motives, bishops were selected out of these clergymen on avowedly political grounds. . . . In the last century and a half the nation was often afflicted with sensual royalty, bloody wars, venal statesmen, corrupt constituencies, bribery and violence at elections, flagitious drunkenness pervading all ranks and insinuating itself into colleges and rectories. The prisons of the country had been in a most disgraceful state; the fairs and wakes were scenes of rude debauchery; and the theatres were, still in this nineteenth century, whispered to be haunts of the most debasing immorality. I could not learn that any bishop had ever taken the lead in denouncing these iniquities. . . ."

And so he goes on through the oppression of India and the sanction of native superstitions throughout the Empire to a crescendo of contemptuous denunciation of the entire Anglican hierarchy.

It was doubtless in such differences as this that John became consumed with his "violent and sullen" rages.   We can
see by what Frank has written that his feelings, also, were
deeply stirred.   Yet, in describing John's inability to discuss
this matter calmly he was quite calm.   How could he in this
be so cool and John so heated?   The explanation seems to be
that they felt with a different set of emotions, and that John's
were by far the more incandescent and all-consuming.   Both
were idealists, but John was basically a mystic or a man of
faith, whereas Frank was basically a moralist, or a man of
good works.   The distinction is ancient, widespread and
vital.   It is not that the man of faith is not a moral man, or
that the man of morals has no faith.   Indeed in some things
John's morality was far more insistent than Frank's, and in
some Frank's faith far more independent of all moral forms
than John's.   It is that in this old rivalry between spirit and
good works, between the religion of transcendentalism and
the religion of good behavior, between a mind fundamentally
Catholic and a mind constitutionally Protestant, priorities
must ultimately declare themselves.   Frank was at bottom a
humanitarian and reformer, John was not really interested in
India, or drunkenness, or prisons, or fairs, or wakes, or, indeed, in human welfare at all.   Catholics rarely are.   Frank
assails the worldly indifference of the Church with all guns
blazing.   John would one day survey the whole panorama of
the corruptions and weaknesses of the Roman Church, and
speak gently of "a vast and ever-growing imperial church
great enough to make flaws and imperfections of no account."   One wonders what poor Savonarola would have
said to that, as he twisted on a rope's end over the fire at the
command of Pope Alexander VI?   What Frank would have
said we may guess.

And, yet, see how unexpectedly all this works out in practice.   As between two such men we might think off-hand
that the more transcendental of the two would inevitably

have the lesser interest in organization, buildings, history, ritual, in all that which the Evangelical calls "carnal religion." It does not go that way at all. The mystic needs a globe to contain his heavenly light. The moral man sees himself as his own vessel. The mystic projects his faith in form; the moralist in reform. So, Quakers are no churchmen, Nonconformists are low churchmen, a Gothic Cathedral is carnal and a tin chapel is spiritual. Yet all will say that our bodies are tabernacles of the Holy Ghost and that God is within us. Again we are watching a slight shift of emphasis in which everything is seen *à travers*.

We may understand now how the brothers could talk on together, and even do church-work together after the breach. They would not see that though they worked side by side they were worlds apart. Their talk henceforth is, as Frank says, only on the surface. On some questions he is overpowered and receives a temporary bias from John's superior knowledge. As he matures he begins to resent what he considers his brother's "fine-drawn and subtle arguments," until his own blunt arguments begin to sound more and more like a prerehearsal for Kingsley.

The upshot of it all was that Frank felt he must only cast himself "on Him who is named the Father of Lights and resolve to follow the light which He might give." The unforeseen and extraordinary results of this reliance on the Father of Will-o'-the-Wisps was, as we shall see in due course, that he became a Plymouth Brother, and went to Bagdad to convert the Muslims to Darbyism.

6

Time made these tensions chronic, and the result was inevitable. Sooner or later every family dies. Nobody notices the symptoms when they occur. Families cannot diagnose themselves. It is only their biographies that reveal

them in the autopsy. For years to come this divided family
would feel itself solid, healthy, happy, unassailable, and if
these years lengthened out to many, and to many, the credit
must largely go to Mrs. Newman, the intermediary between
them all.

Few mothers can have had so devoted a family; as she
often gladly and gratefully admitted. "Dear loved ones de-
parted, and *dears* now possessed who are ever desirous of
sacrificing too much for me." John especially had been "the
silent pride" of her early life. His role now was to be the
guide and comfort of her age. His generosity was bound-
less. Her income was tiny, a bare £150 from her dowry of
£5000 invested in the Funds at three per cent. He be-
stowed so much upon her out of his earnings at Oxford that
she was at time frightened at his lavishness; and he was simultaneously sending his aunt constant doles to keep her
rickety concern at Strand-on-the-Green from following in the
steps of his father's brewery and tavern. He had to cope,
too, with his mother's little conspiracies with Aunt Betsy.
Once, in writing home, he encloses £1 for Cary's *Road Book*
and some Tincture of Spanish Pellitory (*Anacyclus Pyre-
thrum*), which he found soothing for the toothache, and
adds: "I much regret to observe by your not sending it that
you have not the means. I would certainly send something
by this parcel except that I knew that you would at once
part with it, and however much I may *wish* I cannot send it
for the mere sake of assisting in the quarter in which you
would dispose of it"—that is the bottomless pit of Strand-on-
the-Green. He set only one limitation as to what he could
give his family, that it should not prevent him from giving
away, also, one-tenth or one-sixth of his income in charity.

If his kindness to his mother had any fault it was that it
was indiscreetly excessive. He raised hopes that, built as he
was, he could never fulfil. One example will do: his pre-

tense that he wanted to be near her when, as he confessed in the event, he knew in his heart that it would be better if he kept her at a distance. Thus, when he was pressing her, in the summer of '26, to spend his money on making a home for herself all his persuasions were to the effect that he wanted her to do it for *him;* that *he* needed a house; and that Frank did too, though Frank never expressed such a need. She took him at his word—a home to her meant only a home near him—saying of Frank that he was "a piece of adamant" but, "You are such a sensitive being."

She did not see that a man may be kind, and sensitive, and generous beyond measure, and yet have a great and proper egocentricity of his own. Wanting him as much as she did she could not have been so objective. She did not believe him when he tried to clarify his wishes by saying that one reason why he wished her to have a house was his own "selfishness," meaning that he could not afford to lose the Long Vacation. "I *must* be busy. *I must not be idle!*" We know she did not believe him because in the end he had to be brutally explicit about it. Besides, had he not assured her that he was also thinking of his sisters? "Why should my sisters be immured," he had asked, thinking of that crowded, damp little house on the river's edge, "to the injury of their health?" And had he not also said that he was not in his proper element away from them? So, although she told him that she would be perfectly happy anywhere— so long as she had good air, and rustic entertainment, and might enjoy his society "as circumstances permit"—a rather sad little comedy developed between mother and son. He began to look at houses in Sussex. She began to look at houses in London. Tactfully, neither of them began to look at houses in or near Oxford.

The natural result was that while she dutifully compared the houses she and Mary had inspected in Bayswater, Kensington, Hammersmith and Fulham with those which he had approved in Worthing or Brighton, she was still, a whole year later, hesitating between two of his houses at Brighton where, remembering happy childhood days, he had been an assiduous explorer. He was ultimately to lead her to Eastern Terrace, Marine Square, Brighton. She took the house with reservations, to which he acceded: she would sublet it every summer—she needed the money. She never did live there consistently, nor did she make a real home for her girls until she had her way and made it near Oxford and him.

There was, we must feel, one other shadow of blame attaching to him for those family jars. He was, after all, the head of the house. As head of the house there was a frailty in him for which, at all times, especially in later life, he would pay the price of a deep unhappiness. He had the poet's and the thinker's preference for solitude rather than sociability. He was a man of such spiritual and intellectual detachment from the world, whose thought falls on our misty earth like a beam of sunlight between the clouds, a Jacob's ladder into heaven, that it was never easy for him to contact common flesh. Even inside his family circle he was all too rarely gay, flippant, idly sociable. He would have made either a very poor kind of husband, or a completely self-effacing one.

He was so very solemn! When Jem was down in Kent one September enjoying herself with the Rickards he wrote to her, sending his love, and then went on:

"As I am on this subject let me remind you, though you hardly need reminding, that some danger always attends that promiscuous intercourse with society which such visits necessarily involve. We are so apt to be led away, to become fond of worldly things and to imbibe feelings hostile to spiritual religion that it is well to be doubly careful in examining ourselves and watching our thoughts and actions when we are in new and pleasing company . . ."

Very true, one may think. But was it cheerfully timed?

So, when he cries: "Oh, how I love them!"—he confides the dear thought to his Diary. "So much do I love them," he wrote on, in a not unusual mésalliance of humility and egocentricity, "that I cannot help thinking Thou wilt either take them hence, or take me from them, because I am so set on them." An unkind God, this, whom he has, in his terror, conjured up? But how rarely, alas, not more than two or three times, does he write like this for *them* to read!

Possibly none of the Newmans was given to speaking out, as we might gather from the phrasing of one of the few letters in which, after his sister Mary's death, he suddenly burst his dam of silence:—"Dear Jemima, I know you love me much, though your disposition does not lead you to say much about it, and I love you, too, and you (I trust) know it." Some ten years later when his mother died, he wept that he knew well that she had loved him as he had loved her, but "often when I had no means of showing it"; and he recalled, in misery, what happened one evening when he had fainted, probably from over-work and opened his eyes to find her stooping tenderly to raise his feet to the sofa. To her pained astonishment he had started away from her, unable to endure her kind touch: and "endure" is his own peculiar word. "I saw she was hurt, yet I did not know how to set things right. . . ." All he could say was that he "always had some sort of dread or distress" which he could not define, "of being the object of attention." Over and over again he proved his practical love for his mother, brothers and sisters. He proved his utter unselfishness in every conceivable way. Face to face with their love he suffered from some sad inhibition. There are times when, were it not for the poetry in his nature and the lovely delicacy of his sensibilities, one might be reminded of the later Augustine; since, with Augustine, too, there is a mother and that tender, moving scene in the embrasure of the window. Yet, who will ever want to say, "Poor Augustine!" And how often do we not say, "Poor Newman!" His frailty meant that he was doomed always to be buffeted by the sociable iron pots, the gregarious, clubbable, political men to whom such delicate creatures as he are always child's play.

CHAPTER 6

JOHN AT ORIEL

1

ROM the first these sensibilities told against him in Oriel
F where he had begun his career as Fellow after the Long
Vacation of '22. From his letters and memoirs we can see
him vividly in the winter of '23. He presents a Spartan
picture: a lean, handsome, bespectacled figure paddling in
thin shoes down the slushy High, his soft lips closed against
the rain, the wind whipping his gown about his knee-
breeches, his big nose bowed into the storm. All his days
were Spartan. He was still in lodgings. In that snowy
winter when the Cherwell nearly flooded Christ Church
walk, he started work with the dawn. For relaxation he
rode into the country, where the rivers were dangerously
swollen and whole trees were being uprooted by the winds.
The regimen seemed to agree with him. "I am getting fat.
I would not be surprised if I were to come home a monster
. . . Tell Frank the trousers wants airing." His mental
spirits also seemed good. He told the family all his news,
who was visiting Oxford, what elections were pending, what
lectures he was attending, news of his parish-work, what he
was writing. He snatched one day in London to see them
"before I am nailed down in Oxford." In December he told
them that he had moved into the College and dined in the
Common Room. His mother and his sisters would read
those letters of '23, '24 and '25 in admiration. They would

see their big brother at Oxford dining in state with the Provost and the Fellows, bandying philosophical epigrams with them, astonishing them by his apt classical quotations, the coming man at Oriel.

In fact he was the Common Room blight. His arrival there had thrown the Fellows into dismay. They found him as shy and tongue-tied as a village boy. They found— his own admission in his own words about himself—that he had not a grain of conviviality in his composition. What, they must have asked themselves, what on earth had they done to draw on themselves this gauche, silent, myopic, solitary, awkward troglodyte! [1]　A rabid Evangelical with tracts stuffed into his pocket, objecting to the theater, considering drunkenness as great a crime almost as murder, troubled with a sense of guilt when he so far forgot the sanctity of the Sabbath as to breakfast with a Dean! He himself must have suffered agonies, writing miserably in his diary, "I *must* find some way to explain to the Fellows about my wish to keep Sunday holy," so sensitive that "the painful and ridiculous sense of shame I have on light occasions . . . is like a sword running through me." When he gave his first University sermon "I lay on the sofa writhing at the thought of what a fool I had made of myself." The long silences were for safety. The solitary rides were for solace. Never is it more plain that the man was unfitted by his exquisitely sensitive nature to mingle with men, and that in learning how to do it he won a painful victory over himself.

We may as well admit it. More than his sensibilities were against him. His shabby-genteel origins and dim social backgrounds were also against him. We can see it when he admits to "days of acute suffering from the recollection of solecisms, real or imagined, which he recognised in his conduct in society." One curls up for him when the Provost, in the full hearing of the Fellows, leans down the table and says, "Mr. Newman, we do *not* serve sweetbreads with a spoon. Manciple, bring a blunt knife." We cannot fail to relate such incidents to the solitary walks. They remind me of an unlucky friend in a provincial town who was persuaded against his judgment to take part in amateur theatricals and for weeks after would creep about the side-streets murmuring, "Oh, God! Please make them forget!"

He knew well that among all his colleagues and associates he alone was not by origin a gentleman. Provost Hawkins could trace his line back through nine generations to gentle blood. Denison's father had been to Eton. Whately had been born in Cavendish Square. Hurrell Froude's father was an archdeacon, and he had been to Eton. Robert Wilberforce came of an old, wealthy Yorkshire family; his father had been to Cambridge and had refused a peerage. Dornford's father was a writer who had been to Trinity and Göttingen. Jelf, the son of Sir James Jelf, was an Eton man. Keble's father was a learned vicar. And so on. Thomas Arnold had, perhaps, the least distinguished origin of them all—his father a Collector of Customs—but even he had been through Winchester. These, and others not of Oriel, like Marriott from Rugby and Williams from Harrow, were his associates with whom he must mingle, now or later, as closely as men do in a monastery. Being gentlemen they would give no sign; perhaps not in the least care what his origins were; but he would give the signs—as with the unfortunate sweetbreads; he would care; he would feel behind him all the time the Clerkenwell tavern-cum-brewhouse, the dreadful secret of the Bankruptcy Court, so painful to him that he tried to keep it from posterity, the rickety establishment at Strand-on-the-Green, the *House to Let* notice in the windows at Brighton, the fact that he had no steady home where he could freely invite his friends. "After my father's death in 1824 I have had no home but Oxford and Birmingham."

He labored under another disadvantage. It was a very simple one, but in its correction it had a profound effect, one might say a dominating effect on his life. He had never done Logic. Now, the Oriel Common Room, it was said in Oxford, "stank of logic." This must have been largely due to Whately, who was a pioneer in this subject. What this meant, in the experience of it, is that the conversation of these "Noetics," as they were nicknamed, was to those who like that sort of conversation the most brilliant conversation in Oxford; and to those who did not it was a thorough bore.

If we look through the notebooks and memoranda of Hurrell Froude, who was to become John's most intimate friend and who exercised a deep influence over him, lasting beyond the grave, we can form an idea of the sort of conversation into which John was suddenly plunged. For example, Froude asks himself: "Is the absolution of a priest necessary, because comfort cannot be obtained without it; or cannot comfort be obtained without it because it is necessary? Is its expediency the cause or effect of goodness?" Such a question thrashed out in all its aspects would mean an application of logic to mental, or may one say, to spiritual processes, whose subtlety, when he grasped the technique, enchanted Newman—all his dialectic, all his spiritual search is colored by it—but until he found his feet in it he would be tongue-tied.

There is another very charming passage in Froude whose Proustian quality shows us how this analytical habit opened up these men's souls:

"Yesterday, before breakfast, while the vacancy produced by fasting was still on me, and I was reading the Psalms, and craving for a comprehension of things which I could only look on as words, and was worked up to such a pitch that I felt trying to see my soul, and make out how it was fitted to receive an impression from them—Merton bell began to go. And it struck me, I cannot tell why, that if such a trifle as that could give me such a vivid idea, my soul must be an intricate thing; and that when senses were given to the blind part of it, what things would those appear the apprehension of which I was struggling after. This is as near what passed in my mind as I can find expression to shape my memory by. This blindness of heart is what, by habit and patience, it is our work practically to remove. We are to shape our souls for its removal by making it in harmony with things invisible."

This, I think gives a clear clue to the processes of mind and soul not only of Newman but of the whole Movement he was to evoke. It indicates what the Oriel Common Room had to offer him when he had once found the trick of developing and elaborating their logic, of adapting it to his own needs as an artist and a mystic. One of the greatest attractions—perhaps the great attraction of the adult Newman— is this blending of intellect and poetry, of brains and imagination.

In the end the Fellows handled their problem very simply. They handed him over to Whately, who shook his thought out of him as a midwife bangs a baby to make it breathe. Whately to Newman was what Sam Johnson would have been to Shelley. A great talker, coarse in his ways, some of them unfastidious, "nasty" is Burgon's word, such as his habit of keeping a line of herrings on a string, like washing, in his wardrobe in order to pluck one off every morning and throw it on the coals for breakfast. Rough, dogmatic, speculative and original, he used his young probationer as an anvil on which to beat out his own ideas. He knocked him about in lusty argument, he threw work at his head, he discussed with him his projected *Elements of Logic,* so profitably to both of them that when he published the book he particularized Newman as having composed a considerable part of it from early drafts. By these rugged methods he drew his bashful companion out of his shell. Newman puts the date at 1826. "I came out of my shell," he said of that year. "I remained out of it till 1841." The breaking-in

lasted only a few months, but since it was at a time when
Whately was full of the subject of logic—so the published
preface to his *Elements* declares—as a weapon wherewith
to defend religious Truth by sound reasoning, Newman could
say of his trainer, "He taught me to think correctly and to
rely upon myself." It is a sign of the bigness of both men
that they liked one another. Newman did not mind, in
Whately's phrase, being held up by one leg without yelping
like a King Charles spaniel. Whately was soon able to
assure the troubled Common Room that their Fellow, behind
his silence and his shyness, was the clearest-headed man he
had ever met.

His own private notes about his companions are doubly
interesting. They are cool and shrewd. They are also
dimly impersonal. Where a man like Burgon presents
Hawkins and others to us by means of telling details and
graphic anecdotes, as Tuckwell does with Whately, or as
Denison does with Drury, or as Mozley does with Rickards,
Newman is always the abstract intellectual. This is his
picture of Hawkins: "He was clearheaded and independent
in his opinions, tolerant of the views of others, honest as a
religious enquirer, though not without something of self-
confidence in his enunciations." From which we can see
that though he might not know how to touch the confidence
of his colleagues he could understand their minds. Or,
again, we note his old trick of intellectualizing experience
when he writes epigrams on Whately, Hawkins and on himself, in the manner of a 17th century writer of Characters:

"Hawkins is so clear that he cannot enter into difficulties or
sympathise with those who have them. Whately writes for those
who are below him in intellect. Hawkins for those who are
above him. Hawkins and Newman are both acute: but Hawkins
from quickness of sight, Newman from quickness of logic. He is
slow in investigation but is so clearsighted that he has no need of

it.   Newman evolves so quickly that he cannot recollect what his
first sight was.   Newman is cautious for fear of turning out
wrong; Hawkins from coolness of head and dispassionateness."

All of which is good, cool and remote.   Not so remote,
however, as he had hitherto been.   He is slowly ceasing to
be an isolate.

2

If we did not know all this about his embarrassments and
inner struggles, what a deceptively peaceful picture we
might begin to form when he says, speaking of Provost
Hawkins and himself:—"Then during the Long Vacations of
1824–'25, we were day after day in the Common Room all by
ourselves, and in Christ Church meadow."   It is deep summer, the long, unbroken Oxford emptiness.   The two men
are talking softly in the empty Common Room with the sun
slanting dustily across its ponderous quiet, or strolling before
dinner in those widespread meadows whose willow-leaves
John would never forget, past Merton, and Corpus, and the
cathedral's squat yellow and sable tower, and Magdalen top-
ping the trees of Merton Grove,² and nothing to break the
sunlit vacancy of Broad Walk except a nursemaid or a resting
visitor.   It seems a perfect image of what somebody once
called "cis-Paradisian Oxford," before motor-cars, and planes,
and villas, and industries and the Bradmore Road changed
the face of Zion.

We know that these murmuring hours are vocational, in-
tensely lived.   For Hawkins was just as effective as Whately
in influencing Newman.   In that '25 he was thirty-six, the
younger man twenty-four, and the admiration that the
younger man was forming for his senior's intellect is evi-
denced by the fact that two years later he preferred him, as
Provost, to the great Keble himself:

"I have lived," he told Keble, "more with Hawkins than with any other Fellow, and have thus had opportunities for understanding him more than others. His general views so agree with my own, his practical notions, religious opinions and habits of thinking that I feel vividly and powerfully the advantages the College would gain when governed by one who, pursuing ends which I cordially approve, would bring to the work powers of mind to which I have long looked up with great admiration." [3]

Years afterwards he said, "I love him and have never ceased to love him." Those admired powers were a second hone to sharpen John Newman's mind.

One special theory of Hawkins' was vital to his development.[4] As far back as 1818 the Provost had embodied certain views about the nature of Christian thought, in a sermon given from the University pulpit, which stressed the importance of apparently unauthoritative tradition for a full understanding of what Christ had actually said. John Newman had heard this sermon as an undergraduate. Hawkins now propounded its ideas again and gave it to John to read. He tells us in his *Apologia* that these ideas made "a most serious impression" on him. It could plausibly be maintained that his final conversion to Rome stems from that moment.

The core of Hawkins' theory is to be found in nine words of the first sentence of Saint Luke. "Forasmuch as many have taken in hand to set forth in order a declaration of *those things which are most surely believed among us* . . . it seemed good to me also to write unto thee, excellent Theophilus." What Luke meant by "those things," Hawkins explained, is that contextual knowledge about Christ's teachings which successive generations received by word of mouth as unwritten tradition. This was a revelation to John. Like Frank he had been inducted by Mayers into the Evangelicals' exclusive reliance on the printed word of the Bible. He now saw in this broad theory all history opening up new vistas before him, as if in Time's mansion folding-doors were being rolled back before his eyes, century after century, until the lengthening perspective closed at last on the radiant figure of the Redeemer speaking to his first disciples. He saw, in Hawkins' words, how it had been "the general design of Heaven that by oral or traditional instructions, the way should be prepared for the reception of the mysteries of the Faith," and he may well have felt, there in the silent Common Room, or on those broad aerial meadows, that the spirit of the Word was, in turn, being passed on to him. If only, one thinks, Pater had lived in that earlier Oxford—as a boy he, too, came under Keble's influence—what suggestiveness might he not have found in the younger Newman for the later Marius.

They must often have been trying conversations for both men. Provost Hawkins could be a provoking man. Newman often found him provoking, in his love of accuracy that was almost a mania, in his fanatical horror of the least exaggeration, of any one-sided statement, of any shade or atom of conclusion not justified by the premises; though conversely, he would strive just as hard to recognize the least atom of truth in any viewpoint no matter how gravely overlaid by error. So legalistic a manner was not, evidently, as his biographer and all his friends have agreed, winning or even agreeable, unless one had the sense of humor to be entertained instead of irked by this exaggerated terror of exaggeration.

Dean Burgon, one of the Provost's warmest admirers, had this wisdom. Once when he had successfully delivered a carefully prepared sermon on "The Walk to Emmaus" he left the church with Hawkins, not indeed expecting but certainly desiring a friendly little word of sympathy, if not of praise. Instead, to his amusement, Hawkins, after a long silence, turned about and said, "Why did you pronounce it *Emmāus?* It is *Emmăus";* and walked on. Burgon was not deceived: he knew that Hawkins' manner was only deceptively cold.

A drunken undergraduate climbed one night to the leads, fell off into the quad and was killed. The doctor and the Provost were called. When after about an hour the chapel-bell began to toll the frightened and horrified group about the mangled boy saw Hawkins approach through the dim morning light with his bands tied perfectly square, calm, unmoved. But his wife told Burgon what followed. "He is always seeing on his pillow the pale face of that young man dead in the quadrangle." It would take a long time to become intimate with such a man. After twenty years of close and friendly companionship Burgon still found himself regularly addressed as Mister Burgon and offered two fingers, both of which he would as often reject with, "I won't take your two fingers! Give me your whole hand, Provost. And I wish you wouldn't call me Mister!"; at which Hawkins would yield his five fingers, turn up the whites of his eyes, half-amused and half-astonished at such frivolity, and thaw out in ten minutes.

It is significant that Newman loved him. He also knew how to value him:

"He was the first who taught me to weigh my words, and to be cautious in my statements. He led me to that mode of limiting and clearing my sense in discussion and controversy, and of distinguishing between cognate ideas, and of obviating mistakes by anticipation which, to my surprise, has since been considered even in quarters friendly to me to savour of the polemics of Rome. He is a man of exact mind himself, and he used to snub me severely, on reading, as he was kind enough to do, the first Sermons I wrote and other compositions that I was engaged upon."

When we think of the first teacher who influenced Newman, the Revd. Mr. Mayers—an admirable man, no doubt, to whom he was always warmly grateful for drawing his heart towards a spiritual life—and think then of the crude, simple-minded, simple-hearted level of those first stirrings, and think of Newman's inflammable imagination, vaulting and fainting at the thought, so constantly with him, that this world is no more than mist and gossamer, we must tremble first at the extravagances and dangers to which such enthusiastic souls are open, and then feel relieved that his passionate spirit should have received this stern, intellectual mauling of the Common Room and the meadow, like any young Pegasus of the Athenian academy being put into bridle and bit.

Not that this breaking-in meant an end to his habits of solitariness. Thus, November 11, 1828:

". . . My ride of a morning is generally solitary but I almost prefer being alone. When the spirits are good, everything is delightful in the view of still nature which the country gives. I have learned to like dying trees and black meadows—swamps have their grace and fogs their sweetness. . . ."

Again:

"How desirable it seems to be able to get out of the stir and bustle of the world, and not have to have the responsibility and weariness of success. How, if I choose to wish a scheme, and in my solitary rides I sometimes do, I should say, 'Oh, for some small cure of a few hundreds a year, and no preferment, as the world calls it.' But you know this is wishing for idleness, and I do not think I shall have this obscurity, because I wish for it. . . ."

Besides, he concluded, would he—though "I do not know myself"—endure the desert if it were given to him?

Surely not? If it is impossible to conceive him battling in the world of ambitious men it is equally impossible to imagine him as a total neutralist or pacifist. And it is precisely for this reason that we can see him seizing so eagerly on Hawkins' idea of Tradition. It did not enter his mind merely as a notion. He was not quite so abstract or intellec-

tualist as that.　It evoked a living image to which he drew
closer and closer in the years immediately following those
fruitful Long Vacations of '24 and '25.　This was the image
of the common life of the Roman empire in the West and
East during the early years of the Christian flowering.　It
led him in '25 to the reading of the early Fathers.　It would
emerge six or seven years later in his first book, a study of
the Christian battleground during the fourth century in
Antioch and Alexandria.

Surely, the fact of the matter is that we find ourselves only
by creating outside ourselves some desirable image of possible life in harmony with our own nucleus?　John Newman
had been given by the act of God a nuclear sense of this
world as being little more than a symbol or an allegory of
the only real, eternal world beyond it.　This was the clay,
if one can speak of so delicate and tenuous a conception as
clay, which he must mold into his desirable image of possible life.　Mayers had misled him into thinking coarsely
of this world as merely "staining the white radiance of
eternity"; an over-simplification which created in him the
sort of antithesis or dichotomy that the over-simplifications
of Puritanism always create: between a world in which we
manfully live and strive, and a *dégoût de la vie* which makes
the world hardly worth striving in; between the idea of an
Oxford where one nourishes eager ambitions and an Oxford
which one dreams of abandoning altogether for "obscurity."
The Puritan has always resolved this dichotomy in one of
two ways: the way of the ascetic who flies from the wicked
world entirely; or the way of the reformer who fights this
disgusting clod of earth to conquer it for God.　One thinks
of the desert hermits; one thinks of the zealots of the In-
quisition, of Savonarola, of Cromwell, of hosts of well-meaning and utterly objectionable minor reformers whose main
urge is hatred of the very fact of life.　It is difficult to see
John Newman in even the best of this company.　So sensi-

tive, so civilized, so generous a mind would have to formulate some other and far more delicate balance of vision between this world and eternity. From this on, all his adult life will be spent in shaping a vessel to contain and express this synthesis, and he will not come to his maturity until he has shaped or found it, even if it be no more in the end than this flawed imperial image, as full of imperfections as this world of created being must always be. Indeed, one might say that the essential truth about John Newman's odyssey is that he was converted to that imperial image in his heart from the moment when he looked back, at Hawkins' bidding, to the centuries when the last faint and fragile echoes of the Messiah's words were still reverberating in the air; and that all he did, after that, was to spend himself in an intellectual struggle to persuade himself that he could recreate that Golden Age, that, in fact, these years were one with those, that his Church was one with that, that Oxford was one of Peter's children: a dream which he gradually, and to his dismay, realized to be, and always to have been, a dream and nothing more.

3

Hawkins and Whately played an equal part in leading him to other mature conceptions. Both were independent and traditional churchmen. Both had had a long and shrewd experience of people. To them Newman came full of confidence in his simple, semi-Calvinistic, black-and-white notions of Good and Evil, still nourishing some liberalistic ideas, that is, tolerance of sects within the Church (Hurrell Froude for a time considered him next-door to a heretic), and all his old Evangelical ideas of total, personal conversion. Hawkins, in the course of many conversations, gradually impressed on him that people are simply not made that way; that people are never either wholly good or wholly bad; that

differences in moral excellence are a matter of degree rather
than of kind.   Whately, on the other side, was simultaneously
impressing him with the momentous truth that the Church is
not, as the Evangelical tended to think it, a vague, emotional,
subjective fellowship but a solid, organized body, visible,
substantive, historical, divinely appointed, and endowed with
rights and prerogatives and powers of its own, quite independent of the state.   Those ideas he studied in Whately's—
or he believed it to be in some sense Whately's—*Letters of
an Episcopalian,* which set down the concept of an organized
body of faith, independent and indefectible.   Besides, Hawkins' ecclesiastical perspectives carried the logical implication that whereas Tradition teaches doctrine and Scripture
provides proof, it is the Church which carries on the System.
Another blow to isolationism.

How many urgent and painful problems would that not
provoke!   The Church. . . .   What Church?   One Church
or many?   Dr. Arnold, for instance, was not worried if there
were dozens of Churches provided men believed generally
but earnestly in the godhead of Christ; which was plausible
until one remembered what heresies would spring and have
sprung from a multitude of notions about what such words
as "godhead" or "divinity" imply—Sabellianism, for one example, the counterpart of modern Unitarianism which denies
the individual personality of Christ as God.   And then there
would come another blinding idea, that Tradition involves
the *development* of a primal nucleus, by interpretations,
definitions, intellectual expansions and explanations of what
Christ really said or meant.   How far could that idea not
take him?   To the doors of Trent?   Beyond it, to Rome?
"Now if we live," said Keats, thinking also of life as a mansion of many rooms, some bright, some dark, mostly unexplored, "now if we live and go on thinking, we too shall
explore them."

Such discussions and conversations were an absorption of

which John's mother and sisters could know very little, although he was always interested to tell them about his latest ideas, his latest studies, and they were delighted to hear of them and to confide utterly in him; so much so, indeed, that he soon felt a tremor of fear at so much uninstructed confidence, a foretaste of the later, deeper trust of thousands. He wrote warningly to his mother in '26: "Do not be run away with any opinion of mine. I have seen cause to change my mind in some respects, and I may change again." [5] So much honesty from her dear, honorable boy could only induce her to trust all the more in him whom she once called her "guardian angel."

The upshot of it was that John fell into a great trouble of mind before these twin assaults on his Evangelicalism and his Liberalism, and, for the first time, began to make a serious study of the philosophical, doctrinal and historical basis of his religious views, with a view to relating his vision of life to life as it is lived.

CHAPTER 7

THE QUEST FOR THINGS PAST

1

IF WE ARE in the habit of thinking of John Henry Newman
in a purely secular way—the subtle brain, the writer of
marble prose, the delicate but powerful dialectician—we
may, at first sight, be surprised at some of the subjects on
which he trained his intellect, not to say made his soul.
Such a problem as Baptismal Regeneration, for instance, to
which he now began to bend his mind, may strike us as a dull
subject, or an obscure one, or possibly even, according to our
nature, training or general bent, as absurdly trivial for so
powerful a brain. And yet if we should feel like this about
being baptized by holy water, is it not strange that we sympathize fully and understand perfectly when we hear that
somebody has been baptized by fire? I think we often resist
words rather than ideas. The secular man will make no
bones about Fate, or Destiny; he can absorb easily the idea
of the moving finger that writes and having writ moves on;
his experience makes it possible for him to accept the notion
of those great powers that the gods, in an arbitrary selection
of their love for mankind, let fall on some and withhold from
others; when he is strong and confident he does not question
his freedom of will which suffices to "save" him by its own
dynamic power; and in more trying times of crisis, when he
is not so strong and confident, he will feel the need of some
exterior, saving help, which he will call by the name inspira-

tion, or chance, or a woman. But when we talk to him of
the Grace of God, the farthest any such secular-minded
gentleman will go is to say that even if this mysterious thing
exists it seems absurd that we must be touched by *water* to
be a darling of heaven.

Yet the same man will think it right and necessary, that
before a lawyer can practice or a soldier become the King's
man, he must be enrolled with ceremony. And, if he has
some imagination, he will even agree that this enrollment,
far from being a mere decorative ritual, is a form of transformation. He will be able to see it as a movement not only
of thought, or character, or the will but of "the soul"; not
only a practical decision to become another man but the experience of becoming another man, perceived, understood
and remembered for ever—which is the only sane definition
of any real experience. That is all Christians mean by the
Grace of God, received in baptism.

John had evidently not thought deeply about this strange
matter before, or not in this way. No Evangelical thinking
that "Jesus did it all, long, long ago," could think of this
mysterious force as a presence which first sanctifies and then
demands constant effort to live up to the act and ceremony
of transformation. For if this idea of election and challenge
were true, then John himself, as a boy, had not been "saved"
at all! His sisters, his own mother, his dearest friends were
not saved at all—a shocking come-down from his early Cal-
vinistic-Evangelical state of certainty in eternal salvation.
For we must see that nobody ever does become a so-called
gloomy Calvinist, or a so-called sour Puritan, who is not bliss-
fully happy about himself though deeply miserable about
everybody else.

It was one of the several subjects wherein Frank disagreed
strongly with him. Regeneration, to Frank, as to most Evangelicals, meant a conscious emotional experience, a sensation
received in the heart and acknowledged in the brain, and

anybody who pretended that the pouring of water on an infant's bald skull produced this experience was flying in the
face of all human experience and talking vulgar hocus-pocus.
Besides, do we not all try to live the good life, baptized or
not? As between the two men the fact seems to be there is
no bridge between schools so fundamentally opposed. We
are either dealing with brains, bodies and emotions, or we
are dealing with souls and their imponderable and rationally
unintelligible lives. The Frank school talks prose. The
John school talks poetry. Newman was becoming convinced
that in religion he was not dealing with emotions. He was
dealing with mysteries. He was beginning to see furthermore that those who denied the mystery weakened the moral
impulse. In the long run it was the mystery and not the
emotion that ruled behavior. He soon saw from his own
personal experience as a pastor that nothing else did work.
He saw that the purely emotional pattern of Evangelicalism
certainly did not work, as Hawkins and Whately had told
him it could not and did not.

How multitudinously adept at bewildering us the mind is
when it leads us into the realm of religious experience. The
Evangelicals had reacted, plausibly enough, from what Dean
Church has called "the manly school" of Anglicanism, with
its sturdy distrust of "high-wrought feelings and professions,"
and its preference for "cultivating self-command, and setting
up as its mark . . . a reasonable and serious idea of duty."
They had seen how this sturdy, quiet, English reasonable-
ness leads to dryness and lack of spirituality. To correct it
they set out to exalt the hearts of their congregations to a
state of high and lofty enthusiasm. They were presently
caught in an opposite snare. Hearts did, indeed, beat faster
while the gin lasted. When the stimulant died in them the
reaction followed. The Evangelicals made a profound mistake. They either did not plant the religious impulse deep
enough in the psyche, or else they rashly lifted that tender

plant from the shadows of its warm depth within the soul into an unsheltered realm where the gusts of wayward emotion would play hot and cold on its fragile buds.

John Newman made a profound psychological observation when he saw this natural truth. There are secrets which are best left unspoken. Even to feel them is too coarse a touch. They quiver most livingly in the invisible deep. If they must be said, as when Creeds are pronounced, then what we intone is no less a mystery than a prayer. It is as much a poem as an expression of belief. It is at least something more than a scientific definition. It would be years before John fully realized all this, but in the meantime his delicate sense of wonder in the presence of the indefinable began to lead him gently out of the shallows of his youth into an open sea.

So, whereas Frank thought himself wiser in his generation about things like Baptismal Regeneration, more reasonable and common-sensible, more human and down-to-earth, it was John who really saw how the works work, or saw, if one prefers, that nobody can see how the works work. He was thereby the more human and the more humanist of the two. "Calvinism," he wrote, dismissing his past, "is not a key to the phenomena of human nature as they occur in the world." Is this the remark of a philosopher or of a psychologist? So, too, his preoccupation with what at first glance seems a minor matter of ritual led him to reconsider the spiritual mechanism of a host of other major matters about which he had hitherto not thought very deeply—free-will, holiness, original sin, education, popular ideas of those profound disturbances we tabulate so glibly as "election," and "justification" and "good works," until, one by one, he discarded all but the rags and tatters of his original, elementary Evangelical ideas about the way the soul of man works within itself. Or so he thought, or hoped, for early experiences, when they are as searing as his had been, are never fully discarded. The

withdrawn thorn leaves its blot. He admitted that for ten
more years he continued to mingle with Evangelicals on
their various rallying-grounds.

He was thus being led from Calvinism to the Church of
England. He now began to analyze and shape this new
clay. He resumed a love-affair dating to his school-days: his
imaginative interest in the lives and times of the early
Fathers, those first centuries which were now his ideal of
the Christian life. He had been dipping into them since
1825–'26. He began, in 1827–'28, to read them systemati-
cally. He had only a dim idea as to where he was going.

"Will you scold me," he writes to Jem, "if I am bold enough to
think of a work which may take me *t!e!!n!!! years???* perhaps
twenty . . . But what after all is this subject?—it is to trace the
sources from which the corruption of the church, principally the
Romish, have been derived. It would consequently involve a
reading of all the Fathers—200 vols. at least—(you saw some
stout gentlemen in Oriel Library—Austin 12 vols. Chrysostom
13 do.)—all the principal Platonists, Philo, Plotinus, Julian, etc.—
an enquiry into Gnosticism—Rabbinical literature—and I know
not what else—perhaps much more—am I not bold?—it will be
something if I can dedicate my thoughts, studies and efforts to the
cause of truth and the Glory of God—I have some but only some
thoughts of beginning Hebrew this Long Vacation."

What a joyful prospect it was that faced him! He would
happily greet each familiar signpost, pause devoutly at each
familiar scene, rest at many a familiar shrine along that well-
worn path which would lead him, without a single break,
from the pulpit of St. Mary-the-Virgin to the prophet's voice
on the beaches of Galilee. He entered blithely on the long
task. The books came in October. Huge fellows; and so
cheap! "One folio costs one shilling," he gloated, "and all
are in this extravagantly modest way." He carried them off
to his room, the second floor in the far right-hand corner of

the Oriel quadrangle, and spreading their winglike pages wide he launched himself on their leaves into the centuries.

2

Somewhere about the same time his brother Frank also became interested in early, or primitive, Christianity. Frank developed this interest in, of all places, Ireland. He went to Dublin, in '27, as tutor to the son of Chief Justice Pennefather, then and since well known to patriotic Irishmen as what we call a Castle hack, that is a lawyer whom Dublin Castle, the seat of government, frequently employed and ultimately raised to the bench for his vigor in prosecuting rebels.[1] His most famous victim was Daniel O'Connell, whom he tried in '44. Frank lived with Pennefather in Fitzwilliam Square after a brief preliminary sojourn in the Wicklow hills, where he thought the scenery gloomy, but was surprised that everybody could speak English. He found in his employer a kind and generous friend. He also found in the Fitzwilliam Square house an odd-looking man named John Nelson Darby, whose sister Pennefather had married. This man exercised a strange magnetic influence over the whole household, and has his niche in history: he is known as the founder of Darbyism, later to be known as The Plymouth Brethren, a form of Christianity than which it is hard to conceive anything more primitive. Frank found this creed much to his liking and adopted it wholeheartedly.

Its attraction for Frank is evident. It was Calvinistic in tone. It was anti-clerical. The Brethren rejected utterly every form of ritual. They disliked every title except that of Christian, even that of Plymouth Brethren. They believed in personal communion; that is the members handed the alleged sacrament to one another. And each had the right to preach, or rather to prophesy, for they had fixed ideas about the coming millennium. The zeal of the community was, and still is, unbounded. A zealous Plymouth Brother or Sister of our day will have no more notion as to the horrors that are perpetrated in places called cinemas than they have of the domestic routine of harems.

Darby was by this date a physical wreck. He went hobbling on crutches around Pennefather's house, blood-shot, unshaven, in shabby clothes, a virtual cripple. To this he had been reduced by his selfless zeal in God's service. London-born, educated at Trinity College, Dublin, called to the bar in 1825, he had refused to practice because he could not in conscience defend anybody of whose innocence he was uncertain—a somewhat restrictive scruple in 19th, or for that matter 20th century Ireland. Instead he became curate at Calary, in County Wicklow, probably because it was near the demesne of Lady Powerscourt, one of his early devotees. It was a dreary place to live and work, a bleak, upland moor which once connoted to Dubliners a famous Point to Point, and is now no more than a highland heath in whose soothing and solitary vacancy they revel at fifty miles an hour. When this writer lived beside it some years ago Darby's church served two worshippers. These were the curate and the sexton. The lonely National School nearby had about eight pupils. Here Darby labored for Christ as few, if any, Catholic priests needed to labor in 19th century Ireland, roving mountain and moor in all weathers until past midnight, entering the most remote mud-cabins, and finding consistently that the peasants equated every religion but their own with political persecution. The result was that in sheer defense of Protestantism he became an ardent advocate of Catholic Emancipation. These years of toil broke his body, but his spirit still burned so fiercely that all Frank's powers of resistance were shrivelled by its scorching heat.

Would John Newman have succumbed to Darby's magnetism? Yet he had succumbed to Mayers? I think the fact is

that for Frank Evangelicalism had always been a matter of
temperament, whereas for John it had been no more than a
misadventure that by taking thought he would inevitably
slough off in favor of tradition and, finally, authority.   Frank
was an intelligent man dominated by his emotions, John was
an emotional man dominated by his intelligence; though his
intellect was fast becoming so refined as to be transformed
out of its own nature into the nature of the imagination.
Frank's words and career speak for themselves.   He does
not so much progress as oscillate wildly.   That he was subject to his sentiments in religion is clear from his own doctrine: "The Christian sentiment makes, and nothing else
makes, the true Christian."   The "and nothing else" is final.
All else—churches, devotions, priests, pious practices—are,
in his own words, mere "mummery."   Even the sentiment
must have no trappings.   How he raged, for instance, when
John, in a somewhat Carlo Dolci flight of eloquence, said
that "so intense was the Virgin's love of God that it drew
Him out of heaven into her womb!"   He called it "an
erratic, erotic and esoteric utterance."   He could approve
of Christianity only when it was as naked as a jelly-fish.

It is well to bear this contrast between John and Frank in
mind when we come on Modernist admirers of Newman who
find his main contribution to religious thought in the implications of his theory of the gradual development of doctrine
out of the first centuries of oral Christianity: that is, in their
hope of a further development yet to come along the lines
of a more relaxed interpretation of irksome dogmas.   But
would Newman ever have entered the gates of Rome if he
had not simultaneously given his loyalty to the concept of a
substantive Church embodying and defining those traditions?
Frank Newman did not and would not, preferring to all the
colleges of cardinals and all the oecumenical councils that
ever were the wisdom of poor, crippled John Darby.

3

John and Francis Newman were not the only Oxford people at this time exploring the world's distant past. It is exciting to think that while John was lying awake in Oriel pondering Theodoret or Athanasius on the origins of Christianity, Buckland of Corpus may have been lying awake a few blocks away struggling with the origins of the Cheirotherium footprints. John rises to jot down a thought about some passage in Basil or Gregory. Buckland rouses his wife to make paste on the kitchen table, while he fetches the tortoise from the garden to see if those puzzling footprints also were testudinal. John is pleased to see the origin of Unitarianism in Sabellius. Buckland and Mrs. Buckland rejoice when the slanting lamplight on the footprints of their tortoise shows that the impressions of this most ancient of reptiles agree almost identically with the footprints on the geological slabs.

The thought of two such different students, whose diversity must still be frequently replicated in Oxford, is both exciting and depressing. Was no bridge possible between them? How much, how many might have been saved if there had been! After all, if Buckland, as Dean of Westminster, could reconcile science and religion, why could not men as different as the elder Gosse, who timidly prostituted his great knowledge to the idea that the fossils were God's fun, or Keble, who clinched a bitter argument by declaring that "when God made the stones he made the fossils in them," or Pusey, who organized a protest against the conferring of a degree on Buckland's colleague Owen, or Newman, who, according to Tom Mozley, "considered physical science a waste of time"? [2]

It is not as if the scientists were personally unattractive men. Anybody must relinquish with regret so original a

character as Buckland.   At his house visitors dined on horse
one day, on crocodile the second, on mice baked in batter
the third, while the guinea-pig nibbled their toes under the
table, the bear's tongue rasped their hands, the monkey's
arm stole their walnuts and the jackal suddenly yelled fiend-
ishly through the open window.   He must have been a great
man who horrified the priests showing him the bones of Santa
Rosalia at Palermo by saying with the positive decision,
"Goats' bones!"; and who when shown a martyr's blood on a
pavement knelt down, licked it, paused and remarked, "Hm!
Bat's urine.   Definitely, bat's urine!"   But as Tuckwell puts
it in his pedantic buckram way—and how much, or how
little, would that have to be changed to fit Oxford today?—
"In the Thirties the Oxford mind was inscient; its attitude
first contemptuous, then hostile towards the science that,
invita Minerva, was hatching in its midst; a strange, new,
many-headed, assertive thing, claiming absurdly to take rank
with the monopolist Humanities of Donland."

The incubatory period was prolonged.   The most famous
of those early scientists, Buckland, became Fellow of Corpus
in 1809, but he did not arouse domestic fears for the safety of
the Deluge until his *Bridgewater Treatise* of 1836, when
(Tuckwell *loquitur*) "a hurricane of private and newspaper
protests whistled about his disregarding head."   Worse followed when he impeached the Six Days, and the clergy, the
dons and the press all fell on him with a fury that must remind us that the heroes and martyrs of the Oxford Movement were not the only victims of their time.

We must also remember, however, in fairness to Newman
and his friends, that they grew up and spent their most active
years in Oxford well before this scientific movement got under way.[3]   It was not until about 1845, which was the year of
Newman's defection from Anglicanism, that the idea arose of
replacing the old Ashmolean by a proper museum, fiercely
opposed, it goes without saying, by the classicists, the theo-

logians and the economically-minded. Newman never saw
this new building; and those who think him wise to have
despised the "fashionable" studies to which it was raised may
also like to think that he lost nothing by not rejoicing in what
Tuckwell described as a lovely "exhalation," rising under the
paternal supervision of Ruskin, Morris, Rossetti and Burne-
Jones, its every detail "an object lesson in Art," down to the
door-handles, the footboards and the gas-burners; its interior
shafts representing the sequence of British rocks; its capitals
carved by the famous Dublin brothers O'Shea, after plants
brought from the Botanic Gardens; its soaring iron-work
trained by Kidmore into the shapes of spreading chestnut
boughs.

Tuckwell's account of the young Huxley heatedly debating
Darwinism at a first meeting of the British Association with
the blandly contemptuous Bishop Wilberforce (known to
Newman as Soapy Sam) hovers between comedy and pathos.
One is especially grateful for the clergyman who, when the
discussion was at a boiling-point, rose and called for a black-
board, solemnly marked a cross at the top right-hand corner,
solemnly balanced it by another at the bottom left-hand corner and then turned to the audience with a smile of triumph
at this lucid explanation of Creation. One may, pardonably,
though how wrongly, forgive John Newman for thinking,
years earlier, that all this new scientific thing was far too
tentative to be worth while.

Yet does not this very attitude reveal that the strength of
men like Newman lay in their resistance to their period, as
their weakness lay in their being contemporary only by
resistance to it? And even so they were barely contemporary. John Newman's personal efforts to counter the new
scientific scepticism are amazingly feeble. Thus, in his
private notebooks, he counters the objection brought against
the Deluge that no bones have been discovered by considering that "the antediluvians were drowned in the sea, like

Sodom and Gomorrah, "that is in the Indian and Pacific oceans." Or alternatively, he says, "it may be supposed that the immense expanse of interior Africa was their country and that God in his anger has, since the Deluge, covered it with barrenness and drought." The next year he read, or heard, with satisfaction that Buckland had observed the extraordinary fact that of all animals known to exist previous to six thousand years ago—the Mosaic life-time of the world—not one was serviceable to man, though inside this period we find horses, bulls, goats, deer and asses. "How strong a presumptive proof," John joyously writes, "this is from the face of nature of what the Bible asserts to be the case!" Which is chiefly a comment on the slow development of science. Buckland would have been as astounded as Newman were he, today, to visit the Musée de l'Homme in Paris where they would both see paintings and engravings of a man, a horse, and an ibex which have been attributed to the period of Palaeolithic culture known as Magdalenian III, approximately dated 12,000 B.C. John once wrote down his six reasons why the world may be correctly thought not older than six thousand years; including such arguments as the shape of the earth, its destiny, its width at the equator— whatever that may imply—and the scanty population of the globe.

What, then, are we to make of James Anthony Froude's well-known description of him as a thorough-going contemporary, some twelve years later, when he was beginning to be famous?

"Nothing was too large for him, nothing too trivial, if it threw light upon the central question, what man really was and what was his destiny. . . . Keble had looked into no lines of thought but his own. Newman had read omnivorously; he had studied modern thought and modern life in all its forms, and with all its many-coloured passions. . . . He spoke to us (undergraduates) about subjects of the day, of literature, of public persons and incidents, of everything which was generally interesting. He seemed always to be better informed on common topics of conversation than anyone else who was present."

This is impressive from one who met him "now and then" in private and often heard him preach. But can it possibly be true? A man who knew no German, on his own admission not enough French to translate a book, had so little science, had never studied philosophy or examined the biblical exegetists, and held so few opinions on politics that in his published letters, and so far as I have seen in his unpublished letters, we find no discussion of any of the six or seven major events in 19th century England between the Reform agitation and the Crimea—neither of Slavery, nor the New Poor Laws, nor the War with China, nor the War in Afghanistan, nor the Repeal of the Corn Laws, nor the Chartists, nor of the Crimea itself.

In his own field of letters we find some surprising gaps. If he or his family ever read a line of Keats or Shelley they do not discuss them. When Byron died old John Newman announced it sadly to his family and Mary mentioned it in a letter. The only other mention of Byron in the letters is when young John says that "*The Giaour* is my favorite poem"; which is so uncharacteristic that one wonders if he is being facetious, or if he liked the poem merely because it deals with a converted unbeliever. Certainly he far and away preferred Crabbe and Southey. Wordsworth in general he found boring, except for the *Intimations of Immortality*, which bowled him over. He said he knew "one or two things" by Lord Tennyson. He never went beyond the first few pages of William Morris. He was an accomplished musician, yet to his dying day he had barely heard of Schumann or Wagner or—Who else was it?—"I can't remember all those fellows' names," he used to say. He loved Scott,

Trollope, Mrs. Gaskell and Thackeray: sound, elevating
writers. He had a critical admiration for Jane Austen.
("Miss Austen has no romance—none at all. What vile
creatures her parsons are! She has not a dream of the high
Catholic *ethos*. . . .") He had little, if any, interest in
George Eliot. But then, as one of his friends has said, books
to him were moral food; and the editor of his letters, Anne
Mozley, said, "The *ethos* of a book came always foremost in
his critical estimation"; and, indeed, as we shall see when
the time comes to look at his sermons, his views on all reading were sternly utilitarian in the moralist's sense of what is
useful. It is all very much as if a modern churchman of
eminence had never touched the hem of Freud or Jung, ignored the Korean War and the Indonesian War, could not
remember the names of Stravinsky or Bloch, knew "one or
two things" by Yeats, disliked T. S. Eliot, but read every line
of Sir Hugh Walpole, Mary Webb, J. B. Priestley and E. M.
Forster; though it is difficult to find modern counterparts to
the writers whom he liked, and one has the feeling that he
would have disliked them all.

4

But no sooner do we observe the effect of this probing than
we draw back from it. In being aware of what was beyond
his awareness we take him out of his time: which is a biographer's mortal sin. After all if the core of his position was
that he was not of this world is it not unfair, and foolish, to
think ill of him for not being of this world? Besides, we lose
much of the sense of his unknowingness, his simple, inscient
reality, by interposing our modern knowingness between ourselves and him.

To know too much about any moment is to destroy its
innocence. His friends who saw things happening to him,
and did not know what they saw, knew the man as we never

can. Nothing is what it was. Everything is what it becomes. The end changes the meaning of the beginning.
Once ignorance becomes knowledge something precious is
always lost. That contemporary ignorance is so precious
that the mention of it destroys it. It is impossible any
longer to enter the Oriel quad and look up with his casual
eyes at the window of his rooms—in the far, right-hand corner, number three staircase, first-floor to the right as you
climb—because he and all his contemporaries have become
more than they were in his ignorant day: Whately who had
those rooms before him, Charles Marriott who had them
after him, Keble who lived next door, and Pusey next to
him, Froude who was over Newman, Sam Wilberforce who
was under Pusey, Robert Wilberforce in the corner of the
quad looking to Magpie Lane.[4] Their vibrations are explicit now. There is, thereby, a sad loss of contemporary
reality since it is the essence of fame that it is fabulous and
they, for not being fabulous, were simply themselves.

He had, we have seen several examples already, a trick of
trying to extinguish himself by anticipating extinction; to
post-write himself; to be future-minded. He tried in vain.
"Moved into my rooms in college. They were . . . those
of all others I have always wished to have. And future
possessors will succeed me." It is no use. They are not
Marriott's rooms, nor even Dean Church's rooms. They will
always be Newman's. If we ever do glimpse them as they
were it is only when the reference is quite casual. So, Mary
briefly puts them out of the fable with:

> "I wish I *could* see your rooms. Are they generally called by
> the titles you give them? I hope the 'brown room' is not quite so
> grave as the name would leave one to suppose. At least Harriett
> would not be in the number of its admirers. You know *brown* is
> not a great favourite of hers. I had no idea you lectured in your
> rooms."

For this one short moment we do see those rooms as they were, ill-carpeted and indifferently furnished and all cluttered with bookshelves, without the least sign of ornament or drapery, the sole luxury a clean towel to dust the books, and that odd-shaped appendage opening in one corner—the bay of the west window of the ante-chapel behind it, partitioned from the chapel by lath-and-plaster—where he found the last of Whately's herrings moldy on its string, and which he used as a tiny oratory.   Tom Mozley returning late one night to college could hear from the gateway his voice of prayer echoing from it down into the quad.   As one measures the long distance across the quad one thinks: "What a still night it must have been!"   The immediacy of that soundless night only lasts for a moment.   We look at the young man's table to see what he had last been reading, see that it is Irenaeus or Cyprian, and at once the burthen of knowing where all this must lead him—did lead him—blurs our sight by dilating the man as he was into the man he has become, a fabulous image in a fog of fame.

5

Charles Newman is a great help to us to see the Newmans as they actually were.   He, happy man, has little interest in the past.   He also has small hope for the future.   He lives improvidently in the present.   So, in March, 1827, while John is looking back in the fourth century, and Frank looking forward to Aleppo and Bagdad, Charles is at handigrips with the Bank of England.   He is trying to get out of it, perhaps into the Drawing Office, through the help of the Mr. Capel who had got him into it.   But since Mr. Capel had befriended him before and is apparently slow to befriend him again Charles naturally feels the sharp tooth of ingratitude, and says so acidly.   His mother tremulously warns him, "The weakest go to the wall."   Charlie writes back that he does not at all consider himself the weakest. "And no one shall push *me* to the wall!" Patiently he explains the facts to her. They are quite simple, as she may see by the enclosed copy of his letter to Capel. "He believed that I held him in awe, when I regarded him with *contempt!* That I looked up to him in expectation, when I should have been ashamed to receive a favour from him! That I forgot and forgave his breach of faith when I had fresh remembrance and indignation of it!" Accordingly Charles had written him what might be colloquially described as a stinker.

Now, it will be remembered that when the late John Newman was in difficulties with his Alton brewery he had borrowed £1000 from this Mr. Capel, who had already stood by him when the Ramsbottom bank was in difficulties; and though Mr. Capel had never been repaid this £1000 he had nevertheless continued to show a kindly interest in the family after the bankruptcy. An old and loyal friend. He was therefore naturally put out when he received Charles' insulting letter, and came around at once to the bank in a pet. He took the young man into the room where the Directors sit ("with many of whom I suppose he is intimately acquainted"), and there ("assuming a grand air") he told Charles that he had a good mind to take him into the parlor; which, presumably, meant that he felt like reporting him to his employers. This behavior astonished Charles. "For though I am quite conscious that my reputation among the low set to which he belongs"—one may imagine the hauteur of Charles' voice as he says the words "low set"—"is that of being *a fool,* still I had not thought that Capel would go so far." Capel went still farther. He mentioned the £1000. He pointed out to Charles that his education, his very living were all owing to him. At this final insult Charles drew himself up and walked out, and promptly wrote Capel another stinker.

"Your advice of taking port wine," he concludes his report

to his mamma, "I do not neglect. I find air and exercise necessary. The hands in the office are rather friendly. Nor do I form an exception. Some of us are talking of hiring a room for boxing. Or any other purpose," he adds airily.

A month later he has calmed down. He apologizes humbly for having troubled his poor mother with his rigmarole. But like many men who are good-tempered in person but bad-tempered as soon as they take a pen in hand he suddenly proceeds to lose his temper again and cries: "I want no womanish advice as to what method I am to pursue to shake off insult! I think I shall have the satisfaction of seeing him (Capel) keep his distance in future."

Three weeks later he has again calmed down. He is in the dumps. "I doubt whether you ought to reckon me one of you. I am afraid I am a great clog. Besides I do not assimilate with Society, and," getting haughty again, "I do not intend in the least to give up my principles!" Deflating again: "I am afraid I shall always be a misfortune to you as I have been hitherto, but it is not my fault." Brightening suddenly: "I have got a pair of tights which I want to take into common wear. Should I buy a couple of pair of black cotton stockings? Or what sort of colour do you think is neatest for them?" His letters contain many of these happy surprises: as when in a short letter a month later he writes, "I confess I went to sleep three lines back in this letter. I am just waked. But I have received no inspiration in consequence. And so conclude, your loving son, Charles Henry Newman."

That April of '27, his aunt at Strand-on-the-Green came out of one of her periodical financial crises—John advised her to sell out and he would pay any bills left over from what the sale of the furniture would bring in—and had the leisure to plead for Charlie with his mother. Jemima replied that she was only too well aware of "his trials and silent sufferings," as well as of his "particuliarities." If only, she felt, if *only* he would, when he was well, "struggle against that repulsive manner of which he is himself quite conscious!" If *only* he would "for his own sake and everyone belonging to him endeavour to promote his own welfare by a quiet steady perseverance in his duty, thereby in time making friends!" What hurt her most was his constant assertion that he did not want anybody to be kind to him. However, this particular peace-council cannot have lasted long, for Aunt Betsy soon fell into trouble again. Some of her "inmates" had become unpleasant. Presently she had not enough inmates, pleasant or unpleasant. Young Jemima advised her to advertise for holiday-makers from London. "Vacation prime season for bank of Thames." By the summer Betsy was out of trouble again, and once more pleaded for Charles. This time John tackled him. He soon reported to Aunt Betsy that he had no hope.

"His case is truly lamentable. I have no hope at all he will alter his opinions for a long time. Or rather I much fear that he will alter them the wrong way. He is madly rushing along a dark and dangerous cavern thinking he must find light *at the end of it*. But he will never arrive at that end. The Lord restore him in His good time."

Having said which he retired to the fourth century, Aunt Betsy retired to the band-box at Kew, Charles retired to the Bank, and the mother and the three girls retired to . . .

But it is high time we saw what these four have been doing with themselves since their father died.

CHAPTER 8

VAIN FLIRTATIONS

1

SINCE their papa's death, the girls, with their mother, had been living in trunks. When they were not squashed into the little house at Strand-on-the-Green they had been leading that sort of odd, interesting, wandering life, between lodgings, relatives and friends, which is liable to be the lot of any family when the main provider dies. The only income the four had between them was about £150 a year, together with donations, growing in generosity, from John and Frank. Not all their friends could afford to take them in gratis. Board-lodging was sometimes the rule. This gypsy life was their way of coming out; a group, now, of *jeunes filles en fleur*. They seem to have enjoyed it, and in any case it was better than sitting in a bunch at the school-cum-boarding-house in Strand.

They saw less of John than they or he would have liked. In general they met him about four times a year, thrice briefly and once for a longer period which, considering the life he was now leading, was a lot. "Time is drinking me up," he said, and no wonder, between his literary work, on the *Encyclopedia Metropolitana*, his duties as Vice-Principal of Saint Alban Hall, whose muddled accounts "haunted" him of nights, a "Life of Apollonius," an "Essay on Miracles," his parish-work, his tutorship at Oriel, his studies in the Fathers, countless letters and the frequent duty of managing for his family.

We can visualize this busy life, in all its preoccupying detail, only when we come on some worried letter in which, in the middle of his public duties and private interests, he will drag himself to the old task of unravelling the problem of "Where shall the family stay?"—a problem which might make any man reasonably cry: "Why the devil can't they manage this themselves?" In a typical letter (August, 1827) he patiently proposes that if he stays six weeks at Hampstead relieving a friend they can also come. It will help Charles to be with them and will give time for the Rickards to stay also, repaying their hospitality, but then they must all separate, one going to Ulcombe, another to the cousins, another somewhere else for a month until . . . "Let me see? Yes, that will take us to mid-October. Could you, mother, then, in default of some other invitation, offer to pay board for a week or two to Uncle Charles? That will give the house-agent a chance to let the Brighton place. But if he doesn't let it could you go back there?" On the other hand if he does let it could mother try to get lodgings close to town for November? Charlie could join her. "The worst," he sighs tremulously, glancing at the pile of work waiting him, "is the *moving about.*"

How many of us, as preoccupied as he then was, would do as much? How many would, as he did one Christmas morning, post up to London from Oxford to give a sermon, snatch a bite of food and then get into a coach to be in Brighton in time for Christmas dinner? Or, of an April *morning*, leave Oxford at three, breakfast in London, and then catch the coach for the long drive down to Brighton the same afternoon just to be with them for the night? Yet he found time to do still more. He took a hand at trying to get husbands for his sisters.

JOHN HENRY NEWMAN *(Courtesy of The Bettmann Archive)*

JOHN NEWMAN, the father *(Courtesy Mrs. Spilmont)*

Jemima Fourdrinier Newman, the mother, before her marriage
*(From the Fourdrinier family group, in the possession of
Miss Dorothea Mozley)*

JEMIMA NEWMAN *(From a picture in the possession of J. H. Mozley, Esq.)*

HARRIETT NEWMAN *(From the family group by Maria Giberne,
in the possession of J. H. Mozley, Esq.)*

Francis Newman (*From the family group by Maria Giberne, in the possession of J. H. Mozley, Esq.*)

ORIEL COLLEGE, Oxford. Newman's rooms are in the right-hand corner, second floor, beside the windows of the Ante-Chapel. *(From the Oxford University Almanack, 1801, by permission of the Oxford University Press.)*

Top: THE HOUSE AT ALTON, Hampshire *(Photo by J. Butler Kearney)*
Bottom: GREY COURT HOUSE

2

The comedy[1] began at Ulcombe, with the Samuel Rickards, known to them as The Ricks. It is such a fragile, elusive, apparently trivial and yet for one of them at least such a deeply-wounding adventure that the full narrative of its half-acknowledged thrills and sorrows would have filled three volumes for Jane Austen. Regretfully one summarizes the long story, laying aside Harry's letters, with their leisurely descriptions of geological rides with John over the Kentish weald, her comments on occasional visitors, or on the mangled church-music, four parts without timing or harmony accompanied by a single flute, or her amusing accounts of a drive to the demesne of Lord Winchilsea, Rickards' patron, of walks through the fern, of placid nights in the rectory with John myopically bent under the oil-lamp over Genesis in Hebrew, or lifting his head to say he wished he also knew Chaldee, Syriac and Arabic, and Harry wondering would there be a letter from home to break the tedium of mid-morning. During this Ulcombe period the Brighton house would have been economically To Let; as it was again in the next August when Jem took her turn and the others scattered in their usual scrambling way: Harry immured at Strand, Frank gone to Ireland, Mary and mamma housekeeping for John at Hampstead, and Charles down in his city lodgings. It was all highly uneventful until John brought down Robert Wilberforce and, later, Robert's brother Henry.

The first marks and signs of the budding affair are of the slightest; but, then, a courtship like this under the Georges would never be anything but discreet. In an age when girls were not forward they could not be trifled with. Whether we are in the company of Fanny Burney, Jane Austen, Mrs. Opie, Mrs. Gaskell, Miss Mitford, or later Miss

Yonge all these Georgian heroines are immobilized by propriety, sealed off into silence. No masculine attention may be taken seriously in public, scarcely in private; one's own sisters will never be so indelicate as to do more than tease, and never so cruel as not to, even if by no more than the wicked fall of an eyelash. Flirtations are tentative, courtships formal. It often took years of patience to pull it off. One recalls how in *Tom Brown at Oxford,* after the heroine had strained her ankle and Tom had had to carry her, actually carry her—Oh! What exquisite intimacy!—to a nearby cottage, he could not sleep that night, realizing that he had compromised her emotions. In the end he lowered a sprig of heliotrope from his window to hers so that she might know, with relief, by this sign of Constancy—in flower-language heliotrope means *Je t'aime*—that her reputation was in the hands of a gentleman. Obviously the protocol was extremely severe, and anybody who even slightly disregarded it was in danger of being spoken of as "a person." One speaks, of course, only of bourgeois love. "Society" was flamboyant about its love-affairs.

The puzzle is to decide who fell in love with whom. I do not think the girls themselves decided until the very end. In this kind of warfare concealment is a prime rule. Since there were two sisters and two brothers the possibilities demanded immense discretion. In fact the only clear word comes, years after, from John himself: "I introduced another person to you all," he sighed, "some years since with the hope that an attachment might follow between him and Harriett . . . and my mother wished it also." [2] As would happen, it was Jemima not Harriett who first caught fire, and it was "silly" Mary who first noticed it. "I have a great mind," she simpers minxishly, "to say something about RA as you call *it.*[3] Just to plague you, nice little mum. I can fancy how conscious you look! 'Poor nice little mum. She has no art, you know!' That is delightful. I wish I could see that pretty conscious look." This, so far, is the only give-away, apart from their nicknames for the two young men, pussy scratchings that reveal exasperation: Robert, Robert Isaac, R.I., RA, becoming the Owl because he is so solemn, and the AWK because they choose to pretend that he is awkward. "Is not the AWK a fine bird?" He ends up as A.B. And when any young man has to become "A.B." between ladies one may presume that they have a reason for secrecy.

John did not pick Robert Wilberforce for his money; as if such a consideration could ever have entered his unworldly head! Old William Wilberforce, Member for Hull and Yorkshire, is best remembered for his assaults on the slave-trade, "the West Indian interests and the East Indian interests, landowners, borough-mongers, sinecurists and every other interest with the least monopoly or protection." His humanitarianism had lost him most of his fortune by the time his sons were passing through Oxford. They were reduced gentlemen when the Newman girls met them. It was Henry Wilberforce who once said in his mock-diffident, modern way (or is this just the timeless Oxford manner?): "The great use of a country house is to stuff things into it that you don't want to destroy and can't carry about with you"; in other words those hundreds of dear memories that are the making of a family, such as letters, relics, heirlooms, portraits, ornaments, mementoes of persons and events. Henry and Robert found themselves at Oxford cut adrift from the richly furnished world to which they properly belonged, far below the level of comfort on which their father had gone through Cambridge into public life. John liked them, and the girls liked them for their own sakes.

Henry, "nice little Henry" [4] as Mary used to call him, was vivacious and impudent. Robert was quiet and seemed shy. But the girls soon found that "R.W." was less shy than he seemed, and Mary, for all her supposed silliness, soon distinguished the brothers by a process of shrewd equation.

"That nice little Henry W.—what a nice fellow he is! . . . I like them all better and better; and R. W. with all his quietness and gentleness, he is as bad as H. W., and worse because *he* is honest. H. W. says, 'I am impudent, I am a torment,' and he is so. R. W. says, 'I am gentlemanly and timid,' and he is—impudent and tormenting."

In such remarks as these the girls grope their way with H. and R., and distinct characters emerge. Henry comes up the more clearly for his humor and light touch. It was he who innocently told his Oxford tutor on his return from vacation that his papa had exhorted him to go out of college in quest of better company than he found in it. This was the kind of bland impudence that the girls loved in him, and, surely, it is the very stuff of flirtatious badinage? Robert, all diligence and humility, would meanwhile seem a perfect foil to this *enfant terrible* until suddenly the foil discarded its button and they would realize that the "shy" brother was the more exciting adversary of the two.

At first neither Jemima, Harriett nor Robert had any suspicion that they were victims of a parsonical love-plot. But in the late autumn of '27 they must have both realized it. Harriett certainly did when she replaced Jemima as chief victim. What happened then was that Rickards' patron, Lord Winchilsea, was suddenly given reason to believe that he was about to be made governor of New South Wales. He invited Rickards to come as Bishop; who, in turn, asked John Newman to come as suffragan bishop. (One thinks of the first Tracts being scattered among what an Oxford provost of the time used to call "the benighted aborigines of New Guinea.") Rickards' brother-in-law, Woollett Wilmot, and Robert Wilberforce, were also spoken of in this mass-emigration of talent to Botany Bay. John breathed this grave news to Harriett, but he assured her that he would oppose the idea of taking Robert away.[5] Robert could not resist so splendid an opportunity for quizzing Harriett with talk of life among the savages, and Harriett, almost taken-in, was within an ace of exposing her hand and heart. It is obvious that Robert, like herself, had no idea of what John had been plotting. Had he been he could not possibly have been so indelicate as to make fun of her. Harriett must have realized this and looked behind him for the plotters. To her astonishment she found John and his fellow-parson "Samuel Rickards."

At once letters began to fly, the girls' pens trembling with fury, though possibly they were also enjoying it like anybody who laughs hysterically at the memory of a narrow escape. Harriett:—

"There was a rope held out to me to carry me beyond the seas if I would but take hold of it in my first transports. Had I seized it I would have been as much transported with rage as I was with joy when I discovered it. Cowardly wretches all! They have corrupted John!"[6]

Mary:—

"What a shameful affair this is of the conspiracy between Mr. R(ickards), R. W(ilberforce), and John! I know not which is worst. Mr. R(ickards) I think if you were to hear his letter; and the cowardly manner in which he puts it all on John. Harry has just looked up with her Ulcombe curly face and said, 'Really, Robert W(ilberforce) has made no apology! He has used me very ill.' Bag! What a face of displeasure! I wish he could see it. He would not feel very much ashamed of himself. How beautiful she looks when she makes that pretty face! 'Haugh! For shame, Mary! What a shame, Mr. R(ickards)!'"[7]

We may contentedly leave the culprits to Harriett's gentle tongue. "I know," she writes to Jemima, "that you are as angry with these three people as I am. I scolded Mr. R(ickards) well and told him he had been making something of a fool of me and a knave of John." We may also rely on her to give Mr. Robert a flea in his ear. "As to R.W. it shows however quiet and sober a manner he may choose to assume in consideration of his doncial character, he is as impudent at heart as his more honest brother, to behave thus to a stranger like me! . . ." But note the word "stranger." She was not a stranger. And note the word "impudence." It is not an angry word. She is in full retreat under a heavy camouflage. For dignity's sake she must agree that it was, of course, all a joke; but, for honor's sake it must be treated as an impudent joke.

She simultaneously switches to Henry Wilberforce with the same tactic, so lightly that it is impossible to tell if she really has allowed herself to be attracted by him.

"Did mamma tell you," she goes on, "of Henry's imperturbable impudence? I could hardly keep him down though I several times wounded him enough to extort a cry of, 'Miss Newman, you insult me!'; 'Mrs. N., your daughter insults me. Mrs. N. it is your duty to protect me from insults.' Absurd little person, why did he stay?"

"Silly" Mary wondered shrewdly if all this was fire or just fireworks. So, to Jemima:—

"Harry certainly did encourage H(enry) W(ilberforce)'s absurdity! She denies it and says she scolded him and told him he was impudent. But what is this but encouraging him?"

It was probably part of the technique that even jokes could sometimes be turned skillfully dead earnest. Really, no man was safe for a single moment with a Georgian female.

3

Frank had meanwhile also fallen in love. She was a beautiful, buxom, dark-haired, cow-eyed, foolish Juno named Maria Giberne.[8] She had French blood. Tom Mozley called her the Prima Donna of the Oxford Movement. Unkind friends hinted to her that she was really in love with John Henry Newman. It is more probable that she nourished for him the sort of embarrassing *schwärmerei* that it is so often the penance of handsome priests to evoke in emotional women. Besides, she was more inclined to fall in love with young women than young men. She says this in her autobiography, when speaking of a typical attachment: "My passions were in an excessively excited state . . . I was desperately in love with Elizabeth Saunders. Indeed my friendships were more passionate than any love I have felt for the opposite sex." She confesses that if she caught her beloved Elizabeth paying too much attention to her sisters she would suffer the madness of jealousy, pass whole nights awake, all the time fearful lest her sobs and sighs should awaken her sister sleeping by her side. "I was on fire!" Our more clinical day would give a frank name to her disorder.

She met Frank Newman through his and John's Calvinistic friend Walter Mayers, who had married her sister. She was drawn to Frank by a blend of religion and sentimentality. He used to sing with her, talk religion with her, talk logic with her, try to wean her from the Dissenters towards his own as yet undefined brand of tolerant Christianity. That there could have been any least shade of amorous feeling in all this she scornfully disbelieved. She was merely amused when the watchful Mayers prevented Frank from kneeling beside her at the Communion Table. When she took leave of Frank she wept in the coach. However, she met another young girl the very next day, "with whom I fell quite in love." She thought how nice if Frank met her friend and then she could have them both. She says that it never struck her that there was the smallest chance of Frank's having an affection for her. But how did the idea enter her head, even to deny it? Indeed, she thought frequently of him. She wished that he might suddenly surprise her singing in the garden. One Sunday, deciding that she thought too often of him, she "tore the idol from his throne and sacrificed it at the foot of the altar." He came to see her but, she says, she had to leave "for a lecture or something." She strikes us as the sort of person who by luxuriating in her feelings kills all real feeling.

Her first meeting with the Newman girls was not a success. She found them stiff, cold and reserved, even a little bigoted. She could not understand how such good people should not want to talk about their feelings. The fact is, they were the first civilized, religious family she met. They did not talk of God through their noses. When they left her their letters did not begin with scraps of hymns. They told her, rather, all sorts of little news about their daily lives, silly, happy, trivial things which, to her surprise, she found "one likes to know." She was to end by crying out: "O my God I thank Thee for having in Thy Providence brought about my friendship with this dear family." She met John at the Brighton house. We may imagine the impression he would produce on this gushing beauty. She found him "cold-hearted, reserved and dry." He impressed her only by his unusual attentiveness to his mother.

"Has he not," her autobiography wails, in recalling this, "heaped coals of fire on my head by laying me under an eternal obligation to him! Bless the Monk!!!! In spite of my ill-will to him! Oh! Oh! Oh!" Nevertheless, "Je sentis naître tout de suite une espèce de confiance en cet étrange mortal."

The following January '28 she again went with her friend Fanny Young to stay with the Newmans at Brighton. This time she surrendered utterly, indeed in a mood of astonished admiration, to John's great-mindedness, though his talk was not at all of a religious character.

"I began to discover the perfections of his mind and knowledge and the romantic greatness of his soul. I thought him quite a hero. The first thing I heard him talk a long time about was Aristotle, and such eloquence from this hitherto silent personage astonished me."

His talk, naturally, would not have been directed to her. Isaac Williams and Woodgate were also at dinner. Even when Mary suddenly became ill and left the table, and her mother followed soon after her much troubled, Maria had thoughts only for John. She did not think about Mary even when Doctor Rice was hastily called. She sat on, drawing the guests in her sketch-book. In justice to her she could have had no idea that these illnesses of Mary's had been frequent and were dangerous: or that the family had good cause for presentiment. ("As I looked at her," John had written in his Memoranda, under October '26, "I seemed to say to myself not so much, 'Will you live?', as, 'How strange that you are still alive!' ")

Maria records the events of that night and the next day with bitter self-excoriation: her absorbing self-pity that night over a bad toothache; how Harriett and Jemima walked with her to the dentist; how the forceps broke and the tooth could not be pulled; how she was looking forward to enjoying more sympathy from the Newmans when she returned with Fanny Young at nine or ten that night from a dinner-engagement; and how when they alighted from the cab at the door of 11 Eastern Terrace, John met them in the hall and led them quietly to a side-room to tell them the sad news.

He offered them chairs, and then stood back against a table facing the fire, white-faced, his lips quivering, his hands crossed firmly. When he said that the doctor felt Mary could not live beyond morning, Fanny broke into tears, but Maria Rosina could not weep, though she dearly wished she could; fearing that if she did not John would consider her an unfeeling creature. She said, at last, "Won't you pray for her with us?," wondering chiefly whether he knew how to pray extempore, and thinking, "Now I shall see by his prayers whether he is like other religious people who, at such a time, would pour out their feelings at the throne of grace." He replied, "I must tell the truth."

"I, idiot that I was, thought he was going to confess that he could not pray extempore. Just as if he would! Stupid fool that I was!!! Unfeeling, hard-hearted wretch!!!!!! But, instead (Bête, sotte, cruche, pot-à-l'eau, fiend in human shape. Oh!) of that he said: 'She is gone already.'"

He told them a few details of Mary's death, calmed them gently, and wished them good-night, leaving Maria absorbed in admiration of him and hatred of herself. Incredibly, the two visitors stayed on in the house for several more days, deeply edified by the family's restrained grief, which they showed only by an occasional sigh, damp eyes, and John's white, closed lips and downcast eyes. "They thought of us just as if nothing had happened." Every night John used to

read the burial-service. When he did pray extempore Maria
was satisfied. He was a religious man after all.

We will meet her again at this story's end. Her auto-
biographies—she wrote two, in English and in French—deserve publication. In them we see the poor, foolish, lovely,
life-unskillful creature battering herself for years through
endless fears and hopes of salvation, fumbling with problems
far beyond her powers; asking herself in agony, "Am I right
with Heaven?"; thirsting to kneel in confession to somebody,
preferably John Newman; pestering him with letters, all of
which he would answer with an inexhaustible sympathy and
patience; falling into strange excesses as when she used to
flagellate herself with the ropes of her trunk, then go to sleep
on the hard floor, and rise, stiff and cold, three hours before
morning to pray in a red robe with candles, at Matins, in
imitation of Roman Catholics. We are glad to find that she
enjoyed one long, happy period of five years during which
she lived with a young woman named Selina Bacchus in "une
petite maison convenable" at Cheltenham. "We were one
soul, one heart, in two bodies. Chère petite amie! Comme
elle me gâtait! Et comme je la gâtais!" Then the usual
thing happened. Selina married. There was only one God
and Dr. Newman. One alone would have been a lot.

Frank Newman was to carry her image in his heart for
years.

4

The girls met the Wilberforce boys again during the next
summer and autumn ('28), first at Brighton and then at
Nuneham Courtenay, a pleasant little village with a demesne
stretching down to the river, about five miles from Oxford,
where they spent two months in a cottage loaned by John's
friend, Dornford.[9] John writes about it in August to his
mother: "I am led to think you must not wait for the letting

of the house before you come here, and I will tell you why. H.W. (Henry Wilberforce) will be coming." The Inn is still there. The cottage is the one where Rousseau is said to have stayed during his English exile. John's Diary has several references to the Wilberforces about this time. But we notice that there is no reference to Robert for the Nuneham period. The girls' winter letters explain. They are delightfully filled with whispery, pained references to his strange behavior during those two rustic months. His crimes had been that while they waited expectantly for him he had called on them very tardily, and only once; and on another occasion failed to keep a dinner engagement. Some cross words were exchanged, Harriett duly gave him another piece of her mind, umbrage was universal, and nothing was settled. But a new fruitful complex had been established. (This technique may be called The Queen's Quarrel Gambit.) John tried three times to smooth things out and made them splendidly worse, after which he went back, for the time at any rate, to the peace and quiet of the Fathers' disputations, far from these feminine wars.

The misery of this quarrel, from the girls' point of view, was that their friends pretended to take it all as a slight social gaffe on Robert's part—that is the Pownalls and the Ricks and everybody else who knew of their association with the two young men. And what was the good of that? As Harriett wails to Jem nobody has "the most distant idea of the real state of matters. On the terms we are at present with him it is awkward to know what to say."

Their letters constantly revive the subject. It seems, he seems, *they* seem unavoidable; as when Harry visits the Rickards and goes upstairs to her bedroom—the back-room as she had requested—and stands warming herself by the welcome fire; for she looks up to see a shabby ticket pinned against the wall bearing the "abominable long name, only there is an Esq. at the end!": *Robert Wilberforce, Esq. Box and Carpet Bag 2s. Porterage.* She told Jem that as she looked at it she had a mind to pin up her own name as companion on the other side. It is the same that night when they sit together and read two cantos of *Rokeby,* including the song of Allan-a-Dale, a song which Henry and Jemima used to sing together. "It sounded very queer. And nobody knew about it but Cathie and I."

5

They spent the late Winter of '28 and the Spring and Summer of '29 at Brighton, hating it. Mrs. Newman disliked the wind and it pained her head and teeth. One sees them vividly in that Brighton house: Jemima reading *Comus* over the fire, Harry upstairs nursing a swelled head, mamma with her head wrapped in a shawl, listening to the wind and as always longing to be near her dear John. "I have often wished you here and when I argued myself out of that fault I have been glad you were absent." He fixed that they should leave Brighton and come to a cottage at Horspath belonging to a Mr. Talmadge—£10 for three months except that Talmadge would keep one room. Soon they were longing eagerly for it, ordering seeds and geranium cuttings, and begging him to plant some mignonette. He told them there was a Dutch oven, a fish-kettle, and a warming-pan. Mamma begs him to air the beds. In October they shifted from Horspath to Nuneham.

Mrs. Newman kept on pressing gently to be allowed to live still nearer to John. So, this November 16th she agrees that she is willing to return to Brighton but with resigned references to the Easterly winds, and "for Harriett, I hope she is much less susceptible of cold than she was." She pleads openly with him some three weeks later, December 11th: "If we could move advantageously I shd. vote for a nice little cottage with a garden *near you,* as you seem to intend to be a sort of 'monk' for some time." He was obviously in a fix. From his viewpoint Nuneham had every inconvenience: at five miles they were neither near him nor away from him. One of her letters to him gives us the picture in November, '29:—"I am afraid you paid dearly for the pleasure your visit of to-day gave us. I am afraid you had wind, and snow, and slipperiness and solitariness to encounter." Yet, she says she wants to stay on.

She again presses him, in the May of the following year, '30: "We should be coming, I hope, near you for the whole time." In a fright he promptly replies that they have been so much together at Horspath and Nuneham that for the ensuing Vacation he cannot hope to be with them or have them near Oxford. "Indeed, to speak frankly, it would annoy me much to find you near here, for I am sure I could not come to you without serious inconvenience and the disarrangement of my plans."

However, what if they would let the Brighton house *a whole year* and then come quite near? His mother at once joyously seized on the idea of a cottage in Oxford where they could all live together. Within a month she had let the Brighton house for a year, at £180, with an option of a second year. She is next found telling him she "will want the needful for closing and travelling." By August (1830) he is looking at the first of their Oxford homes.[10]

They stayed in three places. The first was a house called Rose Mount, on Rose Hill, which lies between Iffley and Littlemore, looking back on the distant, delicate spires. Harriett speaks of it as "our queer little cottage," but it was not so very little. It consisted of two cottages, originally called Eaton's Cottages, turned into one picturesque dwelling. By June, '31, Harry writes:—

"John has taken possession of his new apartments, consisting of a hall, staircase, study and bedroom. Quite grand is he not? His study is very pretty and comfortable for summer. We have made a large new window in it, allowing him a view of our garden, and a very pleasant look-out towards Oxford."

They were there by October 22nd, stayed about two years and then moved finally still closer to their citadel.

They stayed briefly, first, at "The Cottage" in Iffley, on Tree Lane. This is a steep country lane, even yet rural, and though it is now compassed by urban villas it yields occasional seductive vistas of the city. They were here only a few weeks. The last of these Newman homes nestles into the valley, and has borne various names—Rose Bank, Grove Mount, Iffley Turn House. It is where the bus stops today at Iffley Turn on its way back to Oxford, and is very much as it was when the Newmans lived in it.

So near to Oxford they naturally expected to see their old friends again, and it was not John's fault if they did not. During the Long Vacation of '29 he had ridden out to Horspath every evening for dinner, returning in the morning, often getting wet through on the journey. When they were at Nuneham he used also to ride out there, alone or with his friends. "Our good folks came to us splashed in style, and the walkers in a similar plight." And, indeed, it is a heavy enough walk from Oxford to Nuneham even on modern roads. The two Wilberforces were among those visitors, and the end of the story makes it clear that after '29 Robert renewed his interest in the girls, with particular attention now to Jemima. Thus, Harriett to her aunt, in the winter of '29: "Henry is *my* little friend.[11] You must enquire of Jem for R."

6

The Nuneham visits had been mostly morning calls—the village was too remote for dinner—so that the mother and the two girls must have passed many lonely nights in that cottage by the dripping woods. They hoped therefore to see much more of John and his friends when they moved to Rose Bank, and there they were, in fact, able to enjoy almost as much of Oxford life as if they lived in the city. Pleasantly enough, many of their letters from here are dated in the summer term. *Tom Brown at Oxford* is ten years ahead of us; he evokes the forties rather than the thirties, as when his girls parading Broad Walk during Show Sunday wonder if the dons include the author of "Tract Ninety." But Oxford summers are dateless and we should probably not need to alter for the Newmans an iota of what Tom's "lionesses" saw.

"In Christchurch meadows, and in the college gardens the birds are making sweet music in the tall elms. You may almost hear the thick grass growing. The glorious old city is putting on her best looks and bursting out into laughter and song. In a few weeks the races begin, and Cowley marsh will be alive with white tents and joyous cricketers. A quick ear on the towing-path by the Gut may feast at one time on three sweet sounds, the thud-thud of the eight-oar, the crack of the rifles at the Weirs, and the click of the bat on Magdalen ground. And then Commemoration rises in the foreground, with its clouds of fair visitors, and visions of excursions to Woodstock and Nuneham—of windows open on to the old quadrangles in the long summer evenings, through which silver laughter and strains of sweet music, not made by man, steal out and puzzle the old celibate jackdaws, peering down from the battlements with heads on one side. . . ."

How genial he is! We have from Harriett also a description of Commemoration, that of 1831, which describes in a

rather different tone the same clouds of fair visitors, hints at
the same gentle flirtations, tells of the same sort of American
being given the same sort of honorary degree, the same bois-
terous undergraduates, musical performances, picnics on the
river, promenades at New College, crowded mornings, noons
and nights of which, in some miraculous way, no single moment is missed by anybody. "How it was done," says Tom,
"no man can tell, but done it was and they seemed all the
better for it all." Harriett is not so benevolent. "I wish
ladies would not make themselves disagreeable or absurd.
One might think they might behave like reasonable creatures in Oxford if nowhere else. Everybody was so mad
after all the amusement that there was nothing but fainting
and hysterics, so that the whole house was in confusion."

However, she saw nice little Henry Wilberforce at Commemoration, and breakfasted with Robert. They were, in
fact, gay with dinner visitors almost every day, and when it
was all over "poor Oxford seems quite desolate."

The blow fell some time between this Autumn and the
following Spring.[12]   Then, May 26th, Harriett wrote to comfort poor Jemima, then at the Pownalls' and about to go on
to the Rickards, who had meanwhile moved to Suffolk. For
Jemima is now in a sad state of terror, not lest she should
never see Robert again but lest she should. The news has
become public that he is engaged to marry another girl, one
Agnes Wrangham, daughter of an archdeacon, of Deeside
House, Chester, a landed gentleman—not like the impover-
ished Newmans—with estates at Chester and Hunmanby in
Yorkshire. In her letter Harry makes everything clear, all
discretion dropped at last:—

"I will proceed to relieve you on one point . . . I have had a
letter from L(ucy Rickards). She tells me you will not meet R.
there—for A(gnes) writes word their plans are altered. Tho' the
marriage takes place the 11th they are to stay in Yorkshire and not

reach Suffolk till the middle of July. Now, pray do, dear Cathie, be sure to ascertain—ask if L(ucy) mentioned your visit. I am pretty sure your (*illegible*) visit is at the bottom. Oh, Jemima, I almost despise him! Poor fellow, I make all allowances for an entanglement his marriage may have caused. But is he not to be despised? Really the more the affair presses itself, in its entanglement, into my view the more that sad feeling seems to be just. Yet I am well aware that if he had come I should have had to rouse your spirit by the insult he put upon us and you . . . (*more illegible*) . . . especially, and have urged that the spirit which had the hardihood to dare such a meeting ought not to be spared.

"Yet, I really think, poor fellow, if this is his motive for change of plan how unhappy he must sometimes feel. And if that at such a moment what is there for him this life? Still, that, wretched as is the thought, is not the worst of my trouble, or the one that incessantly wears and rends my heart. It is, simply, his fall—that one irremediable, unchangeable stain—there once and for ever. I will only ask you once again to be sure to hear all that you can. If you can find anything to make matters better do well mark and remember and examine it. You only can now give me this little ease and I ask you, for my sake, to have your wits about you."

The second half of the letter is written by Mrs. Newman. She has read Harry's part; she agrees so perfectly that it would be painful repetition for her to go over the same ground again. "I am glad you are spared the trial I feared so much. If the intended visit was postponed from hearing who was the R(ickard)s' other guest it shows you the truth of what I said in my last letter, that 'conscience makes cowards of the boldest,' and it speaks strong self-condemnation. That is, that the person knows himself to be an aggressor— and he cannot trust to the uncertainty of how far that other person may expose him. It is a sad commencement of life."

Her next and last sentence is meaningful: If we are not happy in our minds "vain are all external advantages": meaning, one takes it, that we are to think of those landed estates, and of the reduced gentleman who has decided to marry into them. We do not know if Jemima replied. There is no word from John. He probably saw that there could be no explanations this time.

CHAPTER 9

THE WORLD BREAKING IN

1

FAR too much has been written about thoughtful, self-examining men like John Newman as if they excogitated everything out of the air, and nothing from their unconscious experience of human beings. John came up hard against human nature, first and last, in his own family. He was coming up against it now in his parish work at Littlemore, where for the first time—since March, '28—he had been mixing closely with ordinary people, Oxfordshire laborers and their families. The parish is not much over a mile from Oxford.

He had written to Jemima, in the May after their sister's death, "What a veil and curtain this life is! Beautiful but still a veil!" In his parish work he was to realize that life is a little more solid than a veil, much as he had begun to realize earlier that a church is something more human than an idea. We can see this in a little passage at arms with Frank over their parish-work. It is recorded so fully in his letters and in Frank's "reports" that it falls naturally into dramatic form:—

Scene: A Summer afternoon in John Newman's rooms at Oriel. Two windows left look into the quadrangle. Opposite them two windows look into Merton Lane. Between these last are engravings of Saint Christopher and *three* portraits of the sainted martyr, Charles I. On the side in which

165

the door opens from the stairs are bookcases packed with the Fathers. Opposite this is the fireplace. On the mantel there is a portrait of his mother and a crucifix from which, in the Anglican fashion, he has removed the figure. It is a dun-colored room and the evening sun has moved from the windows. In the center of the room is a table covered with books. He is seated at the table writing. There is not a sound except his scratching pen and when somebody's hasty steps are suddenly heard on the bare stairs outside. The steps pause and he hears a knock on the oak.

J. H. N.: Come in!   (*Sees Frank, who on finding him busy, makes as if to retire.*)   No, don't go, Frank. I was just finishing my sermon for Sunday. (*Leans back. Smiles.*) I see you've been collecting some of the dust of Littlemore.

Frank: (*Coming in and sitting down.*)   Some of its mortal and immortal dust. Shall I tell you whom I've been talking to?

J. H. N.: Yes, of course. Please do. (*Takes a list from him.*) Now that I look at it I'm afraid it was rather long. Did you get through much of my list?

Frank: Through *all* of it. (*Frowns.*) Some of these people are very difficult, John. Very difficult! However. . . . Well, first of all there was old Granny Phipps. Now she's a *very* difficult woman to do anything with. She makes excuses for everything I say to her. Or else applies my remarks to somebody else. When I talk, for instance, about giving scandal, "Oh, yes," she says, "that's just like old Granny Titcombe, always gossiping." Of course, I try to bring it back to herself, but . . . She's a *very* self-righteous old woman. I'm afraid I could make no headway with her. Then, there's Mrs. Waring. She takes everything to herself. "That's me!" she says all the time, even when I don't mean her at all! And yet she is far from happy. . . .

J. H. N.: I see you spoke to Mrs. Humphrey?

Frank: Impenetrable. I've seen her five or six times. Very stiff.

J. H. N.: Old Phipps?

Frank: He is much better. I exerted myself with him. I said,

"Phipps," I said, "you are walking along the broad way. You are in great carelessness, Phipps, about your soul." I let him have it good and strong. He bore it very well, you know. Made no excuses. In fact, when I was going he said to me, "Mr. Newman, it's *very* kind of you." And he looked thoughtful. I think that was a good sign, don't you?

J. H. N.: (*Leaning forward.*) Tell me! I am waiting for you to come to the case of Mary Bermingham.

Frank: (*Joyously.*) My one success. The case of Mary Bermingham is finished, John! She is saved!

J. H. N.: (*Leans back. Coldly.*) Saved? She cannot be saved until she is dead.

Frank: (*Eagerly.*) Now, John, don't let us get into another dispute about Final Perseverance, and all that. I am merely telling you the facts. What happened to poor Mary was quite simple. This man we know about came into her cottage without being asked. Now, it never occurred to poor Mary to tell him he mustn't come in. And when he did come in it apparently never occurred to her to tell him to go out again. Then, old Miss Hatton—you know her—for some reason or another bolted the door on the pair of them . . . really the incident was *very* confusing. However, I talked sharply to Mary about it. "Mary," I said, "you swore out at this man! And yet," I said, "you didn't think his behaviour was bad enough for you to call out to your brother who was working in the garden?"

J. H. N.: (*Leaning forward again.*) What did she say to that?

Frank: She hung her head. She was ashamed. She began to cry. Her soul was melted. John, I am *sure* she has repented. I am sure she is a child of God again.

J. H. N.: Are you? (*Regards him coldly.*) Or are you quite sure you are not simply applying sweet words to her sins as if they were plasters?

Frank: But she *felt* the Voice! I tell you she is deeply convinced of Sin! She says, poor wretch, that she has seven devils in her. She even says she is too bad to be saved. I spoke warmly, making allowances, of course, for reserve—I mean I am so much younger than she is; and then she is in a lower

order of life. But I could see her heart was stirred. I could
feel it! John, you really must . . .

J. H. N.: (*Rising impatiently.*) Frank, Frank! You are deceiving yourself, or else this girl is deceiving you. No! No!
I've got beyond all that. My only sure ground of hope for
anybody's spiritual state is the sight of a consistent life. The
result of which is that there are very few people I *can* be sure
of—though I feel it's no business of mine to judge them.
No! It is many years now since I took my motto from old
Thomas Scott—"Growth is the only evidence of life." You
say she is a child of God. Where is the evidence? I place
no trust in this girl's words, nor in the words of any man, or
woman, until I see actual *evidence* of a reformed life.
Words are not things, Frank.

Frank: (*Rising angrily.*) You are being hard-hearted!

J. H. N.: (*Quietly.*) Perhaps I am being hard-headed?

And cool-headed? And Frank Newman? Neither hard
nor cool but by comparison much more warm-hearted.
Both of them clever; one of them growing daily wiser; for
though neither yet knew much about men and affairs John
was, by this date, learning fast. This world we see and
touch may be, as he asserted to the very end, a faint *umbra et
imago veritatis,* but it has—he was beginning to see how
right Hawkins and Whately were in this—its own insistent,
practical reality, always confusing because always blending
its colors, as even the most doctrinaire idealist demonstrates
at every moment in the inconsistencies of his own life. Indeed it is not too much to say that John, philosophically
speaking, was moving from a raw, rude Idealism to a mature
and considered Realism, or at any rate, that Realism came
close enough to force from him the admission that this shadowy image of immortal truth is our wheat and our tares to
be reaped, winnowed, ground and kneaded into those codes,
forms and institutions—themselves, it is true, largely cre-
ations of the imagination—which, as he was soon to admit in

one of his sermons, are at least solid enough to be "the very food of faith" and the ground of all human battles.

2

Had there been no parish-work to bring his balloon into its narrow shed it would have been difficult for anybody to be an Idealist with an aunt like Aunt Betsy.[1]   She had for some time now been up to her neck in debt.   All through '27 we see John coming to the rescue; now sending her a stop-gap of £50; now advising her to sell out; now trying to concoct a scheme whereby she would sublet all but one room at Strand—she had, he thought, better not leave altogether "for the tradesmen's satisfaction"; now asking Frank if he could raise £200 for her; now advising her to tell the more pressing of her many creditors that she will settle "something" this month.

Her culminating year of disaster is best summed up in the words of his own private Memoranda: "I have much to try me in the way of money-matters.   Aunt's debts are not far short of £500."   A later additional note rounds this off: "(It was) in the event, £700.   Frank and I paid this sum between us."   His mother closed the story in July, '29 with: "Aunt has met a respectable person near Richmond that she can board with when she leaves Mrs. C's, which I suppose is before now."   She meant Mrs. Fisher, of Hill Street, Richmond.[2]   By September, '30, Aunt Betsy and Mrs. Fisher had gone to Grove House, Marsh Gate.   In '32 we find her at a Mrs. Kershaw's, The Vineyard.   There the family visited her, when they could, and there they wrote to her constantly. She should have been a favored lodger: "Dr. Newman's aunt."   Her life would be a smooth, empty routine.   If she were not too feeble she could, when tired of the gardens and the teashops, the church and the river, revisit Ham, and Grey Court House, murmuring with the rooks, "Twenty-five years

ago . . .   Or, was it only twenty-four . . . ?"   In the end
she went to live with Jemima in Derby.

3

When it was not Aunt Betsy it was Charles.[3]   "Do make
Harriett say seriously and on deliberation whether she does
not think our being near town, and (Charles) having a home
with us would not, in spite of that inward inquietude which
wears him, be a very great comfort to him.   Harriett thinks
and judges more dispassionately and rationally than I do."
It is one of his many efforts to do something for Charles, who
was being unusually tiresome around this time: for he had
written his mother an unfeeling letter when Mary died, and
he had also told her proudly that he had sent a circular letter
of about eight sheets of foolscap to such of his superiors in
the Bank of England as had, in his opinion, been favorable
to him.   John reproved him for the unfeeling letter about
Mary and thereby provoked another rigmarole to his mother
on the lines of—

"Our's is a great loss but why it should cloud you so, I by no
means see.   If you had no other friends it would be different—
but you have plenty.   Did not Mrs. Williams of York St. lose an
only daughter?   When I mentioned it to Mr. Hayes he made
light of it: 'Well these things will happen.'   And very properly
he felt . . .   Do not men of sense drink their wine on the field of
battle with friends dead & dying around them?   Because they do
not believe in Hell or any such superstitions!   It is always my
method in correspondence to put down what comes to the end of
my pen, & if it is not allowed me to do so, if my doing so hurts
your feelings I must decline all correspondence . . ."

There are pages of it, ending, *Believe me, My dear Mother
Your dutiful & affectionate son, C. Newman;* followed by a
postscript which is the only sane bit in the entire letter:

"Aunt did give me John's *Life of Cicero* but I was afraid of taking it to Mr. Mullins lest Fanny should wrap the butter in it & I doubt whether it would have been read I think it would have been lost." '

Then having ignored John's reproval for several months he suddenly came out against him with a bombardment of accusations. One's eyes jump from one piece of abuse to another.

"There are injuries & outrages so unfair & so beyond all calculations as to strike the person injured with dumbness. . . . My mouth has been stopped towards you. . . . You say you are disgusted with the slight manner in which I receive intimations of the good wishes of friends towards me. How do you know what is in *my* mind on these occasions? . . . It is my opinion that my conduct is as sound & well-considered as yours. . . . That I was unpleasant towards you when I came down to Brighton I well knew. Nor inasmuch as you were simply unpleasant towards me in return do I complain in the least. It was what I expected. . . . I will not have my liberty restrained. . . . I meet in my mother's letters many things repulsive to my manner of feeling & thinking. . . . If you complain of me I can as well complain of you. . . . Be disgusted still if you please in the midst of your ignorance. . . . And now I think that in common fairness you should retract your injurious aspersions & intimations towards me. *Dear John, Your affec: Brother, C. R. Newman.*"

We are not surprised that John's patience broke. We could forgive him if he had screamed his answer:—

"Why is it you thus persecute me?, for I can call it no other name. It is hard I may not be left alone. It was *you* first wrote to me in February requiring an immediate answer; now you write again & require an immediate answer. This is nothing new. Years past you have from time to time attacked and insulted me, forcing me into correspondence from which to *you* no good could ensue. . . ."

And he refused to shape a formal reply.

A month later Charles was warmly reassuring his mother that he did not want any pocket-money. He was receiving an "ample allowance" from John.

4

Presages? Knockings at his cloister door? Pluckings at his elbow when he was luxuriating in his "pensive melancholy" or feeling "hungry for Irenaeus and Cyprian"? Gentle and ungentle intimations that if the world is indeed inhabited by angels this is the sort of angel who inhabits it. These private and public insistences rose to a peak between Mary's death in 1828 and his departure for Italy in 1832, which has all the appearance of an emotional flight from the public life which was then confronting him.

He had already taken his first step into public life when he became a tutor at Oriel (in '26) and had to consider seriously whether the life of a tutor is consonant with the vocation of a priest.

Now there are, one here observes, all sorts of priests. Some see themselves as dispensers from sin, some as preventers of sin, some as practicing disciples, some as preaching apostles, some as interpreters, some as vulgarisateurs, some as the generals of their church, some as its rude commandos, some as its executives, some as its administrators, some as God's humble doorkeepers, some as God's consuls, some as God's ambassadors, and some as little gods themselves, some as the protagonists, or actors, over and over again, of the sad heavenly drama, some as its contemplatives, some as its martyrs, some judge us, some are our one friend-at-court, some want only to discipline us, some want only to comfort us, and most, probably, do not consider their role at all. John Newman was in no doubt as to his role. If he was a tutor he was also a priest, and if it meant anything to be a

priest the two roles must meld. He had thought of being
a missionary abroad; he realized now that he would be a missionary at home. He would labor among the savage undergraduates. He would shape their souls.

At first thought this may seem a mere private decision to
reform the world. Then we look at his three fellow-tutors
and allies, Hurrell Froude, Wilberforce and Dornford, and
invoke a famous and fruitful friendship, and another that
came of it, and all that came of it. At this moment Froude
and Newman were not the Achilles and Patroclus they were
presently to become, for Newman was still in Froude's eyes
a "heretic"; that is a Liberal Evangelical, Whately's friend,
the man who had preferred Hawkins to his beloved master.
But they were, in a year or two, to become one another's inspiration; which means that we invoke in turn the spirit of
John Keble, who in working on and through all who met
him—Froude his most receptive pupil—inspired a whole
generation into public service.

That famous friendship, between Newman and Froude,[4]
as Dean Church has sensitively said, was one of those intimacies whose course nobody can ever record: emerging as
gradually as a love-affair out of "unremembered talks, out of
unconscious disclosures of temper and purpose, out of walks
and rides and quiet breakfasts and common-room arguments,
out of admirations and dislikes, out of letters and criticisms
and questions." And in the end, not even the two lovers
could say how it began. But, surely, it must at least have
begun to take some sort of shape in this tutorial war?

"That bright and beautiful Froude," as Harriett called him
after his untimely death, was tall and thin, with, Dean
Church recalls, "a large skull and forehead, delicate features,
and penetrating grey eyes, not exactly piercing, but bright
with internal conceptions, and ready to assume an expression of amusement, careful attention, enquiry, or stern disgust, but with a basis of softness." He was a very different

man to John Newman: a hard cross-country rider, a rough-weather yachtsman, a completely unconventional thinker, impish, mischievous, daring, even perverse, willful, imprudent, challenging, humbug-hating to the point of truculence, hard as nails on himself, yet tender too, and playful and elastic, a fastidious high-tempered aristocrat. He must have been the most lovable and lively of the group soon to coalesce in a common cause, and his influence on John Newman in life and death was incalculable. John admired him from the start: so, in '26, "Froude is one of the acutest and clearest and deepest men in the memory of man." He pays a warmer tribute of love to him in the *Apologia* than to any other friend; as he well might, since no one person, as we shall see, influenced him so powerfully towards Rome. When Hurrell and he addressed one another as *carissime*, the Southern word broke through racial reserve to the truth of their love.

There was no controversy at first when the four tutors began their godly work. To all appearances their Provost, Hawkins, seemed to approve wholeheartedly. Actually he was approving only as a disciplinarian, not as a clergyman. For some time the four freely weeded out the idle and privileged gentlemen commoners, the chronics, the incurables, the dullards and the sluggards, and concentrated devoutly and devotedly on a worthy few. The result was a marked increase in Firsts, Failures and Fervor. Hawkins approved of the increase in Firsts and frowned at the increase in Failures. They led the chosen few through their studies and to church, often no doubt across the street to Saint Mary's, where John was now Vicar, and had begun to preach regularly. But when the four tutors proposed to re-arrange the whole time-table so as to have a still closer moral control over their disciples Hawkins had had enough of Fervor. He had to consider Oxford's clocks as well as Heaven's, and after a prolonged argument stopped their supply of pupils

altogether.   The reformers would continue with those they
had, but their tutorship would then die.

The profit-and-loss account in this affair is that Hawkins
won the round and that John Newman won some precious
knowledge of himself, and of the world.   He had seen the
secular face of Oxford behind its religious mask.   He had
seen that he was not a good judge of character—he had
foolishly preferred Hawkins to Keble.   He saw that he could
lead men, because whereas they, often from a fastidious
modesty, would not formulate publicly what they industri-
ously acted upon, he "when he had a clear view of the matter
was accustomed to formulate it, and was apt to be . . .
irreverent and rude in the nakedness of his analysis, and un-
measured and even impatient in the enforcing of it."   These
are his own words.   He was beginning to know more and
more about himself.

5

He could also act vigorously when he had no clear view of
a matter; and clarify his views afterwards.   He was quite
muddled about the first really public event he was concerned
in.   This was the Peel Election following a Cabinet proposal
to grant Catholic Emancipation in 1829.   He objected at
once.   Not until the affair was all over did he understand
why he had objected.

The situation was simple enough.   Peel proposed the Bill
and honorably resigned, hoping no doubt that a re-election
would endorse his policy.   Hawkins, now become "our med-
dling Provost," had him renominated.   Oxford, and John
Newman, rebelled.   Peel was defeated.   John, crowing as
he never crowed before, wrote like a man who has tasted
blood: "Any of us in the Oriel Common Room would fight
a dozen of them apiece": in talents, one hastens to say.
But when he talked, and he talked much, of the "principle"

thus so gloriously defended against London, Gladstone, the lawyers and everybody else, what principle was he talking about? The fact is, he did not clearly know.

A month before he had said quietly to Jemima: "You know I have no opinion about the Catholic Question, and now it is settled I shall never perhaps have one." He merely saw the giving of the vote to Irish Catholics (though not to all of them, by the way—whole sections, including, among others, the Jesuits, were excluded) as the encroachment of philosophism and indifferentism on the Church of England. "Is not the age evil?" A month later he is sure as a rock and hot as fire. Oxford never changes! We may be mistaken but we are never inconstant! "Our opinion" (he had just recently said he had no opinion!) "of the Catholic Question is a fact of times gone by—a thing done—if a bigoted opinion it remains so. . . ." And he now says clearly, "I am not for Catholic Emancipation." But he does not say why, except that when politicians change Oxford must change its politicians whether it changes its own ideas or not, whether it accepts the inevitable or not. "I would not have lost this opportunity of showing our independence of the world." But they had put up against Peel a man mildly favorable to Emancipation! His only point of principle so far does not seem to be much more than Oxford pride.

In another eager letter, to his mother, he confesses that he has since been thinking about the matter, that his views are much expanded, and that in justice to himself he ought to write a volume about them. (We must note that Peel was defeated on February 26th, and that this letter is dated March 13th, so that it is a patent post-cogitation.) In this letter he says that he now sees that the evil of the day is an untrammelled liberty of thought, independent of church-guidance, a "spirit of latitudinarianism, indifferentism, and schism, a spirit which tends to overthrow doctrine as if the fruit of bigotry and discipline, as if the instrument of priestcraft." He sees opinion setting against the Church; composed of the uneducated, and the partially educated, utilitarians, political economists, useful-knowledge people; schismatics, Baptists, the high circles in London, and the talent of the day. Well, Emancipation was an illustration of all this, for it had been carried chiefly by the indifferentists. Then comes this statement: "All these things being considered I am clearly *in principle* an anti-Catholic; and, if I" (he means, one, or anybody) "do not oppose Emancipation, it is only perhaps because I do not think it expedient, perhaps possible, to do so. . . . If I am" (i.e., if one is) "for Emancipation it is only that I may take my stand against the foes of the Church on better ground. . . ." He concludes by saying that it is pretty clear that Emancipation *is* necessary "because the intelligence of the country will have it." In short he did not object to the actual end (Emancipation) so much as to the frame of mind behind it, the accommodating, unstable, amoral politicians.

If anybody said to him, "This is all very well! But what do *you* propose to do about Emancipation?", he would wave the question aside, calling it "A matter of subordinate consequence." If his interlocutor, excusably irritated by this air of superiority to a nasty, practical problem, insisted that Emancipation happened to be the question before him, he would dodge the question by insisting that it was not the essential issue at stake. If reminded that it was an issue he would admit that in practice it appeared to be "necessary," but declare himself nevertheless resolutely against it "on principle," and actively against anybody who supported it. John Newman must often have been very maddening to practical people in this way. The clue to his attitude is in his anxiety to show Oxford's independence of "the world." It is the Puritan antithesis at work again. Oxford must not be of the world, though in the world, the world being something in the order of the flesh and the devil, in so far, of course, as the world had any corporeal existence at all! It is a common priestly attitude, and it must often drive politicians beside themselves with rage.

It is, all in all, a most illuminating affair, which reveals two important things about John Newman: that he could act, and did act, not on clearly perceived ideas but on obscure intuitions and shadowy feelings; and it shows, once again, that his intellectual post-mortems attempt to rationalize, post factum, decisions prompted not by his intelligence but by his instinct, though they were none the worse for that. But how many of John's other excogitations, one wonders, are post-cogitations? How much of the *Apologia* faithfully records not so much what happened at the time as posthumous rationalizations which had meanwhile merged with the event in his memory?

6

If we must, however, take those ideas of '29, after the event, out of the context of the event they are nonetheless impressive in their own right. They show us the now well-known Newman intellect acutely at work, so seductive in generalization, so fallible, sometimes even repellent in the particular and momentary. We go back over his outline with an intense pleasure in its perception of warring principles whose conflict was already looming ahead, and which can never cease to challenge us when we advert to them.

"The talent of the day is against the Church." There he began: and, one thinks, is it not almost always so? He went on: "The Church party (visibly at least, for there may be latent talent, and great times give birth to great men) is poor in mental endowments. It has not activity, shrewdness, dexterity, eloquence, practical power. On what then does it depend? On prejudice and bigotry." How true! How honest! It is the sort of bold thing Froude might have said. And how his mother and sisters must have stared, as today any equally pious person stares whensoever the same thing is said. "Yet," he proceeds, "I have good meaning and one honourable to the Church." And he develops his thought characteristically: "Listen to my theory. As each individual has certain instincts of right and wrong antecedently to rea- soning, on which he acts—and rightly so—which perverse reasoning may supplant, which then can hardly be regained" (Is he thinking of Frank and Charles here?) "but, if re- gained, will be regained from a different source—not from Nature but from Reasoning, so I think has the world of men collectively." These truths were those given by God, natu- rally, to man; and other truths in the unsophisticated infancy of nations which we call "the wisdom of our ancestors." Now, these truths are carried on from age to age, and are no less true because the men who hand them on are unable to prove them, and may even hold them only through "preju- dice and bigotry"; indeed these poorly-endowed men could be overcome in argument by any clever Cambridge graduate inside an hour. Naturally, then, the talent of the day is always against this traditional wisdom and against the Chris- tian Church which maintains it and, often so inadequately, transmits it. Where, then, will any man who respects "the wisdom of our ancestors" be but on the side of what W. G. Ward was to call "the stupid party"? We might well see this letter as another turning-point in John's life.

It is a persuasive piece of dialectic. But we note that its persuasiveness depends on whether one accepts the *a priori* position implicit in the shifted meaning he has given to the word "talents": a shift managed by means of the sub-sarcasm or irony which was always part of his nature and is becom- ing more and more characteristic of his thought now that he himself has shifted from Liberalism to Conservatism.

For "talents" now is to mean invincible ignorance, and the stupid are alone wise though they are not clever. To describe this method of argument is not to invalidate its conclusion. All argument has to be *a priori*. In cold reason nothing can be assumed as given: not even existence. Everything starts from a hypothesis. The meanings in every hypothesis are subject to agreement on the premises. Why should Newman not shift a meaning to establish his own premises? It was one reason why, later, Kingsley, thinking they were using an identical language, would so little understand him. It is one of Newman's contributions to English to have extended the power of the language by giving it new precisions of meaning in a logician's scepticism as to its commonly having any precise meaning at all.

What was John's *a priori* position during the Peel affair? It was less a position than a prejudice. He was instinctively "on the side of the priest," as he was, and would so often be, instinctively "agin the government." We have noticed those *three* pictures of Charles I in his rooms. When Charles X of France lost his throne in the 1830 Revolution he frothed that the French must be the most wicked nation on earth, and that Charles and his ministers were poltroons not to have stayed in Paris to be guillotined: this after Charles had tried to impose on his people those infamous July Ordinances which dissolved a parliament which had never even met, suspended the Charter, forbade the publication of all newspapers unless they had royal approval, promulgated new election laws and denied the vote to any but the richest landlords. For years after John so hated France that when passing through Paris on his return from Sicily he stayed locked up in his room for twenty-four hours, and saw of that noble city no more than he could by peeping from the diligence. He was, by nature, not so much conservative as anti-Jacobin.

7

In the meantime all but his closest friends must have been somewhat puzzled as to what he was about. His family, certainly, was becoming mightily puzzled.

In that snowy, dreary, frosty winter of '29, when the mother and two girls were isolated in their Nuneham cottage, Harriett might have been found pondering gravely over his sermons[5] by the fire, obviously at a loss to know what he was up to: "We go on very quietly in these parts. . . . I hope you can give us a decent lengthened call. I should like a quarter of an hour's talk with you. . . . We have long since read your two sermons; they are very High Church. I do not think I am near so High, and do not understand them quite yet."

We may well sympathize with Harriett. Here is, for example, a sermon dated September 29th, 1831, on *The Danger of Accomplishments,* which might easily shock the most ardent Newmanite. He gave it on the Feast of Saint Luke and hung it on the fact that Luke had received what, as he said, could be called a liberal education. As if the very adjective has touched off a spark in his mind he asks at once whether what we call "accomplishments" can ever be consistent with a deep and practical seriousness of mind. He doubted it. He thought that accomplishments tend to make us "trifling and unmanly." He even thought them, though not positively evil, dangerous in so far as "an elegant and polite education . . . separates feeling and acting": meaning that the reading of romances and novels, no matter how high-toned, gets us into a habit of feeling excited without any urge to act on our excitement. (Most modern censors of films and books hold the opposite view.) So, he derides all books in which the glory and beauty of Christian behavior is not related to the actual roughness of the Christian Life. It is beautiful in a picture to see Christ washing the disciples' feet, but there is, he observes drily, little that is shining about the sands of the desert. So, too, he derides the habit of showing piety, and talking piety, and feeling piety, which he goes so far as to call dissipation, identical with the most licentious forms of dissipation, being different in subject but the same in nature, and "a strain and waste of moral strength." All of which contains some truth, all of which is as dismal as the sort of bleak austerity pictured in *The Scarlet Letter,* and all of which leads inevitably to the conclusion: "We should never allow ourselves to read fiction or poetry, or to interest ourselves in the fine arts for the mere sake of the things themselves." [6]

A more average example of his sermons would be *The Love of Relations and Friends,* with its hard-headed disbelief in idealistic asseverations of love for all mankind, its sensible preference for the possible and practical love of the one or two near at hand; its shrewd observations about philanthropists full of a universal human kindness abroad but "morose and cruel in their private relations" at home; or the sermon on *The Dangers of Riches,* which is of the order that left another listener astonished at Newman's capacity for entering into what one may call common tradesmen's sins, such as avarice, greed, petty dishonesty, expressed by a recluse as clearly as if he were a practiced business-man; or, for a higher and more subtle thought, his sermon on *The Resurrection of the Body,* which shows us that with his imaginative concept of life as a veil and all time as one moment he would have had no difficulty in accepting the modern dogma of the Assumption.

"Our Blessed Lord seems to tell us that in some sense or other Abraham's body might be considered still alive as a pledge of his resurrection, though it was dead in the common sense in which we apply the word. . . . We are apt to talk about our bodies as if we knew how or what they really were; whereas we only know what our eyes tell us. They seem to grow, to come to maturity, to decay: but after all we know no more about them than meets our senses, and there is doubtless, much which God sees in our material frames which we cannot see. . . . Philosophers of old time thought the soul might indeed live for ever, but that the body perished at death; but Christ tells us otherwise. He tells us the body will live for ever. In the text he seems to intimate that it never really dies; that we lose sight, indeed, of what we are accustomed to see, but that God still sees the elements of it which are not exposed to our senses."

A nice blend, one may think, of the intellectual and the mystic. How brother Frank would have raged at it! And what on earth would he have said had he listened to John speaking of *The Powers of Nature*, wherein the preacher exchanged the dangers of romances and novels for the dangers of those new fashionable pursuits of "chemistry, geology and the like?" Here he suggested that the real reason why rain falls, winds blow, rivers flow and the sun warms us is "that all this wonderful harmony is the work of Angels." Had such a man, one thinks, been born in Tibet or India he would surely have moved through a not very different course: and, perhaps then be read by Frank with interest and sympathy.

"I do not pretend to say that we are told in Scripture what Matter is, but I affirm that as our souls move our bodies, be our bodies what they may, so there are Spiritual Intelligences which move those wonderful and vast portions of the natural world which seem to be inanimate; and as the gestures, speech and expressive countenances of our friends around us enable us to hold intercourse with them, so in the motions of the universal Nature, in the interchange of night and day, summer and winter, wind and storm, fulfilling His word, we are reminded of the blessed and dutiful Angels."

It makes us feel that all these men were, as Keble admittedly was through Wordsworth, more indebted to the romantic poetry of the century than they knew. Nobody would have dared talk like that before 1789, unless we go back to the audacities of the golden age of the English pulpit, to Jeremy Taylor, and Fuller and South and Andrewes and Donne, some of whom were, to be sure, doted on by the romantics and all of whom were well-known to these new Oxford reformers.

8

Darbyism,[7] Frank's favored sect (for the moment), was meantime preparing for its hegira into Persia; a "wild and fearful plan," as his mother called it, which would seem incredible to us if we did not remember that men always behave most oddly when God goes to their heads. A bitter estrangement and fierce quarrels about it broke out at once between all three brothers and completely shattered the peace of the home. "I do not think," poor Harriett wrote to John, "you have suffered in this matter more than I have. I am quite sure that whatever comes I cannot be called upon to endure more than I have already done." The whole family was embroiled; the mother begging John to write to Frank with his old cordiality and brotherly love; engaging Frank himself in a quite learned scriptural controversy; trying to keep the peace when Charles came and the two younger brothers engaged in a stinging, biting, gloves-off argument which must have sent her weeping to her room. Nothing availed. Frank set off for the East.

The funds for the adventure came from one of Darby's best-born disciples, John Parnell, second Baron Congleton, a cousin of the Parnells of Avondale. This young man, in reaction from his worldly parents who were then living apart, sold everything he possessed for the Cause: estates, family portraits, heirlooms of every sort. With him went a Devonshire dentist named Groves; his wife; Dr. Edward Cronin, of Dublin, who was a convert from Roman Catholicism, and a widower with an infant son; his old mother and his sister, Nancy; and a gentleman named Hamilton. A Dublin barrister, named Bellett, is also mentioned as helping with the funds. Groves set off via Russia, and Congleton, Frank and the others, via the Mediterranean, in the Autumn of 1830.

They arrived in Aleppo in January (1831). They were still stuck there in July. They suffered all the trials that the heart of the most fervent missionary could ask for. None of them could speak the language. Frank was brutally attacked by a mob. The accommodation was deplorable because there had been an earthquake eight years before and nothing that fell down then had been put up again. Parnell had fallen in love with Nancy Cronin, but could not marry her until they got to Aleppo. Groves' wife died of the plague in Bagdad, where they had arrived from Russia. Hamilton fell ill and had to return home. Frank took the fever and almost died. Mrs. Cronin died of hardship and old age. Nancy Cronin died; whereupon Lord Congleton comforted himself with Khatoon, the daughter of Ovauness Moscow, of Sheeran in Persia, the widow of an Armenian merchant. As for their missionary work in Bagdad it was a total loss. Groves in his *Memoir of Lord Congleton* says that they found the Mahometans "peculiarly bigoted."

All the time that he was abroad Frank was tormented by the beauty of Maria Rosina Giberne. He had written to her from Aleppo to come out and marry him. He waited for six months in despair and fear lest she had not received his letters. He then wrote in misery to a mutual friend in England, Woodroffe, to act as go-between, and got no answer. He then wrote to John—which is an ironical situation if we remember Maria's devotion to John—who passed the letter on to Harriett, who, with raised eyebrows, passed the story on to Jemima: "He tells me that an affection long suppressed has gained such power over him as he cannot get rid of without supplying its place by another object. (N.B. I make no comment.) And nothing but fear of missing a reply has prevented him from coming over to England." It appeared that after writing to John he had found out that his letter to Maria had fallen into the hands of her papa who had opened it, and assured Frank that the matter would for ever after be kept from Maria Rosina; at which Frank had been about to throw up the sponge when he suddenly remembered Woodroffe! Would Harriett please try and clear up the confusion?

As we would expect, Harriett gave Frank a piece of her mind:—

"You would admire," she tells Jemima, "the patience and temper with which I made things as clear as the sun in noon day. One was to prove that a wife is a tie to this earth. (By the bye, tho', perhaps they do not think so. Mr. Cronin lost his after a few hours' illness and in four months left England in the utmost distress at not affecting a pending remarriage.) At any rate I thought he would confess that there is more responsibility attached to one's movements if others' lives or comfort depended on our actions, for to our surprise he says to John, 'I think you underrate the difficulty of our task for if we attempt to preach to the Mahometans we run the risk of being put to death.' Is it not wonderful? . . . Ah me! In this unreal world how are we deceived and undeceived from day to day!"

Maria Rosina's diary refers to his return home in 1833, something under three years after he had left it. Her French is far from perfect:—

"Un jour au beau milieu de la conversation la porte ouvre et 'M. Francois Newman arrivé de Perse' est annoncé. J'ai cru me trouver mal. Je palissais et mon coeur battait jusqu'à la bouche.

Il ne me voyait pas toute de suite. Ainsi je me remettais vite,
une ami près de moi ayant ouvert la fénêtre, croyant que je souf-
frais de la chaleur. Ainsi j'ai l'entendu causer avec M. Wilson
sans être aperçue. Bientôt j'ai su qu'il m'avait aperçu car il s'en
allait dans un coin, posait sa tête sur une main et ne disait plus un
mot. Il fallait passer devant moi au moment de partir et ma
compassion était trop forte. Je lui ai dit bon jour et il m'a tendu
la main. C'était froide comme la glace. Je crois que j'ai dit,
'Nous demeurons toujours amis.' J'ai fait cela pour empêcher
une répétition de la même chose en cas que nous nous rencon-
trions par chance. Grâces a Dieu qui m'a fortifiée contre cet
union."

It would appear from this that she had received his offer
of marriage and had rejected it.

9

While Frank was far away on his wild-goose chase they
were a happy household, especially when they had settled
into the "queer little cottage" at Rose Hill. John had been
reading deep in his beloved Fathers—"in high glee," as
Harriett said. Every day he would attend to the duties of
his parish; daily he would return to the nest. His mother
and sisters were settled into a routine. They went to morning service in that sturdy old Saxon-Norman church overlooking the river at Iffley; into Oxford for afternoon service
at Saint Mary's. They helped at the school in Littlemore.
They visited the sick. Sometimes they dined with friends
in Oxford, the Puseys, the Hawkinses or the Whatelys. Or
they strolled there, alone but in perfect safety. "We all
agree it is not at all disagreeable to walk at Oxford. London
is hateful for young ladies." The girls kept house, sewed,
painted "coloured landscapes" and read at random—Le Bas'
Life of Bishop Middleton, Scott's *Castle Dangerous, Robert
of Paris,* somebody's *Life of Belisarius.* We must imagine

for ourselves those daily trivial flutterings that give life to a tree. It is evocative to hear from them that the milkman peeps at their notes which he carries into Oxford. We can interpret, too, the hint in John's wry warnings to Henry Wilberforce about the risks of life in a rectory: "I fear the ladies of the house will make you idle. You will be lounging and idling with them all day. There is this mischief attends all familiar society between us and the fair sex. We cannot talk without being idle, but ladies are employing their fingers in a thousand ways while they encourage idleness in us." But Maria Giberne drew a family group which suggests that John did not always let this happen in the Rose Hill cottage. In this picture he sits, hair-tousled, pencil in hand, over a large book; mamma is alone intent on her frame; Jemima and Harry have some needlework on their laps but they are listening to John, not working; and we happen to know that John often entertained them with nourishing drafts of his history of the Arian heresy in the fourth century.

To be sure, there had been breaches of the peace. Nothing could stop John from worrying them by over-working himself. There was a flutter in September, '31, when Whately went to Dublin as Archbishop and John felt that he was likely to be asked to join him—in which his innocence was much mistaken. In a letter to Harriett explaining why he would not go he used some ominous phrases which reveal his state of mind at this period: "The times are troublous, Oxford will want hot-headed men, and such I mean to be . . . I am a reformer." There were more family differences in January, '32, over his new religious ideas: and we know they had not been the first, for he assured his mother of the pain "such accidents" always gave him, and that "sometimes" they brought him to tears. Later when Harriett is complaining in her blunt way of his discouraging manner she will say: "Another difficulty is the great difference I see in our opinions": meaning that, as she would see it, his new priestly

antagonism to "the world" was alien to her spirit of tolera-
tion.

Those family differences were symptoms of a sense of
isolation and dedication growing in himself. He was deliberately fending them off; indeed he was quietly bent on cutting the whole world away. He confessed as much to Henry
Wilberforce in the course of a sad letter evoked by the news
of Henry's engagement, which he undisguisedly felt as a
betrayal:—

"Be quite sure that I shall be free to love you, far more than you
will me—but I cannot, as a prudent man, so forget what is due to
my own comfort and independence as not to look to my own re-
sources, make my own mind *my* wife and anticipate and provide
against that loss of friends which the fashion of the age makes
inevitable. That is all I have done and said with regard to you.
I have done it towards all my friends as expecting they will part
from me, except to one, who is at Barbados. (This is Hurrell
Froude.) *I dare not even towards my sisters, indulge affection
without restraint.*"

In an "Apology for Myself," written long, long after, he
said:—

"It was a great mista' e in all of us, though a very natural one,
to fancy that, if my Mother and sisters came nearer to me, they
would see more of me. . . . It did but involve them in a necessary disappointment, and made it seem as if I did not avail myself
of opportunities of our meeting which they had done their part in
securing.

"When they were at a distance, I went to see them from time to
time for weeks together, for a whole Long Vacation . . . but
when they came near to me they came to the seat and scene of my
occupations, and, when they still found me at a distance from
them practically, as it was not a distance of the body, it seemed to
be one of mind. And, when they, in their kindness, tried, however delicately and considerately, to overcome what was to them

an invisible obstacle, then I got worried. I got worried by their
affectionateness. . . ."

He gives other minor reasons for their differences: such as
that "they did not like" some of his greatest friends any more
than they liked some of the religious principles he was beginning to adumbrate; that the more firmly he defined those
principles the farther apart they drew from him; nor could
they, indeed, not sharing his firm views about dogma, or a
unified Catholic—that is, traditional—Church based on defined dogma, sympathize with his strict judgments on Frank
and Charles.   But over all these reasons it is clear that it is
not they who drew away from him but he who drew away
from them, and that he drew away from them and from
everybody else for one main reason, that he was one of those
fiercely intolerant men who cannot love where they do not
agree.

Apart from those differences their pastoral life at Iffley is a
comparatively unbroken calm until the Spring and Summer
of '32.   By then everything has begun to go wrong.   They
have heard from Frank about Maria Rosina.   Robert Wilberforce has jilted Jemima.   Aunt Betsy is unwell.   When
John's dearest friend Froude comes to stay Harriett squabbles
with him.   And Charles has become unbearable to everybody, including his employers.

10

Charles had for a long time been working up to his Great
Renunciation Scene.   The previous summer he had written
an outrageous letter to his mother, beginning, "Madam," and
ending "Your Obedient Servant," requesting her to "drop all
further correspondence with me. . . . I am a Newman."
This summer he resigned from the Bank, anticipating dismissal.[8]

As we have seen he had been impertinent to one board-member, Capel, and taken to writing wild circular letters to others. By the summer of '32 the Bank could no longer ignore his behavior. The Governor suspended him in August, and a Committee of Inspection duly charged him with misbehavior to his principals. The directors heard the evidence of the Chief Cashier and of a Mr. Hammond of the Cash Book Office, read some of Charles' letters, and then had Charles before them. They found him in what their subsequent reports mildly describe as "a considerable state of excitement," formed the opinion that he was weak in the head, and wrote to his family that he ought to be withdrawn from the service. The unfortunate had thereafter nothing to do but wait in his lodgings at 53, Surrey Row, Blackfriars Road, for the final dismissal, or, as he may have preferred to call it, his order of release from a post which he had with difficulty managed to hold down—and in which his employers must have had even greater difficulty in putting up with him —for seven years. As we read his last letter to the Bank we may doubt if the Bank of England has often had to cope with such an unconventional employee:—

> "Friday morning
> 14 September, 1832,
> 53 Surrey Row.

To the Secretary of the Bank.
Sir,
  Mr. Bock of the Cash Book Office has called on me at my lodgings and informed me that you wish to see me, when I conclude that I am still a Clerk in the establishment. I suppose certain forms are to be gone through. Now I assure you I am quite afraid of forms and all the holy rules; and I have no doubt you would feel as I do, had you been in my place last Tuesday three weeks. The fact is these forms are like ready made clothes, and do not fit me, and I cannot help it, and I am prepared to tell you or any one else in the establishment, be they who they may, that

I think it but fair you should dispense with forms in my case as
much as possible, and I had much rather leave the Bank than
have my feelings hurt.   Having given you this notice as no doubt
I have a right to do, I will wait upon you according to the message.

I am, Sir,

Your obedient Servant,

(Sd.) C. R. NEWMAN."

The Court of Directors accepted this sensitive resignation
a week later.

From that onward he became a lonely wanderer in perpetual search of board and lodgings, clothes, a few pounds a
year, and his independence.   It seemed little to ask but it
proved hard to get.   He did the inevitable thing.   One recalls the words of the college porter to the departing hero of
Mr. Evelyn Waugh's *Decline and Fall*.   "I expect you'll be
becoming a schoolmaster, sir?   That's what most of the
gentlemen does, sir, that gets sent down for indecent behaviour."   He had gone to teach for a while with an uncharted
"Mr. B."   In due course John received a letter from another
address beginning ominously: "I have no doubt I have given
mother very exaggerated ideas of my violence to Mr. B.'s
boys."   However, he goes on, he did them a wonderful deal
of good.   "Their conduct improved amazingly."   And what
if he did break Mr. B.'s injunctions?   They were quite absurd.   As for his family he explains that he has cut himself
off from them not from caprice but solely because he knew
that he cut a disgusting figure before them, and that they
despised him in their hearts.   "I have recovered from that
disease of mind which I carried up to mature years from
infancy.   In short I am not to be pitied . . .   You have
behaved in the most excellent way to me from the first. . . .
Our minds are only partially in our own power."   That was
from Sussex, where he was now working as usher in a school
kept by a Mr. Allfree, at Windmill Hill, near Hurstmonceaux,

in the parish of Archdeacon Julius Hare.   He was dismissed
from this school for biting one of the pupils in self-defense.

John decided that the best treatment for Charles was to
write him a kind letter but keep him at a distance; otherwise
he might become too familiar and quarrel again.   Besides,
how could a priest conscientiously recommend to any teacher
a man holding such odd religious views?   Accordingly he
wrote him a kind but standoffish letter and awaited results.
It drove Charles to despair.   His mother's unguarded love
contributed to the debacle.   She made over to him the
£1000 which he was to receive on her death—his share of
her dowry—hoping that the interest on it would relieve his
needs.   He straightway went up to London, sold the deed
for its market value and in two months squandered it to the
last penny.   The next place we find him is in the Newington-
Lambeth district, No. 7, Hope Place, Bird Street, West
Square, where, in April, '34, a friend of the family, a Mr.
Ellis, discovered him in a state of squalid misery, either
married to or living in sin with a woman whose name is lost
to history.   When Ellis called on him he had been for nine
weeks in the house, which was as bare as a picked bone, and
in all that time had been out of it only twice for the sound
reason that his woman had pawned his clothes for gin and
was in the habit of leaving him locked up while she went
out to get drunk on the proceeds.[9]

"With some difficulty," Ellis wrote, and we may imagine
the feelings of the mother and sisters, at Rose Hill, as they
read his letter, "I obtained an interview.   I was horror-struck
at the scene."   In a room, whose shutters were all but closed,
and whose entire furniture consisted of one chair, Charles
lay on the floor on a pile of straw, dressed only in his shirt
and drawers.   "He appeared in no way disconcerted at my
unlooked-for visit, merely apologising for not having called
on me, but the fact was he did not consider himself sufficiently well dressed!"   Besides, as he explained to Ellis, it

was very awkward that he had no means of washing himself. "His manner, words, looks and actions gave evident proofs of insanity." Ellis begged him to say if anything could be done, but Charles implored him not to trouble himself. He could see that they wanted for nothing. And some of his friends had been *very* kind. His brother had sent him a ten-pound note only the other day. All this while the woman listened and watched in silence. Ellis had brought some money with him, but he saw that it was pointless to give it to Charles, so he left a few shillings with the neighbors at Number Six, people called Dennis, who promised to get some food, cook it and send it in every day. Charles' last words were that Aunt Betsy would be "calling on Monday."

Ellis's news, in a letter to John, dated April 21st, was at once revealed to the mother. But Mrs. Newman was at the end of her tether. She could only suggest to John that they should send an ultimatum to Charles on the following lines: "On condition that you extinguish that person your rent shall be compounded for, your clothes redeemed, and a sum of (blank) per week allowed for the next three months for Board, Lodging and washing, but no money shall be given into your hands. Your affectionate mother, J. N." Perhaps, she suggests feebly, the Dennises at Number 6 would undertake this since Charles was accustomed to them. "Without something of this sort to look to he has an excuse for clinging to this miserable, deceptive object for succour now he has made himself so awfully helpless and dependent." In a second letter she wonders if Ellis, or a friend named Cheesewright could help to separate him from "his Destroyer." A Mr. Morsfield, or Mosfield, is also mentioned hopefully.

While mother and son were shilly-shallying in this way Aunt Betsy sailed in and did the job. It must have been a strange adventure for the old lady, carrying her shocking secret all the way from dear Mrs. Kershaw's reputable guest-house in Richmond down to the purlieus of Elephant and

Castle. She presumably left it to the jehu to find No. 7, Hope Place, off Bird Street, off West Square, somewhere in Newington; or was it in Lambeth? She found the house, braved the Destroyer, collected her nephew, and, somewhere or other—surely not in Mrs. Kershaw's?—brought him, patiently, to himself. When he was sane again Charles confessed that he might as well have thrown his £1000 in the gutter for all the good he got of it. She got some decent clothes for him from John, and some money.

By June he was well enough to write to his mother at Iffley, and she, in turn, was soon writing humbly and pleadingly to John not to *condemn* even if he could not positively *approve* of her plan to have the "poor desolate Being" to stay with her for a fortnight. "I do not pretend to influence your conduct. I am sure you will act up to your character and privileged Profession, and if the poor Wanderer seems desirous of being brought to a right judgement, you will not withhold your assistance." John apparently acquiesced, for the mother is soon delightedly reporting that the "poor fellow" is anxious to perform all his Sunday duties, that they have read together two "very impressive sermons" by John, that he is most grateful for John's attention to his wants, and eager to offer John anything in return that he may find acceptable. It does not appear that John came in from Oxford to visit him, and when Charles, having left Oxford, asked him humbly to recommend him for a job to a Mr. Barnes, of Grove Street, Hackney, John replied frankly by asking what sort of character he was expected to give.

Charles' reply is as frank:—

"You ask what sort of character I require of you. I wish you to say explicitly that you are unable to pronounce me a religious character. Your saying this would not in itself be sufficient to damage my character in the eyes of many people. . . . I did not wish, nor expect you to assist me in a late crisis, but you generously came forward and supplied me with clothes and money;

but, now, if you refuse to speak a word in my favour (for I suppose you consider I have some good points when I am well) you will act as if a man should invite another to dinner and just as he has finished the soup and fish turn him out of the room and say, 'Soup and fish, sir, is better than nothing—be content.' Tell my mother that for the four weeks since I left Oxford I have lived at the rate of 17s. 8d. per week. Pray send by return of post a good character for me, and state your affection and that of my family for me that it may be seen we are on good terms."

John struggled with his conscience. Finally he took pen in hand. He stated that Charles had had a literary turn from youth; that he was always improving himself; that he was a very fair Latin, and he believed, Greek scholar; that he had given much attention to French and German; that his talents were of a high order; and that he knew him to be possessed of the most generous, high and gentlemanlike feelings. . . . Then: "To show that I do not suffer myself to be biassed by the affections of a brother I am obliged to say that he is not a believer in Christianity, but he has promised me that he will neither directly nor indirectly introduce the subject among any persons with whom he is thrown."

Charles got the job. He buried himself among London's millions at No. 1, Liverpool Street, King's Cross. He was out of the job by the next July—the end of term, one notes —and gone on to a Revd. J. Butts, in Bromley. He was soon out of that job and gone on to a Mr. Wilks' at Chippenham. By the next June, '35—again end of term—he was telling John that he was "inclined" also to leave that post, but he held on until the end of the next term, '36, and then he was out of work again. He went on to a Mr. Read at Stroud, Gloucester. By mid-May he was out of that. He went to a Revd. Mr. Gibson, in Upper Town, Boulogne, but soon left that for a post in Bristol. So he wandered for years until his family must have felt almost demented. Once John raised agonized eyes to heaven over a letter in which Charles

blithely said, "I doubt not that I shall become religious tho'
not perhaps in the way you would like"; followed by the
announcement that he was now taking the wafer, as if, John
groaned, religion were a medicine. Once, when Jem became engaged, he had wished to come to Iffley, but even his
mother had drawn the line there. "I could not have him
here to disgrace himself and us." Once he turned up at
Oxford in mid-January, after tramping the whole way without a coat between London and Oxford, indeed without as
much baggage as a change of shirt, because, as he said, it was
good for his health. For like most bachelors, he was ob-
sessed by his health and his letters often speak of it.

"I am not sure that the diet you prescribe may not be good for
me in the long run, though certainly as yet it has not seemed to
agree with me. . . . I am inclined to think I ought to have nice
things in addition. I shd never have got through last ½ year as
I did, in a creditable way, had it not been for macaroons & al-
mond cakes. Often when I have felt quite uncomfortable . . .
these have quite comparatively revived me. . . ."

It must be granted to John that he was infinitely patient.
When Charles lost the Stroud job he wrote, "It is not his
fault at all . . . The truth is this, he will never be settled.
People think him eccentric and will always part with him
after a half-year or two." He was generous with money.
He wrote: "I would gladly give up the whole or part of my
£1000 to get him some situation of permanence." But
though patient and generous—is patience really a virtue?—
he could also write: "I am not unwilling, so that he is not
thrown into circumstances disadvantageous to his *ethos* that
he should do penance some time longer."

As if the poor addled fellow were not his own life-long
penance; or as if it were not his perpetual penance to have
been born into such a holy family! One feels that the only
kind of family that could have helped him would have been

a pack of wastrels like himself whom it would have been his scornful pleasure to have raised up from their mire to his own level: a thought—it would have been silk to Charles—on which we at once begin to float slowly earthwards, far from the coagulated smells of dingy lodging-houses and dormitories pullulating with small boys, towards the odors of godliness, calf-bindings, cinnamon toast and woodsmoke in the house overlooking the sable and gold of that world he alternately envied and despised.

CHAPTER 10

EMMAUS, AND AFTER

1

THERE the most interesting thing that has meantime occurred is that John has been abroad for the first time;
seen the Mediterranean sky supported, as Homer saw it, by
the peak of Atlas; lived in Rome and visited Naples; coasted
by the shores of Greece; wandered alone in Sicily; come face
to face with death, and returned to Oxford a new man.[1]

He was badly in need of a holiday. It had been all very
well for his mother to thank God, when Charles was being
intolerable, that there was one who did not desert them.
"However his Duty is his pleasure." His mother might rely
on him; Harriett might upbraid him; Frank appeal to him;
Aunt Betsy lean on him; Charles abuse him; his superiors and
his friends make heavy claims on him; and he make claims
on himself; but between them all he was worn to a shadow.
And, now, when, for the first time in his life, he saw a narrow
space of freedom ahead, his tutorial work finished and the
Arians virtually off his hands, here was Charles at his worst
towering over him, and new friends like H. J. Rose of Cambridge begging for his cooperation in a new periodical, *The
British Magazine;* and in his mind's eye he must have seen
with a sinking as well as a beating heart what he called
"stirring times" ahead, and the greatness not only of their
possibilities but of their challenges. When, at this moment,
Froude suggested that he should go abroad for six months

with his father and himself, he agreed with alacrity, and fled.

The *Hermes,* a slow ship on the Malta service, steamed from Falmouth into the Mediterranean, slowly along the African coast past Algiers to Malta—seven days from Gibraltar to Valetta—thence slowly towards and alongside the western coast of Greece between the island of Zante and Patras, on both of which they landed briefly; and still slowly northward past Ithaca to Corfu where they anchored for seven days. It rained a great deal in these three places. It was all they saw of Greece. From Corfu they turned back to Malta, where the *Hermes* left them on January 11th. They went into quarantine at once and were mightily uncomfortable as well as unwell, and John saw a ghost there in the Lazaretto. On February 7th they took the *Francisco* for Naples, finding on board "counts and princes without number who spat about deck and cabin without any concern." They crossed to Sicily where they halted, for two days at Messina, and for two days at Palermo, and so came to the end of their sea-voyage at Naples. From there the three friends travelled by road to Rome. After spending some five weeks together in and around Rome the Froudes went on to France and John returned by himself to Sicily. He struck into the heart of Sicily on mule-back, and in May all but died of the fever in the town of Enna. After some three weeks in Enna and three weeks in Palermo he took a sailing-ship, an orange-boat, to Marseilles, was becalmed off Sardinia, hurried across France, and was back at Iffley in early July, '33. He had by then been some seven months away.

In a sense he had not been away at all. England went with him. He had gone via Greece and Italy on a pilgrimage to the heart of England; or one may as truly say that what he had planned as a voyage to the South of Europe became a voyage into his own heart. "England," he says, of the whole seven months, "was in my thoughts solely."

2

Somebody like Charles might easily have laughed at this, thinking that there could be few Englishmen living who knew less about England. And in the social, political, humanitarian sense, it would be true. There is irony in the fact that John Newman began at Oxford and ended in Birmingham, the least likely place in the whole world for a man who had been born into a peak period of the industrial revolution, fought his life's battle against its influences, and never adverted to it. From the whole range of his books and letters one could not extract a single graphic image, not to speak of a general picture of the common life of the century he all but spanned; just as nobody would gather from him that the loathed Whig reformers had anything to reform; or that if they did not reform the alternative might have been revolution. After all, when the peers of the Church voted twenty-one to two against the Reform Bill in '31 the mob—we always call them the "mob" when we disagree with them, the "people" when we agree with them— the mob stoned their coaches and tried to burn down bishops' palaces. His only contact with trade or industry had been banking and brewing, the one respectable, the other almost pastoral. Naturally he was unfitted to relate the ideas of the reformers to the needs of "men and women in their ordinary clothes." By comparison with the dynamite of his religious conscience Newman's social conscience was a squib: for though he gave most generously in charity, it *was* charity and he had no social outlook beyond charity. He was never tormented, as F. D. Maurice was, by the gap between theology and humanity in the Christians' church.

It may be said, it has been said, that his England was the priest's England. It is a feeble defense. Even on the

ground of his own profession we must be pained to observe
that his letters and sermons of the time give no picture of the
urgent need for the re-distribution of church wealth, the
elimination of worldly place-hunters, the adjustment of dioc-
esan boundaries, the forming of new dioceses or parishes to
keep pace with the mounting growth of great new industrial
centers, the reformation of the tithe-system—then payable
in kind, and not, as later, by the landlord but the tenant—
the restriction of pluralists who, as Dean Church put it,
"built fortunes and endowed families out of the Church,"
the development of popular education, of which the first
weak sign was a pittance of £20,000 granted in '33 to various voluntary societies for school buildings: and so on?
Compared with churchmen like Maurice or Scott-Holland
he was totally blind to the need for adapting old traditions
to new times and new needs.

It is not Newman but such men as these, or modern social
historians, who remind us of the many dissatisfactions and
injustices which the reformers simply had to remove since
the Church could not: even such lesser grievances as the
Marriage Act of 1753 whereby no Catholic, Dissenter or Jew
could be married otherwise than in an Anglican church by
an Anglican parson—not that John Newman would have
considered this an injustice, quite the contrary; which would
also be his attitude to Church Rates, levied by law on the
public irrespective of their beliefs, and not abolished until
1868. Even to get his own viewpoint on such matters we
must go to books like George Anthony Denison's vivid *Notes
of My Life* which tells us of the incessant, gallant, hopeless
fight of a typical working clergyman, down in the dust and
smoke of the battle, against what he, like John Newman,
considered to be state "interference" with church affairs. In
education, for example, Denison would not take a penny
piece from the Government once he heard that an Inspector
went with a subsidy. It is from others that we will learn

about state-interference in church revenues; marriage, by which I mean the Matrimonial Causes Act of 1857, previous to which a marriage could only be dissolved by Act of Parliament, or by the Pope; interference even in the jurisdiction of the Church over its own spiritualities, by which I mean the Acts of '32 and '33, which transferred jurisdiction in such things as whether a clergyman must believe in the Real Presence to the secular law-courts.

But even a Denison will merely stonewall—he will never suggest to us that there was some justice in the tiresome and exasperating insistence of the rude utilitarian question, "What *good* are they?" when applied to, say, church schools: he will never suggest to us that it was a fair question in a land which was beginning to hear what Denison contemptuously dismissed as "the march of democracy."   John Newman, likewise, who did not live to hear the hum of Cowley threaten the peace of Littlemore, was pleased that his sisters should help in the school at Littlemore, and saw no reason to think that his poor parishioners could possibly ask for more. As it happened, they did.   Some laborers at Littlemore, then on Oriel property, dared to ask for a few small bits of land to cultivate—some forty per cent of Oxfordshire had been enclosed—with the unwise suggestion that the manors are for the poor as well as for the rich; in other words, they dared to speak of a right instead of appealing to charity.   The result was that they were promptly turned-off by the Senior Fellows of that Christian college.   It would never have occurred to John, so generous, so charitable, so hardworking, so filled with a profound sense of duty, that such men could think, as their like often did think, of the parson as the policeman of vested interests.   It would not occur to Denison; who nevertheless has left a vivid account of how he ordered a policeman, as one might order a pound of steak, when some rough fellows misbehaved in his village, and how the policeman marched them off as quietly as cows to the lock-up to be

transported overseas unless the parson, in his charity, again
intervened. It remained with another type of priest, neither
a recluse nor a *franc-tireur*, to hear the thunder and forestall
the lightning. So, Trevelyan, in contrasting Oxford's flag
nailed to the mast with the wisdom of older hands like
Bishop Blomfield, and others of his kind on the Episcopal
Bench, can record with relief that the total destruction of the
church feared by men like Arnold of Rugby—"The Church
as it now is no human power can save"—was sidetracked,
but only because the chief causes of its unpopularity were
done away with by friendly hands.

To John Newman, for whom England was not so much
England as "Tyre of the West," or else a possible new Jerusalem, such politics were either a closed book or a base betrayal. He lived exclusively in the realm of pure spirit. As
Charles X should have let himself be guillotined rather than
surrender, the Church should let itself be persecuted rather
than yield an inch. So, he would write in Tract Number
One:—"Black event as it would be for the country, yet, as
far as they (the Bishops) are concerned we could not wish
them a more blessed termination of their course than the
spoiling of their goods, and martyrdom." One may imagine
that not every bishop would greet these words with a mur-
mured cheer of approval; nor every clergyman, most of
whom were probably fairly represented by this quotation
from a letter he received from one of them:

"The clergy here, although they look on the ministers as little
better than incarnate fiends, wish to let them have their own way
for two or three years, because they think they will do some good
in a rough way which our Bishops would never do. That is,
they will equalise livings, and look after poor curates, and take
away pluralities and secure the Church from immoral ministers,
etc. etc.; and in this hope they seem content to let the Church
and its rulers be outraged by infidels. . . ."

John took with him, then, on the *Hermes* a frightful, prophetic sense of coming destruction. He saw things passionately, as Dean Burgon saw them in his contemporary description of the reforming agitators.

"The press," Burgon writes, remembering these hottest years of reform and anti-reform, "groaned daily beneath the perpetual issue of pamphlets, treatises, discourses, all bent on the reformation and correction of the church from head to foot. To open one of these disquisitions everything was wrong and required radical change. Nothing could be hoped for except after the expulsion of the Bishops from the House of Lords, the overthrow of the Chapters, the abolition of religion in the universities. The Prayer Book was to be swept clean of supernaturalism descended from the Middle Ages, relieved of professions of belief in the Trinity, the Divinity of Christ, and Divine Providence. In short, the Church of England, without any reference to the wishes of the Bishops, clergy or people was to be remodelled upon the philosophic basis of the 19th century."

And as we read Burgon's or Denison's or Tuckwell's mounting lists of sacrilege, we see, and foresee, the claws of the State stretching out to every sphere of religion and education until, infected by their anger, devotion and gloom, we think that the old traditional England of Chaucer, Shakespeare, Dryden or Pope is crumbling before our eyes. This, all this, with all these limitations, was what John meant when he said that for seven months, whether aboard the *Hermes* or the *Francisco*, in the mountains of Sicily or amid the grandeur of Rome, "England was in my thoughts solely": meaning the coming years that would greet him on his return to Oxford, asking to be spent for England and God. The Liberals might believe in adapting the Church Temporal to the spirit of the age. He believed only in reforming the Church Spiritual and fighting the evil temper of his age.

We, in our time, cannot easily realize how absolute these two attitudes then were. Indeed we can scarcely understand either of them. For it is all over and the game is up. There is in a letter of Hurrell Froude's to Keble, from Devon, in 1831, a sentence which brings this home to us. If any reader casually chancing on it can understand it without first having to stand on his head he must be a rare bird: "Things are still in a bad way down here. The labouring population, as well as the farmers, seem thoroughly indifferent to the welfare of the parsons and the squires." We pull back from that sentence because we have, now, neither Newman's (or Froude's) attitude nor the attitude of his opponents. That Tory-Liberal war is over. Those Liberals have won and those Tories have lost, and they are both gone, and nothing remains but the victorious Spirit of the Age, triumphant among its ruins and its dead.

3

While the foreign scene unfolded past the *Hermes* he entered into himself. "Exchanging as I was definite tutorial labors, and the literary quiet and pleasant friendships of the last six years, I naturally (*sic*) was led to think that some inward change as well as some larger course of action was coming upon me." Again: "The strangeness of foreign life threw me back into myself." Again: "I was still more driven back into myself and felt my isolation." Even while he had waited in the December cold at Whitchurch for the down-mail to Falmouth, he wrote a poem whose "vision"—his own words—"haunted" him daily thereafter; for in a whole series of some eighty or ninety poems which he wrote almost every day while at sea, and in Sicily, except when he was ill, and while on his way back to France, sometimes writing two, or even three poems in a single day, he elaborated it during his seven months' exile. These poems show that his body's voyage followed the trail of a fuse crackling towards his center. The mine exploded when he turned back alone to Sicily. Let us look through those revealing verses. With one exception they cannot be taken seriously as poetry, but their patent sincerity forces us to take them very seriously as personal documents.

The question of that first poem which he had written while waiting for the boat-train sets the theme for them all. Speaking of the Presence he feels in the air about him he asks:—

> Are these the tracks of some unearthly Friend
>   His foot-prints and his vesture-skirts of light,
>   Who, as I talk with men, confirms aright
> Their sympathetic words, or deeds that blend
> With my hid thought; or stoops him to attend
>   My doubtful-pleading grief; or blunts the might
>   Of ill I see not; or in dreams of night
> Figures the scope in which what is will end? . . .

A few days later, at Falmouth, a companion-poem recalls boyhood's certainty that what he calls "the fantasies of sense" are by comparison with this Vision no more than a poor lifeless lying show. For—

> Each mind is its own centre and it draws
> Home to itself, and moulds in its thought's span
> All outward things, the vassals of its will. . . .

He is barely at sea off the Lizard, when he prophetically bids farewell to his dearest human bonds:—

> Ere yet I left home's youthful shrine
>   My heart and hope were stored
> Where first I caught the rays divine
>   And drank the Eternal Word . . .

I went afar; the world unrolled
    Her many-pictured page;
I stored the marvels which she told
    And trusted to her gage.
Her pleasures quaffed, I sought awhile
    The scenes I prized before:
But parent's praise, and sister's smile,
    Stirred my cold heart no more.
So ever sear, so ever cloy
    Earth's favours as they fade;
Since Adam lost for one fierce joy
    His Eden's sacred shade.

This sad little poem our wandering Augustine unkindly sent home to his family.

Then begin the poems on the evil state of England and the impending war. One called "Private Judgement" infuriated Frank by its own positive judgment that all lesser sects without the law are "all wranglers and all wrong." He writes "At Sea" of the faithful few who will stand against the fierce foe. Off Cape Trafalgar his thoughts are still homing:—

My home is now a thousand miles away
    Yet in my thoughts its very image fair
    Rises as keen as I still lingered there. . . .

As the *Hermes* draws away from Gibraltar his thoughts are still flying backward:—

Tyre of the West and glorying in the name
    More than in Faith's pure fame
    O trust not crafty fort nor rock renowned . . .
Earned upon hostile ground.

Off Algiers he looks at Africa and sees the future struggle where "gleams divine edge the distant line." At Malta he is still thinking of England, and again consoled by the belief

that the truth has always been defended by "a few of mean-
est mould." This key, repeated variously in these verses,
was later on to be stated explicitly elsewhere: "Especially
when I was left by myself the thought came upon me that
deliverance is wrought, not by the many but by the few, not
by bodies but *by persons*."

Now the forward-looking poems begin to weigh up his
courage against his fate. Between Malta and Greece he
calls up the spirit of Abraham to strengthen him against the
world. In Corfu he calls on the spirit of Melchizedek to
console him for the lonely lot before him. "Without father,
without mother, without descent; having neither beginning
of days, nor end of life." From King David's scarred and
troubled life his thoughts wander to his own lost youthful
innocence, to the crablike movement of all mankind towards
heaven, to the urgency of his hopes now that England
awaits—

> The second substance of the deluge type
> When our slight ark shall cross the molten surge.

The whole sequence of these poems is rich in high hopes of
success and resignation to the heavenly will. Even when he
is tormented by evil dreams one night, near Naples, he bows
to the thorn of temptation that draws blood from him in
these "trial hours which, save to Thee, I dare not name."

So far, he has seen Corfu, a corner of Sicily, and gone on to
Rome: March, 1833.

4

There is now a large gap, during which we come to his
life's most spontaneous and fated act. For to the victim of
Fate there is no difference between decision and doom. We
may call it his life's one unpremeditated act of passion.

Consider what it was that he did. A young Oxford clergy-man, not in the best of health, sets off with two friends—one of them, the dearest friend of his life so far, in an ailing, one might almost say dying condition—for Greece and Italy. From the moment he leaves England he says he is homesick. He says it so often that he begins to strike us as a poor trav-eller, although as it proved, very few of us would endure a hundredth part of the discomforts and dangers that he en-dured: riding forty and more miles on muleback in a day; sleeping in mean, vermin-ridden inns, or wrapped in his cloak on the deck of a boat; and always intensively pushing on and on without respite. He has come to realize in Rome that he has work to do in England, and that work urgent. He uses the clear word "mission." He is so eaten up by his fears and hopes and hates as a missionary, he has become, he said, "so fierce" that when he sees a French ship in the port of Algiers he averts his face from the loathed tricolor. Now, this man, in Rome, parts from his dear friends. There is no coolness of any kind but he refuses to move homewards with them via France, where, he agrees, there is much that is new and interesting. Instead he turns back on his tracks and strikes off alone for the mountainous interior of remote Sicily, well knowing that it may be very difficult for him to get a boat back to England that is calling him, and in the fullest foreknowledge of the beastlinesses he must endure there. His biographers seem to have taken this willful be-havior as the most natural thing in the world. If he were another man we should be inclined to say that the only ex-planation for it must be that he has fallen uncontrollably in love with a woman living in Sicily and is returning to her.

What, in fact, was the siren-call? The most moving thing about this return-journey is that he himself could never ex-plain it. He could not, because the man who came out of Sicily was very different to the man who went into it, and while there he was in a state of becoming. One illustration

of this is striking. We all know what fierce anti-Roman
polemics he sent home to his friends; at the close of his Sicil-
ian adventure he writes this warm, human and sympathetic
poem on the same subject:—

> Oh, that thy creed were sound!
> For thou dost soothe the heart, thou Church of
>   Rome,
> By thy unwearied watch and varied round
> Of service, in thy Saviour's holy home.
>   I cannot walk the city's sultry streets,
>   But the wide porch invites to still retreats
> Where passion's thirst is calmed and care's
>   unthankful gloom.
>   There, on a foreign shore,
> The homesick solitary finds a friend:
>   Thoughts, prisoned long for lack of speech,
>   outpour
>   Their tears; and doubts in resignation end.
>   I almost fainted from the long delay
>   That tangles me within this languid bay,
> When comes a foe, my wounds with oil and wine
>   to tend.

He tried, in vain, to explain why he was going, or had gone,
to Sicily. "I have lost my companions," he writes to his sister, "and am going among strangers into a wild country, to
live a wild life, to travel in solitudes, and to sleep in dens of
the earth—and all for what? For the gratification of an
imagination, for the idea of a warm fancy which might be a
deceit, drawn," he concludes feebly, saying what every idle
tourist says, "by a strange love of Sicily to gaze upon its cities
and its mountains." Later, having already endured much
discomfort, he writes from Syracuse, giving another reason: "I
wished to see what it was to be a solitary and a wanderer."
Later still, to his friend Rogers: "I had two objects in com-

ing, to see the antiquities and to see the country." On his return home he wrote an account of his illness. It contains the sentence: "In an unlooked-for way I come to Sicily." Years after, when writing his autobiography the willfulness of the thing had gone so completely out of his head that he merely wrote: "I went down to Sicily."

The fact is that he and the Froudes saw nothing of classical Greece; but while briefly at Palermo on the way out they had gone to Segesta. John's account of Segesta in his letters to his sisters explains everything. As everybody knows who has seen the Greek temples of Southern Italy and Sicily—Paestum, Agrigento, Selinunte, Segesta—none are so lovely and so impressive as those honeyed temples at Agrigento, lifted sidelong above the Ionian Sea. These he did not visit. After Agrigento come the ruins of Selinunte. He did not see these either. After Selinunte most people will rank Paestum. This he did see; but, magnificent as Paestum is, its position is as nothing compared with Segesta, and it was the site of that single temple in the lonely valley of Calatafimi that transported him. And, indeed, anybody who has travelled that winding, towering mountain road between Palermo and Segesta, with bare pointed peaks rising far about one on all sides, dim ravines falling far below, the sea bursting gloriously on the view as one surmounts the last pass, and then the entry into a bleak valley on whose slopes one sees, suddenly, one single golden, graceful, ruined temple, will fully sympathize with his awe and delight, especially if, as was his good fortune, that ruin be one's first sight of the loveliness, the dignity and the power of ancient Greece. To him, there was here something specially, personally and irresistibly appealing.

"Little as I have seen of Sicily," he wrote to Harriett, "it has filled me with inexpressible delight. . . . I am drawn to it as by a loadstone. The chief sight has been Segesta, its ruins with its temples. O wonderful sight, full of the most strange pleasure —strange from the position of the town, its awful desolateness, the beauty of the scenery, rich even in winter. . . ."

And, to Rogers about Segesta:

"The temple itself is *very* fine, but the situation—oh, the situation!"

To Jemima he wrote also in admiration of that lonely perch:—

"Such was the genius of the ancient Greek worship, grand in the midst of error, simple and unadorned in its architecture. It chose some elevated spot and fixed there its solitary witness which could not be hid. . . . Doric, six gigantic pillars before and behind, twelve in length, no roof. The temples of later and classical times have vanished. The whole place is one ruin except this in the waste of solitude. A shepherd's hut is near, and a sort of farmyard, a number of eager dogs, a few rude intrusive men who would have robbed us, I fancy, had they dared. On the hill on which the Theatre stood was a savage-looking bull, prowling amid the ruins. Mountains around, and Eryx in the distance! The past and the present! Once these hills were full of life! I began to understand what Scripture means when speaking of lofty cities vaunting in the security of their strength. What a great but ungodly sight was this place of glory!"

To Harriett:

"My mind goes back to the recollections of last Monday and Tuesday (at Segesta) as one smells again and again at a sweet flower."

Every man has his symbol. We must feel that this solitary temple was in some way the image of his heart's desire—a vessel of ancient piety, a tomb of human ambition, a place of

worship in retirement from the world, the evocation of a
nobility of soul that, though pagan, was not faithless, a form
of classic grace. At Segesta all that was thoughtful, devoted
and sensuous in John's being faced him as in a shattered mirror. It was for these harsh hills, that lonely road, those vast
expanses of land and sea, and in the longing to see again that
single ruin that he abandoned companionship and comfort
and returned alone to endure in Sicily, almost to die for it.

He never reached it. At Enna, which he called by its
popular name Castrogiovanni, he fell into the pit of fever.
It is a strange town, lifted up on a single rock towards the
clouds, and in wintry weather lifted wholly into them, so
that the town becomes dank and mist-wrapped, and once
the sun goes down, the lanes and piazzas are dusky and sad
with no sound but the drip of rain, and the shuffling of feet,
and, for all that this is Italy, the few lights browning as
through a London fog. It can be as awesome then as the
drear lake of Pergusa below its cliffs, which Milton described
as—

> that fair field
> Of Enna, where Proserpin, gathering flowers,
> Herself a fairer flower, by gloomy Dis
> Was gathered—which cost Ceres all that pain
> To seek her through the world.

One could not easily imagine a place more lovely in blazing
sun, and perfect health, from which to rejoice in the magnificence of Sicily spread below, far and wide, off towards Cal-
sibetta and Leonforte, or in dull, or wintry weather—he
suffered the sirocco, the maddening South Wind—a more
melancholy rock from which to look, alone, at the face of
Death.

He was at Enna because he was evidently on his way to
Segesta. Only God knows what happened in him there dur-

ing that delirious fever, but it is plain that some final cathar-
sis occurred in him.   He often wept under the force of the
trial.   When, before starting to leave Enna, he sat on the bed
and again sobbed bitterly and could only say to his wondering servant through his sobs, "I have work to do in England,"
Enna was being his Emmaus.   He had, after all, seen his
temple.   He *had* died there and been reborn, and Death and
Resurrection remained in his mind long after he labored on
out of the hills to the blessed sea between Cefalù and Ter-
mini and beside its muttering shore into Palermo.   Four
days later he wrote that poem about the dead who have died
yet are not dead which is remarkable for its image of the
buried faithful:—

> . . . seeds of life beneath the sod
> Smouldering and struggling till the judgement day.

The day after he wrote, to the text, "And He said, It is
finished," his *consummatum est* in which he handed himself
over to Life and Death:—

> Christ will avenge his Bride; yea even now
> Begins the work, and thou
> Shalt spend in it thy strength but ere He save
> Thy lot shall be in the grave.

In another poem the same image of Death and Life:—

> 'Tis the old history.   Truth without a home,
> Despised and slain, then rising from the tomb!

He wrote his finest poem on the same theme, his hymn of
dedication, one June night while becalmed in the Straits of
Bonifacio.   Did the watching pharos come and go as he
stood that night composing it on deck?:—

Lead, Kindly Light, amid the encircling gloom,
  Lead Thou me on!
The night is dark, and I am far from home—
  Lead Thou me on!
Keep Thou my feet; I do not ask to see
The distant scene—one step enough for me.

I was not ever thus, nor pray'd that Thou
  Shouldst lead me on.
I loved to choose and see my path, but now
  Lead Thou me on!
I loved the garish day, and, spite of fears,
Pride ruled my will: remember not past years.

So long Thy power hath blest me, sure it still
  Will lead me on,
O'er moor and fen, o'er crag and torrent, till
  The night is gone,
And with the morn those angel faces smile,
Which I have loved long since and lost awhile.

It is still a favorite hymn of the Church of England. But, surely, its author, in this passionate context of Sicily and Enna, never really belonged in the quiet chancels that now alone hear it? He had too much of the imaginative awe and dread, too many of the flights and surges of pre-Reformation England which nineteenth and twentieth century England disowned or lost. The refined, unemotional voices that still so often raise the lovely hymn will rarely suggest an iota of the terror and the awe that produced its beauty and its faith.

He wrote of Jonah cast up to life from the belly of the whale. He wrote of Lot, who had been led from the death of Sodom by two angels. Still becalmed, madly impatient, he wrote of Christ the miracle-worker:—

  . . . Or should'st thou feel some fever's force
    He takes thy hand, He bids thee rise,
  Or on a voyage, when calms prevail

> And prison thee upon the sea,
> He walks the wave, He wings the sail . . .

Still becalmed in those dull Straits, feeling himself tied as "by a prisoner's chain" he wrote of Zeal, and of Patience, and of Faith.   On June 21st or 22nd the wind blew.   On the 23rd, at sea, he wrote eagerly:—

> But I will out amid the sleet and view
>   Each shrivelling stalk and silent-falling leaf,
> Truth after truth of choicest scent and hue
>   Fades, and in fading stirs the angel's grief
> Unanswered here.   For she, once pattern chief
> Of faith, my country, now gross-hearted grown
> Waits but to burn the stem before her idol's throne.

Four days later they were lying off Marseilles.   He tried to hurry home, but he was so weak that he had to rest again at Lyons.   From there he travelled home at a forced pace, foregoing sleep for six successive nights.   He alighted from the Oxford coach on Wednesday, July 9th, '33.

5

Supposing John Newman had died in Sicily what now would be posterity's measure of his worth?   It could not be very much.   At most an irreverent great-niece might say: "Did you know that I had a great-uncle who went to Oxford? He was at Magdalen.   His name was James Newman.   He died on a voyage to Greece.   I gather he was a bit queer. But papa says he had a very clever brother who was professor of Greek at London University."   Who else would hear of him now?   What would even his closest friends then have thought of their loss—Rogers, Keble, Froude and the rest?

Here nobody will want to list qualities or characteristics. What matters is the blend.   John Newman's close friends were already feeling the force of his peculiar blend: the cool-bloodedness, the hot-headedness; the hard intellect, the soft heart; the mystical faith, the stern morality; a man who could be cold with a brother, weep for a friend; hate that his mother should touch even his feet, but rapturously kiss the newspaper which announced that Rogers had been made a Fellow; a lover of the lonely, the desolate and the sad, a fighter in the public arena. . . . The irreverent great-niece would have been right. He *was* queer. He had a splendid chaos in him. His friends would have admired its genius. He would have left one memorial of it, his first book, the *Arians,* which as they examined it would have made his friends still more sad for his loss. (It was warmly admired by the scholarly at Oxford.) It tells us what he has been thinking for the last five years. It tells us a great deal more than that. For when a man sets out to write a book he sets out on an adventure which will affect him unpredictably. If he is writing anything at all that arrests him, or will arrest others, he is writing himself.

What, then, does this book on the Arians reveal to us about John Newman?

On the surface Arianism was a doctrine of the Father-Son relationship; apparently another entirely abstract subject, like Baptismal Regeneration, but, implicitly, and in political terms overtly, it was, to begin, a battle-ground between Judaism and Christianity. The Eastern empire, under Zenobia, Queen of Palmyra, was for a crucial period strongly influenced by Judaism so that when Arianism sought to elevate the Father above the Son, Jehovah and Jesus fought for supremacy, the old Law wrestled with the New, the East strove with the West, and throughout the long struggle the Empire, under Constantine and others, strove for unity. Unfortunately John had small interest in this fascinating political background. In the human beings who took part in the drama, and who emerge so fascinatingly and vividly from the pages of Gibbon, he had no interest at all; just as he had no interest, or little, in the political personalities of his own England. What carried him away was the teaching, or portions of the teachings, of the Alexandrian mystics and philosophers.

When John had first begun to read the early Fathers he had found himself drifting back to these controversial times under the force of the consideration that "antiquity was the true exponent of the doctrines of Christianity and the basis of the Church of England." From there, he presently found himself being washed up on the shore of the historical center of authoritative teaching in those early times, the great Church of Alexandria. It was of the teachings of the philosophers of that church that he said, "They came like music to my inward ear." They confirmed him in all his old feelings about the world as a symbol of realities greater than itself; they spoke of economies or dispensations of gradual truth embedded in the parable of created Nature; they led him to see the Alexandrian doctrine of the Trinity as the summation of hosts of pre-Christian gropings about the origin of creation, such as are to be found in the Platonic or Plotinian intuitions of a First Cause and of its equivalent agents, so that the pagans now appeared to him as prophets, and the mythologies of India, the teachings of the Magi, the speculations of the Greeks as no more than preparations for the true Gospel. They also intimated a further development of revelation; though even this revelation, embodied in the Church, would never be complete since the Church itself was but another symbol of "those heavenly facts that fill eternity." He fell, thereby, on the idea that there are mysteries which may be adumbrated but are ultimately inexpressible. Superstition, he once said to his sister Harriett, is when we isolate things we should connect; Rationalism is when we ask for reasons when we should not, that is attempt to explain things about which we can know nothing. He must sometimes have felt surrounded by superstitious rationalists, all wildly detaching and connecting everything like a telephone-operator gone mad, until all hope of supernatural communication becomes impossible. One step further, one feels, and he would have denied the validity of reason completely. This pause at a brink marks the *Arians* as a further cross-roads on Newman's Way.

All his life he oscillates between the intellectual, express-ible thing, which emerges from man as law or morality, and the irrational, inexpressible thing, which enters into man as faith or mysticism. The one is known; the other is expe-rienced. The one is generic, the other is personal. One might call the one classical, the other romantic: that is to say, morality is homocentric and generalized, whereas the mystical experience is deocentric and uniquely experienced. Furthermore, in classical minds the object has priority and is finite: in romantic minds the subject has priority and reaches to infinity. It is never possible to say of John Newman that he gives primacy to the one rather than the other. He is perpetually torn between two sides of his temperament, a Hamlet caught between polarities, between the exaltation which overleaps nature, and the intellectualism which would shape, control, reform and legalize it.

Besides, there were certain traditions to cope with. Be-cause he is an Englishman he has the Englishman's reason-able, rational, solid sense of home, and country, and class, and duty and "the proper thing to do": the civilized man of the 18th century. But he is also steeped in the English mystical tradition which has far less sense of home, and country, and class, and duty, and does not care a straw about "the proper thing to do": the spiritual man of the 17th cen-tury and of the Romantic Revival. One might say that he could have blended both traditions? But in his time both traditions were being challenged—he felt being destroyed—by the vulgar utilitarians and irreverent rationalists of his

time, of whom the worst, the most effective, the most super-
ficial and therefore to him the most diabolical, were the
well-meaning Liberal "talents of the day."

If he tried to appeal to Faith alone he was back at the
multi-headed Evangelicals.   If he tried to be satisfied simply
to reason with them he was behind Evangelicalism, like his
brother Frank, who had reasoned himself out of Calvinism
into Darbyism, and now on his return from the East had
reasoned himself into the Baptist Church.   Could he turn to
the Church of England and speak here of the traditional
Faith?   But few Englishmen would tolerate a Church which
did not allow liberty of private judgment, and, here in the
Arians, he had seen the result of that; as Gibbon had seen it
before him, in a more secular way and to a much more limited degree, when he exposed Arius and his followers as
vulgar intruders into delicate speculations which a Plato
might, indeed, whisper to his chosen disciples in the arcades
of Athens, but which he certainly never intended to be
dragged about through the sawdust and the spilled beer.

This perhaps more than anything else drew John deeper
and deeper into the study of Arianism and Alexandria.   For
he, too, was living in a time when all religion was being sub-
jected to the uninformed, vulgar and irreverent rationalism
of the taverns and the clubs.   No part of his book is more
delicate than that in which he develops tenderly the notion
of the instinctive conscience and the instinctive morality as
a plant so frail as to flourish best in the warm shelter of the
unenquiring heart: a thought too wonderful for words, something so ineffable as to be assaulted by words.   In all this
part of his book he is the Newman the world knows, his intellect heated and aerated beyond itself by sympathy and by
pity: as when he thinks how man's instinctive feelings for
the Divine are like the unconsidered love of a child who
does not feel any the less fond of its father and mother
merely because he does not discriminate *in words,* even in

idea, between them and others. True, a child may, as his reason opens, consider the grounds for his mother's love for him, or his own emotions towards her, and find in his own feelings correlatives of her tenderness, her knowledge, her authority; may even come ultimately on the essence of this relationship, a natural bond and debt as deep as life itself. Yet, for all this accession of knowledge, the child will do no more than understand what he has always felt purely and strongly out of nature itself. Nevertheless, he also sees that when this same reason is applied to things beyond itself we incur the dreadful danger not of understanding but of mis-understanding by inadequate articulation. For what have we, in the end, to express any ineffable idea but images from mortality applied to immortality, and what can these temporal images do, no matter how finely we draw them out, but approximate to the reality of things that are of their nature incapable of expression? Instead of enlightening our affections we may in practice deprave them.

So, he finds all creeds and articles, confessions and declarations a regrettable necessity, a sad fatality forced on us by the fanaticism or vanity of men who think everything can be explained; a shallow arrogance leading always to bitter controversies which in turn can end only in tiresome formalisms and technicalities. (Is he here thinking, or may one say sub-thinking, of the Council of Trent?) Inevitably all his approaches to these early controversies are colored by a sad regret for still earlier centuries when felt traditions took the place of spoken creeds, and the acceptance of things ineffable was as simple as the child's unenquiring trust.

Does this mean that he rejects the privilege of Knowledge? He sees it rather as a fearful privilege. Since there have to be creeds now that the line of Tradition has been long drawn out beyond vivid personal memory, become by far too frail a texture to resist the touch of subtle and ill-directed reason, and since what was once accepted without questioning has

now to be protected against excess of questioning by defin-
ings as clear as may be, let us, he pleads, realize that our
finest definitions are no more than shadows of the vision's
object, that their aim cannot reach beyond the threshold of
mysteries that are ultimately impenetrable, and that their
effect can be no more than to tranquillize the inquisitive
mind by a connected rather than, in the nature of their subject, a consistent statement.

One might think that this lands him sprawling at the feet
of the rationalist. His retort could have been that the rationalist, like Cassius, hears no music. His retort is, in fact,
that faith is not a notion. Words are paper. Concord is
the reality. We may formulate light and darkness, but nature has her own fixed courses and unites mankind not by
formularies but by "a sympathy of moral character." A
church, therefore, will speak clearly on matters of doctrine
so that there shall be an end of verbal dispute; and the tests
of phrases thereafter must yield to the test of moral concord.
From which it will follow, as he explicitly develops—throwing at last a bridge of practice across the chasm of mysticism
—that the church must of necessity function as a political
power "whether in Kings' courts or among the mixed multitude"; and if her members can do nothing else they will at
least remind men of the truth by inflicting on them the task
of persecution because of it.

Arianism there ceases to be an abstraction; a tale of something long ago and for ever done with. His topical interest
in this sixteen-century-old controversy is evident throughout.
It was clear in the very title-page which pointedly bears the
quotation from the Psalms: *Fret not thyself because of the
ungodly, neither be thou envious against the evildoers. For
they shall soon be cut down like the grass and be withered
even as the green herb. . . .* Whether he was drawn to the
Arians by latent political and intellectual analogies between
the fourth century and the nineteenth, or whether, as he

wrote, they drew him, the topical parallels crop up frequently in the historical parts of his study. Thus, the temporal quality of Judaistic thought, as evident in its hopes of
a personal Messiah yet to come as in its practical-minded
indisposition for the unexciting mysteries, the more remote
sanctions and the indefinite promises of Christianity, would
lead him to think of the arid formalism of the modern Roman
Church and to consider whether the mere performance of
legal rites does not withdraw the mind from the contempla-
tion of the more glorious and more real images of the gospel.
He would perceive in "the talents of the day" an evident
modern parallel to the sceptical skill of the Arianizing Soph-
ists, so brilliant in dialectic, so unsympathetic to the testimony
or practice of tradition, always reducing the discussion of solemn matters to a literary recreation, always forcing their
rationalism into the realm of the inexpressible, yet always
preferring inconclusion to a decision. How could he fail to
see the foreshadow of 19th century Liberalism in those
fourth century Eclectics who professed to take the best bits
of every system without defining or adhering to any? He
could see about him a thousand counterparts of those high-
brow, religious rationalizers whose all-tolerating philosophy
became "patronised by the imperial court both at Rome and
in the East and spread itself in the course of centuries
throughout the empire . . . until at length obtaining, in the
person of Julian, a second apostate for its advocate it became
the authorised interpretation and apology for state poly-
theism." He did not need to go beyond his own family to
find modern examples of their techniques, such as their habit
of using words like *divine,* or *inspiration,* or *revelation,* or
the like, in ways so ambiguous as to mean nothing more than
the user cared to make them mean from hour to hour. And,
he sighed, those ancient sinners had at least imbibed enough
from old ways to retain enough of substantial truth mixed
with their incoherent system to give it a lofty and serious

character "utterly foreign to the cold, scoffing spirit of modern rationalism."

He saw a topical lesson in those Alexandrians who stood out against the popular heresy, especially the great Athanasius, banished five times by the State, harried incessantly by the Arian court party, sometimes almost a minority of one, never embittered even against his most relentless enemies, always found, one might say rediscovered, in the wilderness, ready for leadership whenever there was new hope or need for it. In him he may well have seen an image of his own possible fate, and found encouragement and inspiration in his example. But, once again, we must go to Gibbon for other personalities, such as that dark-skinned, pearl-toothed, amazon Jewess in whose person he has no least interest; or Constantine, or Julian, or Valens, even Arius himself, who are, to him, vehicles, not people. He could assess friends. He would not measure enemies.

For the rest, nothing was more natural—it was, superficially, the beginning of it all—than that a priest should delight in exploring the origins of his own church, throw a stepping-stone from Canterbury and Oxford across to Rome and Alexandria. That he should throw it so far from the bank on which he stood, throw it sixteen whole centuries away, merely meant that like all historically long-sighted men he foreshortened the intermediate distance. Not that anybody would have expected him then, or would in retrospect now expect him to have considered latter-day Roman claims. For anybody in pre-Emancipation England, when he was working on his book, to take Roman Catholicism seriously was, quite simply, unthinkable; so unthinkable that it is hard to imagine that practical Roman Catholicism can have meant anything whatever to anybody in an Oxford where no Roman Catholic could legally study, in an England where no Roman Catholic could legally sit in Parliament, and where, thereby, every Roman Catholic was effectively outlawed. It is doubtful if, before the Italian journey, indeed before 1835, John Newman ever laid eyes on one of the bestial species, though his mother did behold what she called "that vile viper" Dan O'Connell in Madame Tussaud's, much as we might today see the latest multiple murderer. He could, and did, consider Calvinists, Methodists, Baptists, Unitarians, Darbyites, Bulteelites, Evangelicals of every sort, size and description. . . . But Catholics? Charles Newman became a Socialist and an Atheist, to the indescribable pain of his family. There was only one thing worse that he could have become.

So, the single stepping-stone, so near the far bank, sufficed. The fact that it was only one disposed of Catholic claims by ignoring them. One single step had been enough. One step and he was out of Oxford beside Athanasius and the two Gregorys, Basil and Ambrose, Hilary and the Latin Eusebius, within earshot, almost, of the last faint echoes of the voice of the Founder of the Church of England.

He arrived home intent on proving that every Englishman could and should do the same.

6

The appearance of the person who alighted from the coach in the High Street that July afternoon in 1833 was more than strange. He had no hair. It had all fallen out in Sicily. Frank, who had arrived home from Persia only a few hours before, was struck by his remarkable dignity. Being Frank he added "stiffness." Men looked at him in the street, wondered if he was really Newman, and hesitated to speak to him. Other men noted in him a fierce joyousness, an exuberant energy. The Oriel gate-porter must have looked in some surprise after the bald, emaciated, bespectacled figure loping swiftly across the quad to the Common Room to join the inevitable two or three Fellows murmuring in the dove-

like voices of infuriated dons at the perfidy of the government, the state of the country and the danger threatening
the Church of England.

It would be dramatic if one could say that he sat amongst
them and told them imperiously what they must do. Unfortunately, though more determined than they, he was just
as uncertain. The activity to be known later as The Oxford
Movement had no precise or dramatic beginning, for though
they all agreed in a bumbling sort of way that they must
"unite and associate" in defense of the Church, they had no
clear idea as to what they should do once they were united
and associated, and all through the summer they wrangled
gently about it like a group of ineffectual aunts fussing over
an expectant mother.

Even the proposal to form a Society or Association did not
originate with John though it was he who put it forward.
It happened as follows: On July 14th, the very first Sunday
after he came home, Keble gave a sermon called *National
Apostasy*—the government had just suppressed several Irish
bishoprics—of which, years after, in yet another of his misleading post-cogitations, John would say that "I have ever
considered and kept the day as the start of the religious
movement of 1833." This has doubtless led thousands into
thinking that the sermon was a rousing trumpet-blast. At
the time, however, John recorded it in a fragmentary diary,
saying, "I was low-spirited about the state of things and
thought nothing could be done." But his nature was volatile; he was always liable to ups and downs; and when, in
the following week, somebody suggested to him that they
should form some Society or Association, he at once wrote to
Keble that a League was now in existence for the dissemina-
tion of pamphlets or tracts, and that the other member was
Froude. Keble demurred, but he kept at him. He also told
William Palmer, the great theological scholar of Worcester,
and H. J. Rose, then Rector of Hadleigh, whom he had met

in '32. Both of these thought it a very good idea. In fact, between July 25th and July 29th Rose called a meeting in his rectory. It would be known later on as The Hadleigh Conspiracy, thanks to Hurrell Froude's usual blend of impishness and indiscretion in so christening it. Froude, Palmer and Perceval of Worcester came, but not Newman, or Keble. They discussed various things, including Tracts, but "on the whole," Palmer reported, "the result was disappointing," though they did arrive at the inevitable decision to "unite and associate" in defense of the Church. This, also, Newman's later account has telescoped, saying: "Two things followed from it, a plan of associating for the defence of the Church and the 'Tracts for the Times.'" They followed in time but not otherwise.

It was a prolonged and troublesome birth.[2] Froude suggested a periodical to be given the extraordinary name of *Excubiae Apostolicae.* He sulked when they all sensibly demurred. Anyway Rose already had a periodical of his own, *The British Magazine.* Rose suggested a Lay Synod. Keble demurred. He saw the government would appoint it, though it might, perhaps, be used for bargaining purposes? John now demurred, asking, "Is it lawful to compound?" An Address or Petition to the Archbishop was mooted. Keble demurred. After many tiresome vicissitudes it went through. Froude suggested that they should revive the monastic system. As far as we can gather they all demurred. Golightly, now in the group, was for the separation of Church and State. John demurred: it was a happy anomaly.

Palmer next drew up "Suggestions for an Association," but Bowden said people ask, "Who *are* they? Where *are* they? They might be operatives working from an alley in London," and John was now, so he says in his Fragmentary Diary, "strongly against an Association, i.e., any body in which a majority bound a minority." This clash broke out violently

in mid-September. However, on October 2nd we are astonished to find John saying, "We are getting on famously with
our Society." The split was still undecided in November,
at the end of which month, John records, in bewilderment,
that "the questions became frequent: 'How are we to act?'
and to myself, 'Do you approve an association or not?'" In
the same month Froude is reported as downcast, and begging
John to stir up the rest "into a fury," [3] Keble is gently irritated at the changes being made in his papers, John has "no
confidence in anyone," Palmer has "scruples." Froude is
cross at their "milk and water" Petition, Rickards is jibbing
strongly, Miller is "full of cholers and tremblings of mind,"
worried about the Athanasian Creed. The only bright spots
are that donations of ten pounds are "flowing in," and that
behind all this dithering and confusion John himself had,
since the first week of September, been issuing little four-
page leaflets on his own initiative, with the result that in the
midst of his autumnal depression we suddenly find him blazing with enthusiasm and good humor.

To his friend F. R. Wilson he declared that—

"Rose has almost been advocating a Republic in the last number of *The British Critic*. The monarchy and the aristocracy
should be our instruments of influence, but if these powers will
not do we turn to the people. The King has tied his own hands.
He has literally betrayed us. . . . Therefore expect on your return to England to see us all unflinching radicals. We have set
up Church societies all over the kingdom, or at least mean to do
so. Already the seeds of revolution are planted in Oxfordshire,
Berkshire, Devon, Gloucester, Kent and Suffolk. Our object is to
maintain the doctrine of apostolic succession and save the liturgy
from illegal alteration. . . . We have begun to print tracts."

From then on, tract after tract began to pour out of Oxford,
fluttering down like manna on every parsonage in England;
so many passionate appeals to embark for the Promised

Land, in italics, in leaded type, in brief sentences—Newman
as well as being a scholar and an artist was a first-class
journalist—so many learned prospectuses of the New Canaan
of a revivified and refurbished Church. By September he
had put out three Tracts. Seventeen more followed before
the end of the year. He had written nine out of this
twenty. Thirty more came the year after. By the start of
'36 there were seventy-one.

The yet-to-be-famous tracts were insignificant-looking bits
of things; in white paper; no covers. As far as appearance
went old ladies still shove similar pieces of paper into letter
boxes every day, and young men hand their like about in the
streets. They became more impressive-looking later, swell-
ing from a two-page leaflet to a four-page, to sixteen-page
and twenty-eight-page booklets, and Pusey, who had to have
space in order to speak according to his weight, presented .
them in '36 with a fat book of four hundred pages. But the
little mosquitoes kept on flying between the leviathans and
their stings were probably far more effective.

The trouble about these leaflets was that they were hard
to distribute. Parcels were simply sent off to friends who
were asked to hand them around whenever and wherever
they could. Tom Mozley describes how he got on his pony
with a bundle of them and went from rectory to rectory.
This was so irregular, so very casual a method of publication
that, at first glance, it is hard to see how they ever succeeded
in making a noise. The fact is, they were being handed
about chiefly inside a closed circle, not to the public at large
—their ideas were meant to seep from the top down—and
those who received them spread the ripples in their talk
about them, to the limits of the circle. It would have meant
a great deal to these country parsons that they "came from
Oxford." The reformers may also have taken example by
the methods of the anti-Slavery campaign, which had set a
headline in propagandist methods: they opened a depot in

London and instituted a bureau for newspaper influence. "We have about twelve country newspapers in our eye which are open to our friends." Moreover swiftly-written pamphlets could be topically effective as books never could. When a rumor broke out that the Marriage Service was to be altered to please the Dissenters, John at once told Keble to write a tract on that service. When Froude wrote articles about Praemunire—the law which gave the State power to command deans and chapters, bishops and archbishops—news came from town that the Archbishop had stopped certain obnoxious promotions, stiffened by these signs of the rise of a party of talented rebels against "State Tyranny."

Besides, these men were all zealous missionaries.

"Golightly has promised £50. . . . Pusey circulates tracts. . . . Mr. Jeune of Pembroke joins heartily. . . . H. Wilberforce has been back here and working most vigorously; wherever he is he distributes tracts with all his might. . . . At Christmas I hope to make a missionary tour to Derby, Leicester, Huntingdonshire, Suffolk, Northamptonshire, etc. . . . The Duke of Newcastle has joined us 'in life and death, so that we are true to ourselves,' and Lord Arden, Lord Kenyon, Sir W. Heathcote, Joshua Watson, the Bishop of Winchester (I hope), Gladstone, etc."

Moreover, the tracts themselves appealed. They were, at their best, vivid, daring, personal and plain. When John's old friend Rickards objected to an extreme statement in one pamphlet John simply remarked ironically that things written in the style of Richard Hooker or Isaac Walton would have been classical and a failure. He said: "Willingly would I be said to write in an irritating and irritated way if in that way I rouse people . . ."; and as for the extreme statement which pained Rickards because it expressed a belief in Transubstantiation he was reckless about the consequences: "I expect to be called a Papist when my views are known."

The opening lines of the first Tract (his own) set the tone. It is frankly personal, proclamatory and propagandist:—

"I am but one of yourselves—a Presbyter; and therefore I conceal my name, lest I should take too much on myself by speaking in my own person. Yet speak I must, for the times are evil, yet no one speaks against them. Is this not so?" the leaflet goes on. "Do we not 'look upon one another' yet perform nothing?" Must we, he asks, stand idle and allow the bishops to bear the brunt of the battle, though, indeed, "we could not wish them a more blessed termination of their course than the spoiling of their goods and martyrdom."

("Maria, do listen to *this!*")

The tract is sheer journalism in its appeal through what a modern newspaper editor would describe with satisfaction as "the personal touch":—

"If the Government casts off the Church on what will you rest the claim of respect and attention which you make upon your flocks? Hitherto you have been upheld by your birth, your education, your wealth, your connexions; should these secular advantages cease on what must Christ's ministers depend? Is not this a serious practical question? We know how miserable is the state of religious bodies not supported by the State. Look at the Dissenters on all sides of you, and you will see at once that their Ministers, depending simply upon the people, become the *creatures* of the people."

The argument that dependent priests become creatures of their flocks is, of course, utterly fallacious, as every Irish Catholic well knows; but the English rural clergyman of 1833 would not and could not know it; and since John Newman also could not he rubs it in. He tells his colleagues that if they are thrown over by the State their influence will depend solely on their popularity, and surely it is their office not to please but "to *oppose* the world?" Then comes the core of his leaflet: "On *what* are we to rest our authority when the State deserts us?" The answer is given in capitals: ON APOSTOLICAL DESCENT.

"Therefore, my dear brethren, act up to it in your professions. . . . A notion has gone abroad that they can take away your power. They think they have given it and can take it away. They think it lies in the Church property and they know that they have politically the power to confiscate that property. They have been deluded into a notion that present, palpable usefulness, producible results, acceptableness to your flocks, that these and such like are the tests of your Divine commission. Enlighten them in this matter. Exalt our Holy Fathers, the Bishops, as Representatives of the Apostles and the Angels of the Church, and magnify your offices as being ordained by them to take part in their ministry. . . ."

And in capitals again he rounds to his conclusion as oratorically as a candidate for parliament. "CHOOSE YOUR SIDE!"

But though it is sheer propaganda, nicely balanced between appeal to self-interest, political feeling, religious faith, at its center is the clear intellectual proposition that the Church of England is the Church *Catholic*, basing its authority on its direct descent from the Apostles. The historical perspective has been opened up; the challenge to England and Rome is implicit; and we are not surprised to hear that religious men read it, laid it down, and wondered for the first time if it were really true that the Church of England rested its authority on its pedigree from a few oriental fishermen.

When tract succeeded tract and it became evident that a concerted movement was on foot, when big names became bruited about, and men asked who was behind it all, and the press took it up, and rumor flew, and fuss made fuss, we are not surprised that men should have paused, remembering the Peel Election of '29 and Oxford's power. For although the thing became known at first as the Tractarian Movement, and later, as the chief promoters' names got abroad, the Newmanite Movement, or the Puseyite Movement, its general final designation became the Oxford Movement. By February 1834, it was already established. Then Henry Wilberforce wrote, in high glee: "It seems Ministers are fairly frightened and have quite abandoned any notion of spiritual reform in the Church. For this we may thank the Movement."

How splendid this young enthusiasm is! Taking no least account of the immovable, stubborn weight of the *Zeitgeist;* of the sceptical, longheaded men; of the rational, compromising men; of the indifferent, unsympathetic, material-minded men; even of the well-intentioned, serious-minded, sympathetic but politically-minded men like, say, that young Gladstone whom John had hailed as an adherent. For when we turn to Gladstone to see what he really felt about all this, how very different the picture is!

"The Oxford Movement, properly so called, began in the year 1833 but it had no direct effect on me. I did not see the Tracts and to this hour I have read but few of them. Indeed my first impressions and emotions in connection with it were those of indignation at what I thought the rash intemperate censures pronounced by Mr. Hurrell Froude upon the Reformers. My chief tie with Oxford was the close friendship I had formed with Walter Hamilton. I do not think he at this time sympathised with Newman and his friends. . . ."

His biographer, John Morley, denies that he and Newman were ever intimate or had any friends in common; and at the end Gladstone wrote that Newman stood in the general view as a "disgraced man." One of his latest comments on the reformers arose from his reading of Dean Church's *The Oxford Movement*, of which he said that there was a "per-

vading sense of soundness about it which Newman, great as
he was, never inspired."

One could cull other examples of the false impressions on
which these ardent young men built their hopes of sweeping
Oxford and all England before them.   Not that they dreamed
insanely; as they would today, when "England" means not a
ruling class of rank, privilege and intellectual repute, but a
vast, levelled, semi-illiterate, impenetrable mass.   One Tract,
then, by an Oxford scholar, could exercise as much influence
as the whole of England's popular press today.   One Gladstone—if only they had "got" him—would be worth a million miners.   One Newman could, and did, lead, though he
did not effect, a Reformation.

Yet, even within this closed circle they must fail, though it
would be a splendid and inspiring failure.   The leaves of
rumor that accumulate in the corners of clubs and drawing-
rooms and vestries can evoke widespread passion, feeling,
inspiration, create great reputations, even build fame—and,
indeed, all lasting public repute spreads by the narrow ways
of private report and personal memory—but these methods
do not create a system, and though systems do not create
ideas they contain ideas and make them become realities.
The Oxford reformers never "got" the system.   They did
not, for one thing, get the bishops, who were in a cleft stick
ever since the Evangelicals began, as Dean Church says,
"after long disfavour to gain recognition with men in power
and ecclesiastical authorities of a different and hitherto
hostile school."   These eager Oxford reformers did, indeed,
exalt the *office* of Bishops, but they also presented them with
disturbing doctrines and constantly urged them to resist the
State which appointed them and paid them.   So, Dean
Church records "the bishops let the movement run on by
itself."

"Sharp sarcasms, worldly-wise predictions, kind messages of approval, kind cautions passed from mouth to mouth or in private

correspondence from high quarters, which showed that the movement was watched. But for some time the authorities spoke neither good nor bad of it publicly."

After all, the reformers did, as we saw, successfully organize a Petition to the Archbishop of London in '33, one of whose objects was to strengthen His Grace against Dr. Whately. But, in '36, when it was necessary to choose a new professor of Divinity in Oxford, and the Archbishop of Canterbury came to Lord Melbourne about it, it was not the reformers but Archbishop Whately whom Melbourne consulted, and it was Whately's choice whom Melbourne approved—that Dr. Hampden whose appointment Rose, writing privately to Newman from Lambeth, described as "this evil," and whom the entire body of Tractarians would assail most violently without, however, dislodging him. On that occasion they went so far as to send a Petition to Lambeth for presentation to the King. Lambeth simply pocketed it.

Inside Oxford the Heads of Houses were almost to a man against them: a stubborn, lazy-minded, obstinate, short-sighted, but immovable dead-weight of conservatism and prejudice. The Martyrs' Memorial in Oxford, erected at the height of the Movement, and as a gesture against it, stands as much as a permanent sign of opposition to Newman as a memorial to what he was felt by so many to have betrayed. But the most striking instance of their impotence is that it did not pay to be a Tractarian, as Mark Pattison and James Mozley presently found out when they hoped for Fellowships. Sometimes it did not pay even outside Oxford, as Atkinson, a Fellow of Lincoln, found when he was turned down in York for holding "Oxford opinions." We may say that these were petty revenges. They will suggest much to everybody who has had to do with universities, and who knows with what ruthless circumspection and cautious attention to self-interest politics are played within those apparently unworldly cloisters.

It is right and necessary to think of these things in that they remind us of how utterly unworldly the reformers were, how totally devoid of the merest shadow of self-interest, of any concern but to elevate their university and their Church. This bitter opposition will remind us, too, not only of how they throve on the challenge and revelled in the fight, but of how they wore themselves out on it year after year. One of the commonest notes in John's letters is in this vein: "Do come here sometime and we will have some quiet talk together—my hand is too tired to write letters unless I am forced. Literally, my hand is in a continual ache." This from a letter-writer whose epistolary remains now fill shelves upon shelves in the Birmingham Oratory. Or, again, John to Jemima, about one of his books:

". . . I write, I write again: I write a third time in the course of six months. Then I take the third: I literally fill the paper with corrections, so that another person could not read it. I then write it out fair for the printer. I put it by; I take it up; I begin to correct again; it will not do. Alterations multiply; pages are rewritten, little lines sneak in and crawl about. The whole page is disfigured; I write again; I cannot count how many times this process is repeated."

Or, again: "My hand is so tired I can but scrawl." No wonder, between endless correspondence, endless controversies in the press, the Tracts, his lectures, his sermons, his books, all on top of his normal duties as a hard-working parish priest.

Is there too much emphasis on one man's work in all this? If there ever was a one-man-made Movement it was the Oxford Movement. John Henry Newman did not, to be sure, create it. As Burgon shrewdly phrases it, the spirit of the

Movement was not created; it was evoked; and this spirit "afloat," as Newman described it, was to be found, and had been found for several years, in many men. Newman brought it to a head by giving these scattered men a lead. He was a born leader. He clarified their confusion. In his insistence that no great work was ever done by a system he cut across their conventional wishes for committees and councils, gave individual leadership and evoked individual exertions. The Oxford Movement was an accumulation of individual passion led, canalized, encouraged and driven on for years by the example of one man. It is inconceivable without Newman. Which is why, when he fell, the whole fabric groaned and tottered; and which, also, is why in the end nobody can properly speak of the Oxford Movement as having either failed or succeeded. For what Newman and his friends did for thousands upon thousands of people cannot be measured in terms of political success or failure. It was not until his noble voice was stilled that people felt in the awful loneliness of that void how much courage and happiness he had given to them, and we feel, with them, how deep and wide his influence had been, and that as it was rich it must be lasting.

CHAPTER 11

THE FAMILY SCATTERS

1

LIFE is becalmed at Rose Bank. "How fast autumn has come on!" Jemima sighs, gazing out of the window. "The trees in Oxford are all turned." Henry Wilberforce is staying. Eliza Fourdrinier is on a visit. But there are no more happy teasings about R. W. She is twenty-five. Harry is in her thirties. If something does not happen soon they will never go to Moscow. Charles has got a new job. John is being cold with him. Frank and John are hardly speaking to one another. "I had got into disgrace," says Frank, almost good-humoredly, "because I did not accept the shibboleth that Christ is Jehovah." Harriett is simmering because John is neglecting them all. Before the winter ends she will break out at him openly:—

"I wish you would a little more show in your manner towards us the affection and tenderness which I know you feel in your heart. How much happier we should all be! Oh, how I wish you would open your eyes to your mistakes in this respect. Perhaps even you are not aware you are often apparently wanting in manner to us. And though it may be weakness in me I do not see why, my dear and only left brother, you should not pay regard to it. Make all allowances for a severe headache. . . ."

It was not the first time she had spoken about his manner, "which I cannot always understand." [1]

239

One by one they are all beginning to fall away from him now, except Jemima, who will remain his one last confidante within the family and from whom he will have no secrets to the very end. Even his mother is losing sympathy with him, as he will presently have to confess to Jemima:[2]—

"Of late years my mother has much misunderstood my religious views and considered she differed from me; and she thought I was surrounded by admirers and had everything my own way; and in consequence I who am conscious to myself I never thought anything more precious than her sympathy and praise had none of it."

It was then that he at last saw what a false step it had been ever to have wished her at Oxford.

They have all come to differ over religion: John with Frank, and the mother and Harry and Aunt Betsy with John, and John with them, and Charlie with the whole bang lot of them. In fact John cut off Frank completely for six years, never writing to him or speaking to him because he considered him an indefatigable and to-be-abhorred schismatic.[3] And had his sisters or his mother done what Frank did he would assuredly have done the same to them. If this sounds fierce nobody knew it better than he who uses this very word in describing his behavior during those years; though when he speaks of this fierceness, or of his recklessness, or of his imprudence and wantonness as he drove ahead without a care for the anger of the dull, the fears of the prudent, or the sneers of the conceited, exulting in his strength, full of confidence in his cause, we do not need him to tell us that his fierceness was a form of joy, or that, for seven heavenly years, between '33 and '40—though I would put the end of his joy much earlier, in '38—he was more happy than he had ever been before; or would ever be again.

One likes to see him in these years walking out of Oxford between the hedgerows of the Iffley Road, or perhaps by the footpath beside the Isis along Meadow Lane, seeing in field and river and spreading country whatever divine analogies will occur to him, or weaving a phrase about a turn of thought, or heads together with some unceremonious friend like Rogers or Keble, whom he is bringing to Rose Bank, unannounced, to share a Woodbury pheasant with his mother and sisters. And then, in the darkness back to work into the late hours in Oriel, ending with those prayers which he would so fervently utter that men returning late to college could hear him, as they crossed the quad, murmuring over their heads. He had everything: peace, war, love, loyalty, a large repute, and the zest of constant discovery like an alchemist in search of the magic formula that will turn the dross of life to gold.

2

By the summer of '34 he had finished Tract Number 38. It was the Formula. He called it *The Via Media*. He followed it soon after with another tract on the same subject, and between that and '41 in lectures and letters he elaborated the idea. This Middle Way was his image of what the reformed Anglican Church would or should be like: a rock standing midway between Protestantism and Rome.

Outwardly the reason for Tract 38 was that he and his friends could no longer ignore the fact that the public at large suspected them of being crypto-Papists. Earlier in '34 he had already faced this suspicion when he began giving weekly lectures on Romanism and popular Protestantism in Adam de Brome's chapel, a Lady Chapel then detached from St. Mary's, merged now into the church. He next published in '35 Tract No. 71, *Against Romanism*. He kept at the question in '36 and '37.

This decision to "take on" Rome was crucial, and, as we can now see, ultimately fatal to the Movement. It had three unforeseen results. In the minds of the more sympathetic it deflected the proper business of the Movement from the constructive idea of a spiritual re-reformation of the Anglican Church into an Anglican-versus-Roman fight. It angered the bigoted by being a fair and intelligent criticism of Rome; with the result that they responded with the devastating cry of "Popery!" much as their counterparts in politics today cry "Communism!" as the easiest way of meeting any argument that challenges thought or conscience. As for the end of the affair it was always bad enough when any ordinary man was deceived by the arguments or wiles of Rome; but for one's champion, who had so often demolished the enemy, to be found, after it all, languishing in the arms of Delilah, about to be bound and blinded, was total disaster.

The polemical reaches of *The Via Media* will always be of general interest. They are well beaten by the feet of converts passing between Rome and England. Indeed this part of the Middle Road now looks like little more than a narrow right of way between two opposing edifices where there is no room for a third. His constructive proposals for reforming the Church come far nearer to our interest in so far as this theory of a reformed Anglicanism represents his intellectual efforts over several crucial years to rebuild his house for his own soul-stuff, as well as for the faith of others. It is in his approach to this problem that we come closest to his breathing.

3

In approaching the *Arians*, as we have seen, his thought had gone directly to the source of his interest, by-passing Rome. In making this vast leap he had also by-passed the Reformation. Now he comes nearer to his own times to throw another stepping-stone into the intermediate stream for the sake of his weaker or doubting brethren. What is most striking is that he approaches the task without pleasure; unhappy that it should, after all, be necessary to appeal to the intellect of people instead of "stirring up their pure minds by way of remembrance," as he had stirred his own in his readings of the Fathers; deploring bitterly that he must direct his readers to modern articles of faith whose essence should have been their starting-place, or treat as mere conclusions what in other ages had been assumed as first principles. It is almost as if it feels that he is himself doing what the rationalists about him are doing with another aim; that is, reducing things absolute to a secondary or rationalized condition, lowering them to a state of mere derivatives of thought. He would have preferred, as all men should, to rely on revelation which supersedes reason, disclosing to it what it cannot of itself reach, saving it in any event much labor where it might weakly avail, and sanctioning "the *principle* of dispensing with reason in all cases." Instead, he goes on scornfully: what do we do?

"We seem at this day to consider discussion and controversy to be in themselves chief goods. We exult in what we think our indefeasible right and glorious privilege, to choose and settle our religion for ourselves, and we stigmatise it as a bondage to be bid take for granted what the wise, good and many have gone over and determined long before, or to submit to what Almighty God has revealed."

And all to what result? We succeed in making doubtful what had been certain. We raise clouds to hide the sun. And so are deservedly left to grope our way by the dull wick of reason as best we can.

We have learned to be wary of his post-cogitations, and therefore will read with reserve his letter of many years later (1846) to Henry Wilberforce, in which he speaks of his "flagging zeal" as he pursued this task. But we may believe —since the impression which this '37 volume leaves on us supports the conclusion—that he thought all reasoning a weariness of the flesh.

And yet the first thing he does is to assail Roman claims under the head of Infallibility! Why does he thus attack authority, which we should, rather, have expected him to uphold? It seems to him that this false doctrine rests upon the false idea that any degree of doubt is incompatible with faith, and therefore an infallible assurance is necessary to exclude doubt. Proof, or certainty, will then come from reliance on the God who cannot lie, and on His organ the infallible Church. He resents the idea strongly. He feels that it produces a theology which is distastefully complete, since there are so many questions which no man's reason can determine, but which Romanists delight to handle, such as, for example: "What change occurs in the consecration of the Eucharist?" Furthermore, a too highly articulated system lowers the standard of Gospel obedience. We become engrossed in the System and forget the Author.

In short, we can feel the anti-rationalist side of him at work, resentful of the whole inherent idea of unbounded knowledge and unlimited certainty.

In any case, he insists, Infallibility is neither arguable nor argued. Men generally act, not because they are convinced but because they feel; and so it is with Infallibility, which is to Roman Catholics no more than a symbol of their Church as a reliable teacher. Therefore the only proof their Church needs to establish her Infallibility is to act frequently as if she were in fact an infallible teacher, until her very audacity influences the imagination at the same time that the completeness and consistency of her doctrine tends to create a simultaneous trust in her unassailable wisdom. Infallibility is an immense delusion.

We remember how in the *Arians*—following one of his earliest teachers, Butler's *Analogy*—he had developed the thought that faith is not a notion but "a character of mind," uniting men by moral sympathy. He does not see this emerging from a religion in which an infallible theology pursues every mystery to its most secret lair to tag it with a final authoritative label; leaving to human nature a lesser reliance on the moral evidence for God's administration, and a lesser interest to cooperate with Him in it. (This is evidently another echo of Butler—the Third Chapter in the *Analogy*.)

So: "It requires little knowledge of human nature to perceive how readily a doctrine will be embraced and followed which sanctions a secondary standard of holiness and which allows the performance of certain duties to make up for the disregard of others." The result, indeed, of such a doctrine must be that people will be encouraged in indulgence and feel absolved from the duty of sacrificing their whole lives to God. Dean Church summarized all this very clearly when he said: "Men must transcend the conditions of our experience if they want the certainty which the theory of Infallibility speaks of." But, most men, in objecting to Infallibility, we notice, do not say this. They say, "Reason is too frail for any man to make so immense a claim"; but they do not then go on to admit that the Spirit transcending matter can achieve an assurance beyond Reason's power.

This is where Newman's approach reveals the man. Two things about Infallibility seem to frighten him. He cannot help feeling that there is in it from both points of view too much vainglory. On the one hand it contains a suggestion of a hyper-rationalized ontology, assailing the Unknowable. On the other hand he feels that this over-articulation, demanding verbal assent to this, that and the other decreases man's responsibility to bear witness in other, more creative ways, that is in his whole moral and spiritual life. Do we detect herein a relic of his early Puritanism or Calvinism?

I think that he would have paused a long time if he had heard Berdyaev's daring apothegm, born of a rather finer

concept of godliness, of humanity, and of human liberty:—
"The idea of God is the greatest human idea, *and the idea of
man is the greatest divine idea.*" As I have intimated, in
comparing him with his brother, Frank was more humanitarian, but he was the more humanist, because Frank believed that it is the carnal emotion that works, whereas he
believed that it is the incarnate mystery; in other words, that
men live, as men—in his, or any civilized man's idea of what
is meant by "live"—by supra-rational values. With his
nuclear doubts about the reality of this world he would
therefore have easily assented to the first half of Berdyaev's
proposal. But as for the second half, that unfortunate Calvinistic conversion had profoundly tainted him with a sense
of man's pitiable weakness. We will remember that frightening sentence from the *Apologia* about the human race being implicated in some terrible aboriginal calamity. As his
sense of evil is pervasive his awe and love of God are im-
measurable. He could, therefore, never reach that summit
of daring in which Berdyaev became aware that "on man
depends not human life alone but divine life as well." His
mystical side would have understood it, but his moral ob-
session would have shrunk away.

4

Taking his ideas at this time in bulk there is, throughout,
an attractive nobility and a fine moral fiber, but, somehow,
his exposition is dry and narrow, ungenerous and inhuman.
His natural sense of poetry, his larger vision seems to have
been frozen by the ice of the very rationalism he assails, as
we shall realize fully only when we compare all this with the
superb handling of the same subjects in his great book, perhaps his greatest, *The Development of Christian Doctrine,*
where his reason becomes, as it were, air-borne, sublimated
by his mystical urge. Even on the ground of polemics too

much has been left out; as when, for example, in contemplating the repellent completeness of Roman theology he confounds what we might disrespectfully call the vast body of free-lance opinion with the comparatively rare pronouncements of the Church; and, for that matter, he ignores their variety which gave Pascal so many opportunities for wicked irony in *Les Provinciales*. He does not appear to have done sufficient historical or theological reading; and he shows no sign of his usual technique of advancing to meet objections; that is, of impressing us with the force of his own drift by the amount of wash he raises in opposition to his prow.

Somehow, whether it is that it has all become stale stuff now, or that it was becoming a little stale already in his own hands from being worked over so much in tracts and lectures, this polemic does smell a little of "the weariness of the flesh." Even the assaults on Rome smell of the brief sincerity of the journalist, flogged up for an occasion:—

"Let us be quite sure that Rome is our enemy and will do us mischief if she can. We must deal with her as towards a friend who is visited by derangement—with, to be sure, all affectionate and tender thoughts, with tearful regrets and a broken heart, but with a steady eye and a firm hand. For she is a Church beside herself, abounding in noble gifts but unable to use them religiously: crafty, obstinate, malicious, wilful, cruel, unnatural as madmen are. She is her real self only in name, and till God vouchsafe to restore her we must treat her as if she were that Evil One which governs her."

Perhaps the fact is what will do well in a tract, or impress as a lecture, leaks away between the covers of a book.

It was all, however, exciting and disturbing in his day. He put in the preface to the *Prophetical Office* the words of the Irish divine, Bishop Bramhall, proclaiming his love for his Church, "Bees, by the instinct of nature, do love their hives, and birds their nests." But to many men he was already beginning to foul his nest, and more and more of them felt in agreement with the opinion of the German scholar, Christian Bunsen, who had said that if these new reformers succeeded they would be introducing Popery without authority, Protestantism without liberty, Catholicism without universality, and Evangelism without spirituality. There is a Gaelic proverb which hits off the fate of the *Via Media* formula: "Whoever comes off safely in a quarrel, the man between never does."

5

It was while these controversies were at their height that Charles was found in the lower depths of Newington-Lambeth with his drunken woman; and that Mrs. Newman brought the poor wreck to recuperate at Rose Bank; so that if John did not give him, at that time, much attention we can understand his preoccupation. At the same time the walls of his new church at Littlemore were rising. His mother had laid the first stone in July, '35, and by September, "The arch of the door is finished, the windows are finishing and the roof is making." It is not quite the same church that we look at today. It has been added to, and the whole place has become green and, at the same time, populated. But the barn which he later converted into a sort of presbytery or conventual house is not much changed on the outside, and one can easily imagine its rude simplicity among the Littlemore fields and, with its image, evoke beside it the simple building whose fate it has been to become the Anglican shrine of Anglicanism's most famous deserter.

Still happier things were coming the Newmans' way. For the girls the R. W.–H. W. pattern repeated itself with the Mozley brothers: sons of a comfortable Derby printer and banker, both Oxford men. Jemima's new friend was John Mozley, whose brother Tom had first met Harriett as long ago as '29. This time, too, there were coy advances and retirements, but not by the two suitors, and Jemima's and Harriett's hesitations were no more than the minimum demanded by the protocol. So, when Harriett "spars finely" with Tom we will recognize the Queen's Quarrel Gambit all over again; and when Jemima wanders about the house groaning about John, "How provoking that I should be found out by the only man who could make me hesitate," or "How shocking to give him and his family pain!" neither her mamma nor Harry is deceived. We get it all in Mrs. Newman's delighted letters to old Aunt Betsy at Richmond, and in the letters of the Mozley sisters to Jem, pleading for their poor, love-sick brother. "Poor John looks very anxious and spoke hardly a word yesterday after he had whispered to me that he had put a letter into the post." Maria Mozley crosses Anne's letter to say that she is just as anxious about the outcome of John's "application" as he is himself; which is saying a good deal "judging by his looks sometimes." She tells wickedly how, after dinner the other evening, Anne had been playing something on the piano, and "poor John" had been standing about the room listening, but "not with his eyes so earnestly fixed on the player as I *have* seen!" and when his sister ceased playing he had said, innocently, "The music sounds rather poor!" A nice example of how brothers give themselves away to watchful sisters.

We will see Jemima with flushing cheeks reading and re-reading these two dear letters in her bedroom, hesitating whether to accept or to refuse "poor John." But downstairs, Mrs. Newman has no doubts. She writes exultantly to Aunt Betsy: "Happy prospects await dear Jemima . . ." True, Jemima will heroically decide to refuse John Mozley. But, of course, "he could not consider *that* a final answer." And, sure enough, back will come a letter asking permission to plead his cause in person, which he is graciously permitted to do: "a woeful-looking creature, dreading every word she

should say, lest it disclose some insuperable obstacle."
Within a few days he is on the coach back home to Derby
joyously addressing the post-boy:—"Post-boy! Look around
you! Behold before you a happy lover."

Further bubbling letters from Mrs. Newman to Aunt Betsy
enlarge agreeably, with the proper Newman-Fourdrinier
touch of snobbery, on the comfort and wealth of the Mozley
household. "He is in partnership with his brother Charles
and has the whole management of an *invisible* Concern."
Mr. Mozley did, it is true, show her some warehouses, and
printing-houses in a back-street, but:—

"I suspect his father has little to do with the Concern but to
take the interest for his Capital and to see the books weekly so
that all goes straight. He, Mr. M., is one of the Partners in the
Branch Bank. Their whole arrangements are wealthy without
ostentation, everything respectable, gentlemanly and economic.
Their house, for space and style of building may be termed grand.
They make up not less than twenty beds which are frequently all
occupied. The Drawing Room is 35 × 24 × 14. It looks into a
five-acre paddock and lawn, an improved 'Farm,' taking it altogether. They have the luxury of their own cows. I think I
may say Mr. and Mrs. Mozley and I are good friends, and I hope
I shall value them as I ought."

Harriett begs leave to add a word to this wonderfully
newsy letter. She raises her head to think.

"There is a beggar standing before the window who prevents
me from writing. . . ."

"Mamma, may I read your letter?"

"Mamma won't let me read her letter, which is very cross. I
have a great mind to ask you to tell me. . . ."

There was more good news that winter of '35–'36. Frank also was marrying. He was now a classical tutor at Bristol College, and while on holidays the previous June he had met a Plymouth Sister, a delicate beauty, Maria Kennaway, living in the little Devonshire village of Ottery Saint Mary, the daughter of Sir John Kennaway, an East India Official. The course of their love had not been smooth. In Mrs. Newman's words, to Aunt Betsy, the repository of all such confidences: "The false representations of persecuting, worldly, self-created Prophets at Plymouth have been torturing Frank and her almost to frenzy." The Prophets, it seems, considered Frank—now a Baptist—as a heretical backslider from Darbyism. They were married on Christmas Eve and in March Frank displayed his beautiful bride to his mother and sisters; first writing ahead in a vein that poor Charles could not have bettered at his worst:—

"Maria has no insuperable objections to attending the Church of England, but I cannot take the Lord's Supper there. . . ." However, "to disavow what I think evil it is not necessary to absent myself altogether. I even might attend Roman Catholic worship occasionally, with respect and solemnity, and in the hope that *some* of the worshippers might be accepted with God in spite of their mummeries. . . ."

With all this afoot at least one family in England that Christmas was not mightily concerned about Tractarianism. Charles alone was out of the fun; for it was then that his mother sighed to Aunt Betsy: "I could not have him here to disgrace himself and us!" Even John took a brief rest from his battles. He went down to Richmond to visit his aunt, and while there walked over to Ham to see his old childhood home. There he found that the old house had become a school and that the beloved trees on the lawn had been felled. He remembered sadly how he and his father and

Charles had last revisited the place some twenty-three years ago, and how the gardener had kindly offered them three apricots, and how his father had said to him, "Choose!" The grown man winced to recollect that he had taken the largest. But there were other grave things, as well as those happy betrothals, to distract him. His mother was poorly. His dear Hurrell was dying.

He might well feel a sense of the dissolving world that April when he attended Jemima's wedding. Frank was not there. Charles did not come. The company would provoke memories and, perhaps, premonitions. "Old Ogle," was there—James Adey: it must have seemed ages to him since they two used to star-gaze from the tower of Trinity Chapel. They were less intimate now. Presently Ogle would be cutting him. Golightly was there. But they had already fallen out and he would soon find him one of his bitterest opponents. Isaac Williams was still on his side, but with deep-rooted reservations, and that friendship would also presently break. Of the three Mozley men he would break with James and say sharp things about Tom, at that moment performing the wedding-service.

If he had any premonitions they were justified. Jemima and John were not well gone on their honeymoon, to Windsor, London and Richmond, before his mother began to flag. Three weeks after the wedding almost the same group gathered for her funeral. The young bride was now wearing black. John had to cling to Isaac Williams' arm for support. Anne Mozley remembered long after how, when it was all over, he remained kneeling at the altar "lost in prayer and memory." Charles did not come, but a letter to his dead mother arrived from Chippenham, where he was teaching at a Mr. Wick's. It was dutiful but a trifle odd. He had kept all her letters, and he was glad of it, for otherwise he might not remember how good she had been. "Tell her," he begs

John, "that my prospects are improving and," he adds ominously, "if I leave here it will be with a high character."

Harriett returned to an empty house. She was thirty-
three. Her younger sister had married before her. Would
John ever come out to Rose Bank now for the slice of beef
or the chance pheasant? What was there to attract him?
She must have had some bad weeks facing her future. Then
in July Tom Mozley asked her to marry him. We notice
that it was not she but Jem who told the news to John. He
loyally helped to ease Tom into a cure at Cholderton, in Wilt-
shire, a small parish of some seven hundred souls, ten miles
from Salisbury, in the middle of that bare and uninteresting
country of the plain, rain-beaten and wind-swept in the winter, where a coach passed by for half the year and the house
was built of mud—"The best of materials I hear," Harriett
wrote cheerfully, "very warm and dry." He also gave them
his mother's plate and furniture and all the money he had,
which was £30.

"Try hard," he wrote to Jemima, "to make H. easy with herself
—she talks of her 'fate' being to do what she is doing. My dear
Jemima I have long thought she has in such matters talked of
feeling and *taste* in a way which was likely to interfere with *duty*,
and while I rejoice to see she has, when the case occurred, preferred duty, yet I cannot help thinking it is providentially intended for her good that she *should* be obliged to do so. I mean
as a kind of merciful discipline."

Jemima wrote back defending Harriett from the charge of
nourishing romantic visions or fancies. He replied, using an
unfeeling phrase:—

"As to visions and fancies they are not my words. I did not
think of them but if I were obliged to think and give an opinion
it should be this—that I can fancy Harriett to have wished some-

thing to turn up to get her out of her difficulty—nothing more—
but I may be wrong here and I certainly did not mean it in what
I said."

To his chagrin Harriett wrote to him that she intended to
marry within three months. He wrote at once to Jemima
protesting that he was much pained that the marriage should
be so soon:—

"I cannot help saying so and think I ought to say so. I do not
think my mother would have been pleased from what I have
heard her say and do not think it will be a pleasant thing to look
back on twenty yrs hence. Perhaps it would not have happened
if I had been consulted. Perhaps I am superstitious about these
things but I do not like it."

They were married in Derby, at Saint Werburgh's, even
earlier than Harriett had at first planned, on September 27th;
when their mother had been barely four months dead. After
the marriage whatever little intimacy remained between
brother and sister gradually withered and finally died completely.

The truth is, John had the celibate's dislike of seeing his
colleagues marry. We remember his pained sense of betrayal when Henry Wilberforce married and how Wilberforce had been afraid to tell him of it. His friend J. F.
Christie, of Trinity, now said something to him about the
effect of this marriage on Tom Mozley and he answered:—

"You must not fancy about Mozley—at the same time be sure
of this, that everyone when he marries is a lost man—a clear good
for nothing—I should not be surprised to be told Mozley would
not write another letter all his life."

He had, we feel, expected too much from Tom—he always
expected too much from everybody. He seems to have de-

veloped towards Tom a mingled feeling of pity, condescension and near-contempt.

He did visit at Cholderton, but it was not an entire success. Christie of Oriel and Copeland of Trinity were there and they would keep on nagging at Tom for "breaking up the bachelor party." One can imagine the donnish jokes, amusing at first, then boring. Copeland, whom everybody found sweet and good-tempered, was easily handled, and it even entertained Harriett to "spar" with him and put him down; but Christie had a heavy touch and when Golightly came and heard him taking things so "tragically" he said: "Mozley never offended anybody in his life; but I fear Christie will provoke him to settle the matter by a rude speech." The man would keep on making such arch remarks, like: "How quiet these married men look!" Then John turned up and in the most inconsiderate manner nothing would do Christie but to discuss with him the "propriety" of Tom's marrying Harriett! When we remember John's feeling about Tom Mozley and that hasty marriage we must sympathize with both brother and sister.

Besides, Harriett, though determined to live her own life, was not an insensitive woman, and would know well what John, and perhaps others, had been thinking; and they both might well have thought that after all her years of tireless devotion she had not been over-lavishly rewarded. She had no carriage, which meant no visiting about the countryside; they had no cook; the church was small and mean; and Harriett had already observed that in point of society the place was virtually a desert. This, after the interest and variety of Oxford! Her salvation would lie in frequent visitors; which meant more housework. She even had Charles to stay. Once, when Tom had to go away for a week, she declared herself "bored to melancholy." As John left her, for the companionship of Oxford and the excitement of the battle, he may have remembered, with some surprise, that he, too, had once longed for a small parish and for obscurity, and, his heart softened in sad affection and old memories; he may have thought that, perhaps, she had had some reason to speak of her "fate."

It was at Cholderton that Harriett began to write her stories, probably out of boredom.　She had one child, a girl who married and emigrated to Australia.

CHAPTER 12

REASON *versus* RATIONALISM

1

IN February of '37 John began holding a weekly salon at Oriel; a far cry from those tongue-tied days when the Fellows could not get a word out of him in the Oriel Common Room. This means that his reputation in Oxford was becoming established; not to speak of his widening notoriety. It is the sort of fame that still can fall overnight on any Oxford lecturer, picked suddenly out of the mass by a series of brilliant appearances, reported on the grape-vine with the speed of Rumor. The undergraduates were already imitating his very mode of speech, heads tilted a little to one side, long pauses between their would-be pregnant sentences. They would draw aside as he passed by unseeing—he could only see clearly straight ahead through those small silver spectacles—his gaze fixed on some secret vision of his own, his tread as swift and noiseless as an apparition, while they nudged and whispered, "There's Newman!" Gossip had begun to build him into an Oxford character. He was said to wear a scarf embroidered with a cross; he kept candles lighting day and night in Littlemore Chapel; his surplice bore a rich, illuminated crucifix; if the bell was tolling when the London coach passed by, the driver would point with his whip and tell tall stories to the outside passengers. He enjoyed hearing about these things: his humor had a sardonic taste. "I heard yesterday that the Master of University had

been assured by a lady at Cheltenham that we offer sacrifice
every morning. She knew for certain that we killed something, she did not know what. Query. Little Children?
Or each other?" His big nose would soon be found in
Punch. He was attacked by Lord Morpeth in the House.
Gladstone defended him. O'Connell patronized the Tracts.
Wherever opinion counted, the Movement was well-known:
too well-known, perhaps for Newman's leisure. In a letter
to Tom Mozley about this time he mentions that he had just
had six callers: two old pupils, a Presbyterian clergyman
from Dublin, a politico-ecclesiastical friend of Lamennais,
and two Ashantee princes.

"June, '38," he recorded, "was the zenith of the Tract
Movement." "The Tracts are selling faster than we can
print them." "We sold above 60,000 Tracts altogether last
year." But he was, though so well known in public, a lonely
man whose family had scattered, who would never marry,
whose friends, though dear, were few. He felt this loneliness and sought an explanation for it. "I think I am very
cold and reserved to people, but I cannot realise to myself
that anyone loves me. I believe this is partly the reason; or
I dare not realise it." The words *realise* and *I dare not* are
touching. By *realise* he means, as he always does when he
uses the word, making a thing emotionally real. He had
also not "dared" to feel his sisters' affections.

After the zenith, he did observe, on looking back years
later, a "change of fortune" in August, '38; but he felt that he
overcame this, and he declared that by the Spring of '39 he
was again riding the wave and that his position in the
Church was at its height. "I had supreme confidence in my
controversial status and I had a great and still growing success in recommending it to others." He does not allow that
he suffered any other shock until late in '39. Here his memory is at fault. He has left out one thing that is so important
that, in a sense, he has, in omitting it, left out everything.

We have seen more than once that his post-cogitative
memory is not always to be trusted. No memory, least of
all the memory of a subjective intellectual, can be accepted
implicitly; so that to follow the course of his adventure by his
own map of it is dangerous. When he later admitted with
his intellect, post-cogitating on the results, that a shock to
his security took place in the winter of '39, he ignores a tidal
change which had in fact occurred much earlier in the deeps
of his being. This is revealed by matters about which his
memory says very little, at whose center we constantly find
the posthumous influence of Hurrell Froude, working on him
since his death in February, 1836.

2

First, the outward sequence of events. In the spring of
'38, when the Movement was approaching its zenith, a very
important tract appeared, Number 80, by Isaac Williams on
Reserve in Communicating Christian Knowledge. This imprudent tract, in Dean Church's words, was "like the ex-
plosion of a mine." There is hardly a word about Tract 80
in Newman's published letters, or in his *Apologia*. Yet it
produced for years the most savage attacks and bitterest
sneers at people who advocate concealment under the title
of Reserve, and the hiding of their full thoughts under the
pretense of what they call Economy; and Charles Kingsley
will, in due course, throw some of his loudest thunderbolts
of scorn at this alleged principle of calculated deceit as a
means of leading innocent young men on and on to the verge
of Rome.

Next, in June, '38, Dr. Faussett, of Magdalen, Lady Margaret Professor of Divinity, fired off at them an attack particularly directed at Newman's dearest, lost friend, whose
views on the Eucharist he found obnoxious. John wrote in
high good-humor about this to Jemima. "Old Faussett has

been firing off at us. He is like an old piece of ordnance which can do nothing but fire, or an old macaw with one speech." (This is, surely, a happy childhood memory of Lady Parker's old macaw next door at Ham?) "He fired off at Milman, and against Hampden, and now against us. He can do nothing but fire, fire. . . ." But, in practice, he took the attack most seriously and wrote a long, passionate and fine reply. We will pay careful attention to this little-mentioned document which reveals his unconscious but swiftly accelerating tidal turn, but which he passes over so lightly in the *Apologia* that he only gives it about five lines.

This reply to Faussett produced a third striking event, to which his memory also pays little attention. It was the least predictable thing possible: a breach with his dear friend Keble, with Keble's brother Tom, and with other colleagues. Associated with this tiff over Faussett was his plan to have the Roman *Breviary*, which he had received as his last memento of dear Hurrell, translated and published.

He could not ignore the events of August—the "change of fortune" date. His Bishop then came out with a Charge so unsympathetic as to shake him badly. He actually offered on the head of it to stop all the tracts. Meantime Hurrell's *Remains*, which he and Keble had been editing, had begun to appear, and both he and Dean Church recorded that it was the book which "made the most stir and caused the greatest outcry of all"; a fact which must have pained Newman deeply. There is no doubt that he was gravely harassed in '38.

We note, finally, that in January, '39, he collected all the strong things they, but especially he himself, had been saying against the Church of Rome and published them. He says in his *Apologia*, that utterly truthful book which no biographer can trust implicitly, that he did this to silence the popular clamor rising about him in '38. I believe that he

was trying to still a rising clamor in his own heart, dating
from much earlier.

Now for the inwardness of these events, and for Froude's
connection with them. "March, 1836," he had written in
a note of that date, attached to a bundle of letters, "is a
cardinal point of time": for nine reasons. Of these the first
is Froude's death, and the third, "My knowing and using the
Breviary." He fell in love with the book; it lay constantly
on his desk; it lies there to this day. He wrote a Tract on
that *Breviary* in July, '36. It frightened his colleagues but
sold amazingly well, which he took for a portent. He received Froude's manuscripts in the summer of '36. They
were a revelation to him. He found in Hurrell's private
papers things he had never suspected of the living man.
Some of them, he said, "have made my head whirl." They
revealed a secret ascetic in the gay, ironic, intrepid yachtsman, mountain-climber and cross-country rider. It was as if
he had found a hair-shirt on his friend's dead body. He
found that on many days this man who had for years been
dying by inches of consumption, used to eat nothing but a
piece of bread, and that he used often sleep on the bare floor.

Moreover, the accumulated papers showed a boldness of
thought—Arnold, on reading the volumes, called it an "extraordinary impudence"—which, to a mind like Newman's,
slow, cautious, complex and considered, must have come like
the lightning-flash that at once illuminates and simplifies a
landscape. We can imagine how Hurrell's passionate clarity
of feeling, his directness of speech, his daring way of taking
his fences must have spurred any sympathetic reader. From
one so dear, so mourned, so deeply longed for, it must all
have had the effect now of—"This is what we really have
been thinking, Carissime, isn't it?" For example: "Really I
hate the Reformers more and more!" Or: "Why *is* the opinion of the English Clergy entitled to be called the teaching

of the Church more than that of the Clergy of France, Italy, Spain, Russia?" Or: "We cannot know about any seemingly indifferent practice of the Church of Rome that is not a development of the apostolic ethos; and it is to no purpose to say that we can find no proof of it in the writings of the first six centuries. They must find a *dis*proof if they would do anything." Nobody else in the Movement had dared speak so bluntly.

Fascinated, John began to transcribe the papers. He was working on them through '36, '37 and into '38. Still in close communion with his dead friend in '38 he began to get two of his old pupils, Wood and Williams, to translate the *Breviary* for publication. Then, as we have seen, Faussett attacked Hurrell; and then it was that Tom Keble not only protested strongly against the *Breviary* plan, and took objection to certain ideas in the Faussett reply, but used unmistakable expressions denoting lack of confidence, such as that he heartily wished that Newman "would go out of Oxford somewhere or other for a while," and forget all about Faussett. And there was mention of people who "used to sympathise" with them all.

This double attack on him, over his desire to publish Hurrell's *Breviary*, and his defense of his dead friend's ideas, disturbed Newman more than anything he had hitherto experienced.

The alienation lasted openly not more than three weeks, but he was still feeling its effects in January, '39, when he said to Jemima: "It is only when friends fall on me that I am touched." And while the tiff lasted he had poured some of his hurt on Bowden, who had no part in it, for when Bowden asked some questions about early corruptions in the Church he received the curt reply: "I am so bothered and attacked on all sides by friends and foes that I would much rather say nothing, and had I my own wish I certainly should say noth-

ing and write nothing more. I mean I distrust my judgement and am getting afraid to speak. . . ."

How can we fail to be struck by all this? Especially when
he attached to these letters, when published, the remark that
after the date of this tiff he could never again "prefer a claim
for (Keble's) *confidence.*" And in one of his December letters to Keble there is this passage:—

"When others protest (I do not mean Low Church, but men
like your brother) I feel a sort of bad conscience and disgust
with what I have done. . . . And yet if I *am* to speak I cannot
speak otherwise than I do. . . . My constant feeling when I
write is that I do not realise things, but am merely drawing out
intellectual conclusions, which I need not say is very uncomfortable."

Is it to read our foreknowledge to hear a certain undertone
of insecurity, if not actually of fear in—*I do not realise
things.* . . .

3

And now, why had his fugitive pamphlet on Faussett
caused so much pother?

I suggest that it was because its passionate tone and its
turbulent longings took them by surprise. The *Breviary*
scheme threw further light on these secret longings. The
pamphlet is certainly not written by a Protestant. Newman
has completely taken over Froude's anti-Reformation attitude and will henceforth reject Protestantism consistently as
an uncreative, schismatic, perhaps even heretical negation.
But Tom Keble apparently began to wonder if the man who
wrote the pamphlet was even an Anglican, and he threw up
his hands when he came on a passage in which Newman declared that it passed his comprehension how divines holding
to the Apostolical Succession could believe Rome to be "the

mother of harlots"—as Tom Keble firmly did—followed by
a generous defense of Rome and a stern criticism of the
Church of England.   It is to this date (the summer of 1838)
that I would relate what Dean Church observed a year later
—the subtle but decisive, and by then visible, change which
altered a Movement that began by defending England and
assailing Rome into a Movement which ended by assailing
England and apologizing for Rome.

The pamphlet is in part a denial that they are reviving
Popery.   It is in part a defense of Froude in particular
against this charge.   It is in part a defense of the right of
Anglicans to believe whatever is not expressly denied by
their Church.   It is in part another and more than usually
passionate reminder of the liberty of Catholic opinion once
permitted in the Church, and of doctrines held once by
Hooker, Andrewes, Laud, Montague, Hammond, Bramhall,
Taylor, Thorndike, Bull, Beveridge or Ken, and now denied
or constricted by men who have become more Protestant
than the Protestants themselves.   It is in part the usual Tractarian appeal to the practices of the ancient Christian church,
so that those Anglican divines assemble in the mind of the
reader with Ignatius and Irenaeus, Tertullian and Origen,
Ambrose and Jerome.   But the core of the pamphlet is an
effort to protect with Froude for Anglicanism the reality of
the great central ceremony of the Christian church wherein
bread and wine are miraculously made the Body and Blood
of Christ as against Faussett's position that the ceremony is
merely a meager, a commemorative ceremony and that the
bread and wine are but symbols of "absent" Body and Blood.

Doubtless not one reader in ten-thousand-and-one whose
eye falls on such a volume in a library would think of taking
it down.   In this aversion to theology the ten thousand are
generally justified.   Newman is exceptional.   A human interest attaches to everything he wrote not only by association
with his story and because of the peculiarly delicate quality

of his mind, but because he is not primarily a theologian or
a philosopher but an artist.   The boy who first saw the world
as a dream; who emerged from his first elementary ratioci-
nations as a Calvinist moralist; who passed through the intellectual training of Oxford into a realm of thought where
thought was, so to speak, civilized by experience of men and
aerated by an imagination cultivated and refined out of its
first credulity; who extracted from the history of early religious controversies the discovery that the intellect is after
all a dangerous and fearful privilege; who then applied his
intellect *terre-à-terre* to religious controversy in his own day,
is here applying thought on yet another level, and with such
further skill and delicacy, that—as if in conformity with his
own growing scepticism about the reliability of the normal
processes of the intellect—we are hard put to say whether
his thought conveys a sensation of ice or of fire.   But, then,
as we shall see before we finish with him, in his last flight of
all, in some of his *University Sermons* and in *The Development of Christian Doctrine,* he will so analyze thought as to
fray it away between his delicate fingers until we feel that
we are left with no more of the intellect, which intellect has
reasoned away, than a pinch of dust in the palm, like ash
falling from a burning sky, or the dust with which the priest
touches our foreheads on Ash Wednesday, murmuring, "Memento homo quia pulvis es et in pulverem revertiris."   This
apparently fugitive pamphlet on "old Faussett," this apparently dry-as-dust essay into theology is a courtship between
the Imagination and his Reason, aiming to do that which he
will later define as the aim of all development in thought—
to crown an early impression on the Imagination as a system
or creed in the Reason.[1]

If anybody feels this is a dull adventure he can never have
experienced the ecstasies of applying language to the refine-
ment of thought in the effort to capture some philosophical
concept at once abstract and material, evanescent and per-

manent, or even to define some historical event. If we
doubt this we might ask, say, some philosopher to explain the
meaning of the word Existence; or ask a learned Rabbi to
discourse on the historical misinterpretations of the phrase
"God's Chosen People"; or read Newman's efforts to put into
words what happens to God and to bread in the mystery of
the Eucharist. The experience, according to one's nature,
will be amusing or terrifying, or even disgusting, in its revelation of the powers and vagaries of reason falling into unreason, and unreason masquerading as reason, and reason
sensibly aware of its limitations and functioning within them;
and, perhaps, in the end, we will feel that the only certainty
is with the artist or the mystic for whom all language dilates
ultimately into a symbol.

4

It seems to me that when Newman began thinking like this
he came to the last bridge between the outlying islands of
Protestant schism and the mainland of Christian thought.
Tom Mozley once asked himself—and he was the average,
not-too-bright, not-too-dull, not-too-zealous, working country clergyman—what were the chief Protestant objections to
Roman Catholicism; and he gave three presumably average
answers: Truth, meaning that Rome is a fabric of lies; Loyalty, meaning that in England a Roman Catholic's loyalty to
the state is—as it then was—suspect; and Superstition,
meaning that the whole ambience of Rome partakes of the
miraculous, the supernatural or the credulous, and is to solid
John Bull just plain, damned, disgusting irrationalism. We
may nowadays omit the appeal to patriotism. As Tom said,
in effect, it took a few thousand conversions before England
realized that converts also serve their king. The charge of
irrationality and the charge of untruthfulness seem to merge,
and they remain. It *is* the distinction between Rome and

England that for a Roman Catholic the truths of reason are never more than relative; to be respected, indeed, but never to be relied on to take us farther than within sight of the shore. One must always expect to have to jump in and swim the last bit.

It is profoundly revealing of Newman that it was the artist in him and not the intellectual that finally admitted defeat in considering the mystery and the miracle.[2] For, in this pamphlet on the Eucharist, he observed the great truth that any miracle is not against reason, but against imagination. That is to say: we can easily accept a miracle in our brains— such as the existence of God: we can posit the idea, and argue about it; and come to a conclusion about it; we can declare the fact of the existence of God as any Greek philosopher might arrive at the idea of a First Cause; we can lay it down as a firm intellectual concept; but we cannot imagine, or, in his sense of the word, *realize*, this ineffable Being, or any of His processes.

This defeat takes us to the heart of the mystery of life. For while it occurs in the field of the imagination it reacts on the field of intellect. Like a battle that is lost in the hills and reacts on the palace, it unsettles the throne, the government, the executive arm, the merchants in their shops, the people in their homes. Once we discover that we cannot imagine what we understand we rush through the streets crying chaos, tear down the palace, guillotine the king and his ministers, fall at last into despair and enthrone in the temples a harlot called the Goddess of Reason, who can hardly read or write, and who falsely tells that this defeat would never have occurred if we had only had enough sense to realize at the start what she has always known—that there is no mystery or miracle in life at all.

The message of Newman is that the reason is not defeated, though it can be unsettled when the imagination fails. When Napoleon falls France does not fail. It was he, as

Léon Bloy said, who was the superb Failure, the colossal
Weakling, in his original imaginative lust to reign at any
price. But when Joan of Arc is burned she is not defeated.
We cannot defeat a vision. It is her judges who lose the battle. Of course, as the world wags all this is nonsense, and
France did fail with Napoleon, and England did triumph over
Joan, and the rationalists are the only sane people in the wagging world. But, as we have seen, by a process of *reculer
pour mieux sauter* Newman's intellect has, since boyhood,
been rising up and up out of the space and time of this world
wagging like an old crunching clock on the wall of eternity to
where the Imagination on the very brink of heaven seems
alone fit to rule . . . and there he stops. There his Reason tells him that Imagination will not do and that the last
flight is with Faith. So he kicks away both his ladders and
sits on a cloud at heaven's gate. In that world of faith, as
Léon Bloy insisted, there is no history in our sense, there are
no final battles, all time being a timeless part of a divine war.

So, in this argument against Faussettism the "what happens" of the Eucharist troubled Newman hardly at all: there
is a Presence, and he was content to rely on the divines of his
Church for that. As for the "how it happens" he wished, as
far as reason could, both to defend his dead friend and to
exalt the mystery by his disquisition on the possibility of
believing that a personal God could in some manner be
simultaneously and personally on earth and in the heavens.
But here the words begin to dilate; and later, when a Catholic, he will annotate with further words, from Billuart and
Bellarmine, to indicate that a distinction between local, substantial, sacramental or real presence is a difference that is "a
mere matter of words," with the implication that definition in
such matters is, in fact, beyond language.

Essentially his argument is that there is no such thing as
objective space; that space is a subjective idea; and that
words which convey the contrary are misleading, and that, in

any case, no words can possibly convey the results of this idea of spacelessness.   It is a pleasure to read this argument —even if one only reads it as one may watch a ballet-dancer performing some highly delicate and difficult figure; abstracting the performance from all material relevancy; as one must indeed always abstract the absurdity of a ballet-dancer's behavior from common sense to enjoy it.   One *must* abstract his argument, since it is patently false in common life.   Ask any lover separated from his mortal love whether there is such a thing as space.   Though, indeed, even a lover may write: "You are always beside me."   But ask a prisoner or an exile!   Yet, listen to him:—

"First, as to material things, what do we mean when we speak of an object being present to us?   How do we define and measure its presence?   To a blind and deaf man that only is present which he touches.   Give him hearing and the range of things present to him enlarges; everything is present to him which he hears.   Give him at length sight, and the sun may be said to be present to him in daytime and myriads of stars by night.   Presence, then, is a relative word, depending on the channels of communication existing between the object and the person to whom it is present.   It is almost a correlative of the senses.   A fly may be as near an edifice as a man; yet we do not call it present to the fly because he cannot see it, and we do call it present to the man because he can."

If this be theology who shall say that theology is dull?   He goes on:—

"But we must add another element to the idea expressed by the word in the case of matter.   A thing may be said to be present to us which is so circumstanced as immediately to act upon us and to influence us, whether we are sensible of it or no."   Perhaps, then, he suggests, the god may be *present* in the sense that though far away, he acts personally, bodily and directly on us, though we cannot tell how, "as a blind man cannot conceive the results of eyesight."

"We know but of five senses, we know not whether human nature is capable of more; we know not whether the human soul possesses any instruments of knowledge and moral advantage analogous to them; but neither have we any reason to deny that the soul may be capable of having Christ present to it by the stimulus of dormant, or the development of possible energies. As sight for certain purposes annihilates space, so other unknown conditions of our being, bodily or spiritual, may practically annihilate it for other purposes. Such may be the sacramental presence. We kneel before the heavenly throne and distance vanishes. . . ."

He sees, then, the risen Christ—risen with what Saint Paul calls "a spiritual body"—in the heavens, yet subject neither to laws of matter, nor confines of space, nor dependence on its conditions, and that His modes of being present on earth may be as different to the modes of locomotion natural to human bodies as spirit is different to matter. Why may He then not be present in the Eucharist, even though not locally present?

"We, to whom the idea of space is a necessity, and who have no experience of spirits, are of course unequal to the conception of such an idea and can only call a mystery what is as transporting and elevating to the religious sense as it is difficult to the intellect."

Evidently we are far, by this, from the common materialist objection to the idea of carnally consuming Christ!

"And hence, whereas He is unseen and His presence ineffable and known only by its outward signs . . . when we touch the one, with our spirit we touch the other, when we eat the one we eat the other, when we drink the one we drink the other. And whereas what is spiritual has no parts and what is spiritual cannot receive in part, therefore when we speak of eating Christ's body with our souls the words cannot be grossly or absurdly taken to mean a partial or general communication of so heavenly a treasure as happens in carnal eating, but in some unknown way the soul becomes possessed of Christ according to its nature, and as bodily contact is the mode in which bread nourishes our bodies, so the soul, and the motions of the soul, and faith which is of the soul, as by an inward contact, is the mean and instrument of receiving Christ."

Thereupon calling on the language of the Homilies, and of Hooker, he arrays against the minimal, unimaginative rationalistic thought and language of Protestantism that passionately poetic spirit of Anglicanism which the enthusiasm of the Oxford Movement at its most intense so often succeeded in blowing into heat and fire again:—

"Let disputes and questions, enemies to piety, abatements of true devotion, and hitherto in this cause but overpatiently heard, let them take their rest!   Let curious and sharp-witted men beat their heads about what questions themselves will; the very letter of the word Christ giveth plain security that these mysteries do, as nails, fasten us to His very cross, that by them we draw out even the blood of His gored side; in the wounds of the Redeemer we there dip our tongues, we are dyed red both within and without, our hunger is satisfied and our thirst for ever quenched. There are things wonderful which he feeleth, great which he seeth, and unheard which he uttereth whose soul is possessed of this Paschal Lamb and made joyful in the strength of this new wine. . . .   This bread hath in it more than the substance which our eyes behold; this cup hallowed with solemn benediction availeth to the endless life and welfare both of soul and body; in that it serveth as well for a medicine to heal our infirmities and purge our sins, as for a sacrifice of thanksgiving. . . ."

At this, fired by Hooker, he cries out at Faussett:—

"What a contrast do glowing thoughts like these present to such teaching as has been too much in esteem among us of late years! What a decrepitude has come on us since Hooker's day! How has the fine gold become dim! How has the promise of the spring played us false in the summer! How have the lean kine eaten up the fat kine, and the thin ears choked the full ones! What a spiritual famine, or rather what locusts and cankerworms are our portion! The olive-tree can be content with its own fatness and the fig-tree with its own sweetness, and the vine reckons it much 'to cheer god and man'; but the thin and empty ears of Zurich and Geneva think it scorn unless they devour and make a clean end of the pleasant and fair pastures of Catholic doctrine, which are our heritage:

> *Interque nitentia culta*
> *Infelix lolium et steriles dominantur avenae."*

Having read him we can now understand better his agonized feelings that late Autumn and Winter of '38 when Tom Keble having read this pamphlet wished he would go away out of Oxford and leave old Faussett alone, and deplored the *Breviary*, and spoke of people who "used to sympathise" with him. We may feel how deeply he has ploughed his soul in loving communion with his dear friend. We may feel, too, that it is only natural that the change from defending Anglicanism to upbraiding it, which Dean Church saw in '39, should have been on the way long before then. We may feel, lastly, that the fatal shock which Newman will sustain in '39 at Wiseman's hands was prepared for long before by such unsettling experiences as these.

5

He had said, "Let matters take their course freely and trust in God's providence for the issue." It had been only two years before, in May, '36, that Hugh James Rose had solemnly warned Pusey and Newman against this.[3]

"All that is in antiquity is not good, and much that was good for antiquity would not be good for us"; and he told them that if they persisted in travelling far and wide and deep into that ancient world, "where we shall get to seems hard to tell"; and, in a later letter, he protested that "we are going on no voyage of discovery" taking "our chance of finding a new Atlantis." Newman and Pusey had replied jointly on a single sheet of paper, with this very quotation that John used again in '38, saying:—

"If a person be sent into any one field to bring all he can out of it he will bring the *infelix lolium* as well as other things, and perhaps be more taken with it than good seed; the *steriles avenae* being constantly the tallest. But if he be told that he is to look for certain herbs which have been planted everywhere and that he is not to bring away things which he does not find in every part of the field—why a volatile labourer will soon lay down the business altogether and an ardent one will be sobered."

And, farther on:—

"This is what I meant by saying that we must spread our sails, not knowing whither we should be carried."

Hurrell Froude would have liked that image. In his conversations with Keble he may have fathered it: talking of cruises to Guernsey, with each wave in succession washing the deck, his only compass the sun, or peeping through the clouds for Lyra and Cassiopeia chasing one another about the Pole; or of wild night-crossings from Plymouth when the yards hummed frighteningly, and it was with a breath of relief that he would manage the entry into the smooth sound at Dart and see on the hill the lights of his father's home.

CHAPTER 13

THE SCHISMATICS

1

A LL through '39, as in '37 and '38, Newman's spirit and
Froude's continued in close communion. With Keble
he was preparing the third and fourth volumes of Froude's
Remains for the press, completing thereby the publication of
all his friend's papers, finished and unfinished notes, journals,
letters; the two editors even included some of his most casual
remarks that they remembered from occasional conversation.
They annotated it all in such loving-kindness and with, one
feels certain, such a sad recollection of many a vivid discussion that no close relatives could have more carefully
presented the remains of a dead son or brother to, as it tran-
spired, an irritated public and, as it appears, an indifferent
posterity.

To read these volumes is to be surprised at the number of
ideas that John Newman and Hurrell Froude had held in
common, or, perhaps, owed to the stimulus of one another;
as well as to be struck by the number of finger-posts point-
ing the way that John was to follow, or, at least, the way
that, in fact, he did follow in and after '39.

We are familiar with some of the common stock of ideas to
be found in the *Remains*. They were partly the development of other men's ideas, such as Provost Hawkins' theory
of Tradition, and partly their own ideas, such as their insistence on the apostolic pedigree, or their devotion to the

spirit of the antique church, or their love for all its institutions, or their resistance to a dry intellectualism in religious
matters.   Even these ideas might be traced to other sources,
and the probable truth is that they were all part of the general Oxford fermentation, and are to be thought original to
them only in that they were more thorough in developing
and more bold in applying the latent conclusions to notions
that other men threw out in the *vague*.   To illustrate this
interweaving, all that John had said in the *Arians* about the
defectibility of language is in Blanco White's *Observations
on Heresy and Orthodoxy*.   In reviewing that book Froude
made use of his friend's book on the *Arians* to reject Blanco's
idea that there can be no such thing as a reliable church authority.   At the same time, in the same review, he employs
against Blanco's theory that the Thirty-Nine Articles are
articles of faith (rather than articles of discipline), arguments which Newman will, in turn, take up and develop in
Tract 90.   But some of these same arguments had long been
held by Stillingfleet, and Bramhall, and the Bishop of Peter-
borough, and we can be reasonably certain that more than
one Common Room had, in any case, brought those views
into argument before either Froude or Newman took them
over and applied them as part of their general thought.

There is, nevertheless, a striking concordance, too strong
to be a mere coincidence, between John's behavior, in '39
and after, and the thought and spirit of these *Remains* of
Hurrell Froude that had come so frequently before him over
the past three years, beckoning him, one might say, to pursue still their common road.   They are especially close on
two salient counts: the unworthiness and unreliability of the
English Reformers; and the shallow Rationalism that has be-
devilled the English Church ever since the Reformation.

We do not know for certain whether Keble alone, or Keble
with Newman assisting, as I suspect, wrote the Preface to
the 1839 volumes; but both are as one in agreeing whole-

heartedly with Froude's contemptuous references to the Reformers.   As for the shallow Rationalism of these men, and
their inheritors, Froude's third volume opens with a long
Essay on Rationalism, and Newman opens the year '39 with
two University sermons on the relation between Faith and
Reason; to be elaborated more and more in the following
years, in his great book, *An Essay on the Development of
Christian Doctrine,* and finally in *A Grammar of Assent,* into
what we might call his dialectic of faith.

It all links up.   That Newman would pursue the ghostly
finger beckoning in this special direction might almost have
been presumed from the Faussett affair.   That clash, entered
on in defense of Froude, had been a head-on collision with
Rationalism under the title of Protestantism: for what Faussett had smelled in Froude was that supernaturalist mentality
which Tom Mozley had picked out as one of the salient
marks of Rome, and he had replied to it with the natural
weapon.   In his position he was quite right; for if men were
to persist in this high-falutin', mystical way of reinterpreting
matters on which the sanity of the English Reformation had
spoken, they must, in the process, wipe out the English
Church as a Church.   Faussett saw, that is, that the whole
theory of Apostolic Succession cut across the Reformation.
The editors of Froude's *Remains* also saw it, but from the
other side of the fence.   John Newman saw it.   If that
"painful, invidious, indelicate" topic "lay not only *in* but
across their way," and if its appeal was indeed to Reason,
then both the essence of his difficulty, and its solution, lay
in the rational basis of faith which he must, in turn, analyze
and expose.

We will look at his approach to the intellectual basis of
belief not in the *University Sermons,* where he first employs
this new technique, but in its most considered statement, the
Development.   Although he will not actually begin to write
this book for some five years we are not, in looking at it now,

anticipating his thought, in which there is, in any case, a certain inevitability from start to finish.   This principle of development had been adumbrated by him in *Home Thoughts
Abroad,* in '36; had come to the surface of his mind in Italy
in '33; he had introduced it into the *Arians* in '32; he had discussed it with Hawkins, as Tradition, in the Long Vacations
of '24 and '25; and he had first heard the idea mooted in a
sermon by Hawkins in 1818 when a mere boy.   What is new
and illuminating in his treatment of it in '39 and afterwards
is the analysis of the actual intellectual process itself by
which, as we imagine, we rationally forward the development of ideas: and even this critique of impure reason might
be held to be the development of another earlier idea—
namely, his long-standing suspicion that the too-too-clever
"talents of the day" are not as clever as they imagine.   What
is not at all new in it is that his assault on "reason" is, in
effect, an assault on "reality"; and that was something about
which he had had the gravest doubts since childhood.   It
was, in a sense, the core of his philosophy.

                                   2

   Newman's attack on Reason is as swift as a drawn knife:
"It is," his first sentence declares, "the characteristic of our
minds to be ever engaged in passing judgement on the things
which come before us."   Then begins, in his second sentence, a brilliant piecemeal dissection of the wilfulness of
thought:—"We allow nothing to stand by itself: we compare,
contrast, abstract, generalise, connect, adjust, classify; and
we view all our knowledge in the associations with which
these processes have invested it."
   With this one word, *association,* bang goes the simple notion that "facts are facts"; for facts are thereby only to be
called facts when they are isolated in our minds.   And are
they ever isolated?

The supposedly rational judgments resulting from this process of association are now led to the rack and gently torn limb from limb:—

"Of the judgements thus made, which become aspects"—Aspects!—"in our minds of the things which meet us some are mere opinions which come and go, or which remain with us only until an accident displaces them, whatever be the influence which they exercise meanwhile. Others are firmly fixed in our minds, with or without good reason, and have a hold upon us, whether they relate to matters of fact, or to principles of conduct, or are views of life and the world, or are prejudices, imaginations or convictions. Many of them attach to one and the same object, which is thus variously viewed, not only by various minds but by the same."

He points out that at times these judgments lie so near one another that each implies the others, that, at times, our judgments are inconsistent with one another, apart from the fact that they happened to originate in the same way, that, at times, our judgments are not only mutually incompatible but falsely associated in our minds with incompatible objects which we think the same object. "In any case they may be nothing more than ideas which we mistake for things." Yet, how else can we think and reason except by means of ideas?

Here he opens up the complex nature of any idea, which must, inevitably, refer to many aspects of everything we consider. For instance when we walk around a statue we see its manifold aspects. But the very variety of these aspects becomes an argument for that statue's essential oneness, integrity, solidity, originality, its individual, indivisible power. Therefore the multiplicity of these aspects is crucial in that while, with our inadequate intelligence, we can only discuss them one by one, we chop into portions what is a unity. The statue remains indivisible. We do not break up the indivisible unity of God though we discuss Him as if we could.

The result is evident. Any idea which is arresting will be seized on by a million minds in a million moods, and discussed by them in a million aspects. Every idea will be discussed in relation to other ideas, each with its many aspects. It will live on as a subject of discussion for generations. It will intermarry. In each generation it will be fecund. It will as a living, fecund idea affect all life, creep into our social codes, affect public opinion, impress itself on public order. It may gradually emerge as an objective institution or institutions. It may grow into an ethical code. And yet all this multiplicity is, in the end—if there ever is an end to the process—the maturation of the procreative plasma of one original nuclear premise. This process is what he calls Development. "To live is to change and to be perfect is to have changed often."

After all this has been allowed it is easy to see how in religion a body of dogmatic statements must reduce what had been a primal impression on the Imagination to a concrete system in the Reason. True, these creeds and dogmas live only in the primal idea which they are trying to express— just as our multiple remarks about the statue lived only in the indivisible object before us. But these fissurated statements, or creeds or dogmas, are none the less necessary and justifiable, however weak and relative, because though the human mind cannot reflect upon any idea except by piecemeal, "cannot use it in its oneness and entireness or without resolving it into a series of aspects and relations," there is no other way, inadequate though it is, to discuss and to teach any doctrine.

So it has been with Christianity. Its original documents do not determine it; for the ideas of Christianity are in the reader and writer of the revelation, not in the written text, and only in time can they hope to be clarified; just as Christianity, in its external or political framework, must expect to conform to the general methods by which the course of things is always carried forward in this mortal world. We have only to open the text of Scripture to see that this is true. *"The Word became flesh."* What prolonged investigations, what discussions those three vocables—"Word" and "became" and "flesh"—must involve! And then consider the whole of Scripture! What an inexhaustible catalogue it is, so unsystematic and so various, so figurative and so indirect that "to the end of our lives and to the end of the Church it must be an unexplored and unsubdued land. . . ." In short, the idea of Christianity is not to be contained temporally or locally. It is the grain of mustard-seed.

An authoritative guide for the amazed explorers among these far-spreading ideas is, then, to be as probably expected as it is evidently necessary? In this part, he goes far from the elementary arguments of *The Prophetical Office* of '37. For what now is this probable Infallibility but a certain body of truth, traditionally held, "pervading the Church like an atmosphere . . . partly written, partly unwritten . . . poured to and fro in closets and upon the housetops, in liturgies, in controversial works, in obscure fragments, in sermons, in popular prejudices, in local customs"—all these to be arranged and authenticated by some authority external to their course, with the presumptive power to decide between major and minor, essential and less important truths. This presumption does not, indeed, mean that our reception of the doctrine of Infallibility guarantees total certitude. All certitude is only a probable certitude. "I remember for certain what I did yesterday but my memory is not infallible." Yet you will believe me on the probability, will you not? In practice, you must.

In all this, of course, he was at his old, old bugbear "the talents of the day": the ever-enquiring, clever, sceptical, restless rationalist who because he must have scientific proofs, signed, stamped, sealed, and delivered for everything, arrives at no certain conclusion about anything; or, rather, does, of course, in practice choose to arrive at "conclusions" about some things, such as the winner of last night's boxing-match or the Derby of 1851, though purely by a weight of probabilities which he illogically prefers not to acknowledge in other things.   Do we accept, let us say, gravitation only on proving it, each man for himself?   When we hear Falstaff babble of green fields do we demand documentary proof that Shakespeare, rather than Theobald, wrote these words?   (It is in fact impossible to produce.)   In reading Cicero's letters to Atticus do we scruple to explain an obscure passage by a more explicit statement in another text?   But the sceptic who does these things will not approach the historical question of the development of religious ideas in a mood to do the best here also with what is given, or to look for aid from any quarter, such as the traditions of ages, or the prescriptions of authority, or analogies and parallel cases, or to be patient with difficulties, and apparent objections, or to interpret what is obscure in certain portions by such portions as are clear.   Rather, he prefers to mass the weakness of every individual argument (which is nevertheless an argument) into a—to him—satisfactory impression of total dubiety.

In sum:—

"Our dearest interests, our personal welfare, our property, our reputation we freely hazard, not on proof, but on simple probability, which is sufficient for our conviction, because prudence dictates to us so to take it.   We must be content to follow the law of our being in religious matters as well as secular."

And if, finally, we declare that all probability is here at a loss when we find "bishops against bishops in Church history, Fathers against Fathers, Fathers against themselves," we must not only agree that such differences are naturally involved in all intellectual development, but agree to fall back on the recognized organ of teaching, the Church itself, who has never contradicted her own enunciations; who teaches *quod semper, quod ubique, quod ab omnibus.*

Here, surely, we are to enjoy the irony of an unforeseen influence. For when we go back from Newman's essay to Froude's essay, which is its evident inspiration—he echoes it clearly—and seek the likeliest source for both we will find it where it was least intended to originate—in Whately's *Logic* and *Elements of Rhetoric,* or, behind him, in books like Hume's *Essay on Miracles.* Glance at no more than Whately's exposure of popular notions about such ideas as *Certainty* and *Experience* and we come at once on the deception of the senses (How Newman must have delighted in this!) and the fallacious inferences of reason from illusory experience—as when the King of Bantam "knew" from "experience" that water cannot become solid; or—this is one of Froude's examples—as when all men before Galileo "knew" by their senses that the sun moves. Surely, Whately must have groaned at the use that has been made of his cynical opinion that most men, in describing any state of affairs, first extract from their senses, at all costs, some minor premise, and then extract conclusions from it in favor of some instinctive major premise which they have secretly nourished all the while. His opinion has resulted in Newman's decision that the too-great burthen of Revelation implies trust in some saving guide as to the conclusions to be drawn from it, so that we had all better yield to the presumptive authority of the Church, there being no other; which is what is meant by accepting Infallibility.

When men had said that the Oriel Common Room "stank of logic," how could they ever have thought that logic would one day transcend itself to this result!

3

Logic was to have its revenge. Within a few months he was to be shipwrecked on his own logic. That phrase *quod semper, quod ubique, quod ab omnibus* which the Preface to Froude had called, so challengingly, "the great principle of Catholicism" was to topple to the ground the whole edifice he had been building up in the *Via Media*.

For in the summer he began to study a fifth-century schism, the Monophysite. And the story of the Monophysites made him uncomfortably aware of the enormous, indeed universal power of the Pope in those pure days he so adored. It was a dose of medicine, or an "alterative," as he called it, that he did not at all like. While thus disturbed, one day in August, Robert Wilberforce, when passing through Oxford, drew his attention to an article in the current issue of *The Dublin Review*[1] by Dr. Wiseman, based on another schism, the Donatist, which likewise involved the principle of the universality of Catholicism. Newman got a copy of the periodical, took it to his rooms, read it, and, his own word, it gave him "a stomach-ache." It was another "dose"—also his word—on top of the Monophysites. He confided in Rogers: "It does certainly come upon me that we are not at the bottom of things. At this moment we have sprung a leak." He concealed from himself for a long time that he had done more than spring a leak, that he was, in plain truth, sunk. But four years afterwards, in writing to Harriett he pin-pointed the date and the fact:—"My present views were taken up in the summer of 1839 upon reading the Monophysite and Donatist controversies. I saw from them that Rome was the centre of unity and judge of controversies." This is the shock to his security to which he refers in the *Apologia*. I have pointed out that the softening-up process began long before.

4

Wiseman's principle, granting his premises—which the Oxford Movement freely granted—seems irresistible. It was of the simplest. It was that in religion secession is impossible. A man can desert from his army, but he cannot without permission secede from it. If he wilfully decides to leave it he is a traitor, and there is no more to be said. He may set up another little army of his own. He is still a traitor. If his little army becomes a great and universally powerful army, which persists in its power over such a vast period of time that he can now invoke the *quod semper, quod ubique, quod ab omnibus*, then he may cease to be a traitor. But where, Wiseman gently asks, with a soft flash of his amethyst ring, is there in history such an example within the Christian system?

Consider these Donatists of Africa, these traitorous Africans, as one might say these traitorous Anglicans. What was their story? There had been two parties, who may be termed extreme and moderate. The moderates, to forestall the extremists, had elected a bishop named Caecilianus. The extremists promptly elected a rival, Marjorinus, whom Donatus succeeded, declaring that the moderates were all schismatics. These extremist Africans were very powerful; indeed they lasted on for three centuries, and at one time numbered almost as many bishops as the moderates. Against them the moderates insisted that they alone were Catholics, that they alone were in communion with the universal Church, that they alone held to the Chair of Peter, and that the extremists were merely attempting to establish a local or National Church. On the other hand the rebellious Africans claimed that they alone by their glorious "Reformation" were the Apostolic Church, and that everybody else was corrupt. The reply of the moderates, whose most fa-

mous protagonist was Saint Augustine, was that the Church
is one; it cannot be one with all heretics and schismatics; it
must therefore be only in one place. (*Restat ut uno loco
sit.*)

"Thou, Brother Parmenianus, hast said that it is with you alone.
Therefore, as it may be with you in a small portion of Africa, in
a little corner of the land, with us in another part of Africa it is
not? In Spain, in Gaul, in Italy, where you are not it is not?"

Hereabouts comes the sentence that pulverized Newman:
"Saint Augustine," said Wiseman, "has a golden sentence
on this subject which should be an axiom in theology.
*Quapropter securus judicat orbis terrarum bonos non esse
qui se dividunt ab orbe terrarum in quacumque parte orbis
terrarum.*" "For the whole world (of Christianity) securely
judges that those men are not good men who divide themselves from the world in any part of the world." For months
Newman heard that phrase ringing in his ears and could not
thrust it from him. It echoed his footsteps. *Securus judicat
orbis terrarum. . . .* It whispered with the autumn leaves.
Orbis terrarum. . . . It faced him in his Bible. "In thy
seed shall *all* the nations of the earth be blessed. . . ." Or:
"He shall rule from sea to sea and to the bounds of the earth."

Besides, if the Roman church were corrupt whence did
this African church come? "From what earth," cried Augustine to Donatus, "did he spring up? From what sea did
he emerge? From what heavens did he fall?" As for so-
called corruptions, the very fact of any practice being followed or tolerated in the Church is a sufficient vindication
of it; and whenever a separation takes place from the body
of the Church on the ground of such being corruptions they
are safe who persevere in those practices while *the pretended
Reformers are at once to be rejected as having no mission or
commission for their schismatical undertakings.* The whole

matter of alleged reformations, or secessions, is, in one word, not in the least a question of a right but of a fact; so that although men in one place or time may have to endure evil men—and the Roman Catholic Church has had many evil men—no good men can on their own account separate, for that reason, from the good living elsewhere, "far off and unknown."

Wiseman hammered home the analogies. You men of Oxford say that you did not secede; that it was the Catholic Church at Trent that apostatized. (This had been the burthen of Tract 15.) But the Donatists used this very same argument! As others who secede from you—the countless sects of England—say to you that it is you who have apostatized! And where is this Church that you proclaim, outside your own small region? You are not in active communion or intercourse outside your own region, except, perhaps, in North America; just as the Donatists were not outside their African stronghold. What Augustine said to the Donatists might also on another count be said to you Anglicans: "What schismatics did you ever spare, you who too impudently wish to be spared by the entire world from which you yourselves are schismatics?" That drew blood from Newman, who had never spared his brother or any other schismatic from the English Church. He heard with awe the voice of Augustine say to him across the centuries: "If you ask me by what fruits we know you to be rather ravenous wolves, I object to you the crime of schism. . . ."

When Newman laid down *The Dublin Review* he was in his heart a Roman Catholic. His mind still denied it. He confessed to Rogers and to Henry Wilberforce—he confided in nobody else for almost two and a half years—his agonizing fear that "perhaps I might break down in the event that perhaps we were both out of the Church." He exposed his fears to Henry Wilberforce while they were walking side by side one October day in the New Forest. Looking before him down a long vista between the trees, he paused and said, "A vista has opened before me, the end of which I do not see." He would walk on, then, for some time in silent musing, and say: "One thing I am sure I can promise you, that I shall never take such a step unless Keble and Pusey agree with me that it is a duty." At another time he said: "I wonder whether such a step would be justifiable if an hundred of us saw it to be their duty to take it with me?" In recalling this terrible moment Wilberforce admitted that the words as he remembered them might not be quite exact but that the deep wound which they branded on his own inmost soul—"fear came like a thunderstroke"—made it impossible that they should not be correct in substance. Newman said to Rogers: "If things were to come to the worst I should turn Brother of Charity in London. . . ."

Years afterwards when Wilberforce read his friend's novel *Loss and Gain*—in which Newman is only mentioned once or twice, under the name of Smith—he was struck by the ominous remark of one character about Smith: "He has shifted his ground." By this is meant that Newman temporarily restored his tranquillity of mind—in January, 1840, when replying to Wiseman in *The British Critic*—by retreating to the ground that "Rome is the Church and we are the Church, and there is no need to enquire which of the two has most deflected from the Apostolic standard." But it was no use. *Haeret lateri lethalis arundo.* His letters thereafter say everything by saying so little. The evasions begin, the hints, the understatements of a man secretly fighting off a conviction. So, to Jemima, Wiseman's article is "striking." Or, "The question of the Fathers is getting more and more anxious." Or, "Certainly the way good principles have shot up is wonderful but I am not clear that they are not tending towards Rome. . . ." Or, in a hint to Bowden, thrown out so lightly that it is hard to think he could have caught Newman's idea. "The only vulnerable point we have is the

penitus toto divisos orbe ["wholly divided from the world"].
It is the heel of Achilles, but a person must be a good shot
to hit it." And there were hints of his retiring from Saint
Mary's.

5

Nobody took any of these hints. Why should they? As
far as everybody but his two intimates, Rogers and Henry
Wilberforce, knew, the same storm was still raging and the
same heroic Newman stood firmly in the center of it. But
an avalanche begins with a small thing and far in distance
from its final ruin—a fall of rock, a movement in a banked
mass, slowly growing as it advances, gathering up detritus
like the snowball we roll on the lawn to make a snowman,
crushing down whole woods, absorbing great trees and rocks
as the snowball absorbs twigs and leaves, and not until its
terrible mass rumbles at last, it may be at the dead of night,
on the inscient village in its path, is its existence known at
large. When he wrote his last and most famous Tract,
Number 90, in '41, the public heard the rumbling. They
must, by then, or could, by then, have surmised the land-
slide that had begun earlier and elsewhere.

There still are, no doubt, in England some few people who
would regard any minimizing interpretation of the Thirty-
Nine Articles with the same horror that the many regarded
Tract 90 in 1841; just as there are people in England who are
sincerely horrified if one of the Royal Family goes to the
races on Sunday or pays a formal visit to the Pope. They
are our only guide towards understanding the feelings of
disgust the tract aroused, unless we turn to odd books like
Walsh's muck-raking *Secret History of the Oxford Movement*, with its revelations of how Tractarians go to Mass
secretly in disguise, or how Sister Mary Agnes was cruelly
whipped in "a ritualistic convent," or how Dr. Pusey hears

confessions "on the sly," or how Newman once established a monastery; all jumbled up, like the Chamber of Horrors, with scraps about Faber kissing the Pope's foot while still an Anglican and Manning kneeling in the mud in Rome while still an English Archdeacon; and all of which has no value or interest whatever except to intimate that Tract 90 infuriated people because it was trying to remove the last stockade of security from the path of a ravenous apocalyptic beast.

Tract 90 is a modestly worded document. When Newman explains, for example, what historically had been meant by indulgences he says that these indulgences were relaxations from the severity of canonical punishments or penances whose discipline in the primitive church lasted at times for several years, and which could be indulgently reduced or even abrogated. He explains, quietly, that the modern use of the word merely means a gracious indulgence from temporal penance equivalent, in terms of time, to those old penances: e.g., "One thousand days' indulgence." He agrees, certainly, that this method of description may offend, as if prayer or good works can be measured, tagged and tally-kept mathematically; so must the abuse of the idea offend, as when indulgences ran to fantastic lengths, e.g., to "One Thousand Years' Indulgence," or even to "Ten Thousand Years' Indulgence"; or when indulgences attached payments of money to their acquisition; so that the idea became vulgarized in the minds of the ignorant or gullible, and the unscrupulous made political use of the idea, as when it was employed to forward Crusades, or when people fostered a number of absurd apocryphal indulgences. All of this, he points out, is alone what the Reformers denounced, and the Council of Trent after them: not the simple idea of an indulgence in itself. By similar arguments he disposed of other obstacles to a Catholic interpretation of the Articles.

The whole Tract, as we now calmly read it, seems plausible enough to have persuaded any detached reader of the time that it was true. His readers mostly found it far too plausible to be true. And, is it not more plausible than true? For whatever were the intentions of the framers of the Articles—in their wish not to offend the susceptibilities of the mass of the people, and gently to attract the many in whom the old leaven had gone deep—this was not, by and large, the manner in which their descendants regarded the creed founded on those Articles, or the Church to which they felt them to be opposed. The reception the Tract received meant that whatever Englishmen once desired they no longer approved a primitive interpretation of Christianity. They did not want to go back to the early Church at all.

Why Newman wrote this Tract at this date is not easy to understand. It was a suicidal thing to have done, and allowing all we can for his natural imprudence, indifference to danger, his rashness and fearlessness, we must also allow that he has never before been so rash and wanton. He says, of this time, that he used still utter fierce things against Rome as a form of "relief." One can only think that in this trying time it was a relief to him to invite destruction. It was not realistic of him to say that he was merely trying to prove that any Anglo-Catholic could subscribe to the Articles and remain a Catholic, because the Articles could be historically regarded as not unCatholic. For it is one thing to say this in a general way and another to set about proving, point by point, that one is not, as an Anglo-Catholic, compelled to disbelieve in Purgatory, in Prayers before Images and Relics, in the Invocation of Saints, or in Transubstantiation; and he barely stops short of admitting the supremacy of the Pope; and he does not, in fact, deny that His Holiness may have "a primacy of order" in the Catholic world, and he admits that the breach with Rome did involve individual sin while not affecting the Church of England as a Church. It was more than English flesh and blood could stand.

The Tract is dated February, 1841. By March 30th the

matter was finished.   The Heads of Houses condemned him,
and his Bishop both declared Tract 90 to be objectionable
and wished that the writing of Tracts should come to a stop.
Newman, to whom the authority of the Church was a sacred
principle, obeyed.   The best opinion in Oxford was that he
had behaved with dignity and meekness.   Popular opinion
wrongly held that he had at last been exposed as a traitor to
his own Church.   But it was right in deciding that the
Oxford movement was dished.

6

It was at this time of crisis that dear Charles, with his un-
failing genius for seizing the wrong moment, decided to
enter from the wings.   While teaching at Boulogne he had
begun to lay it down as a claim in justice that his brothers
should support him, and now, possibly influenced by the
Socialist atmosphere of Bristol and the Hotwell Road, where
he had got a small job as secretary to a Statistical Society, he
renewed his claim in the form of a low threat to Frank: "If
John and you do not like to keep me going what I should
do would be to apply to the parish."   They sent him some
money.   "We were," John told Jemima, "continually sending him money.   I suppose he gave it away."   In August
he uttered a cry of total distress.   "I have got thruppence,
and as I have some bread and butter in the house I can make
this last two days."   Frank and John, thus brought together
by Charles in self-defense, agreed to pay him £1 a week by
way of giving him time to look about him, but as John sighs
to Jemima: "Up to this he has done nothing.   Or, rather, he
sets his face against doing anything, and sends me rigmarole
letters about philosophy."   In the following month Charles
wrote to John: "Yesterday I heard a man saying, 'Never mind
him!   He's silly.'   Now there is a degree of truth in this.
Frank is insinuating I could do fifty things!   He is telling me

to make bricks without straw!" John to Jem in October: "Charles has at last turned sharp upon me and I don't know what will come of it." Charles to John in October: "The idea of my competing with others is absurd. I hope you will leave off blaming me."

John was by then in no state to blame anybody. Charles to John in November: "I am much in arrears!" John, at that moment, in the thick of a Tractarian fight to get Isaac Williams elected to the Chair of Poetry, presumably again bought Charles off. There then seemed for a moment to be hope of a longer peace, for, in December, Charles got a post teaching for a Dr. Fripp, Tripp, or Cripp. By January he had lost it and was again on Frank's and John's hands. This time the two harassed brothers decided to do something final with, for, or to Charles. A small legacy from a friend coming in *à propos* they pooled their money and sent him bumbling happily off to Bonn University to get a doctor's degree. They fondly hoped that when he got it he would sail far away to America and torture a new world.

CHAPTER 14

THE SURRENDER

1

AFTER Tract 90 Newman seems to act in a dream. It either took him some time to realize that his career as a public man was finished, or else he must, subconsciously, have known before hand that this was the fate he was wilfully and recklessly inviting and yet been stunned by the reality of the experience. We could almost see Tract 90 as a gamble, or challenge to the gods: a *responsa sortium*. If he won this game he would persist; if he lost, it would be a sign that there was no hope. Though, had he got away with Tract 90 one feels that he would have gone on, and on, throwing out more and more daring challenges to the Anglican powers, and been satisfied only when the judgment of their thumbs agreed with his instinct that he was not one of them.

He nevertheless continued, for a while, to take counsel with his friends about the next moves, as if the campaign were still in progress, and he still preached at Saint Mary's; but, in February, '42, the strain of holding in public a position which his heart secretly denied became too great for him. He made open acknowledgment of his defeat by appointing a curate, his friend Copeland, at Saint Mary's, and by deciding to retire to Littlemore. Everybody read this sign clearly enough, though he feebly pretended that it was nobody's affair but his own. As well might Gladstone have suddenly retired and said to his party and the country: "This is purely a private decision with no political significance whatever." It was only by degrees that he realized his enormous responsibility. When he did it filled him with dread. "The shock, surprise, terror, forlornness, disgust, scepticism to which I am giving rise; the differences of opinion, the division of families—all this makes my heart ache."

To his friends he said, with a sort of jesting flourish, that he was setting up a monastery in Littlemore; more prosaically to Aunt Betsy that he was "fitting up a pretty parsonage." So, he packed up everything at Oriel and transferred his belongings some two miles out on the London Road: chiefly his books, worth, he remarked, between £1500 to £2000. From that on, except for occasional walks into the city, he ceased to be part of the life of Oxford. He was downcast at first, but, once settled into Littlemore, he might have been happy enough, in spite of his great trouble of mind, if there were not so much public curiosity as to what he would do next.

The place itself, and the life he lived there, though frugal to the point of austerity, was not unpleasant. He was out of the public eye of Oxford. His duties as priest kept him absorbed. The cottages were not uncomfortable. They looked, and still look, like something between a couple of ordinary wayside cottages or almshouses and a converted barn. They formed an L-shaped group, with the dining-room which gossip insisted on calling a refectory, fronting the country road, divided by a passage from what tradition still insists in believing was his chapel in spite of the fact that he denied firmly that he ever had a chapel. A red-bricked passage led in from the door, with geraniums set along one side at intervals. This hall or passage opened to the right on four rooms, which gossip liked to call cells—he had himself jestingly called them cells—and to the left was the garden in the oblong space within the L. Here we can still see an ilex which he is said to have planted, and from which pious visitors take leaves as mementos. As one stands beside the tree, it is hard to believe that it is so long ago since he left it. The present caretaker's mother-in-law, old Granny Titcombe, remembered him vividly, though no sage word of his has come down from her through her surviving relatives.

Unfortunately people would not let him alone in his retreat. One thinks what he would have to endure today from the popular press! But though he suffered miserably from this insatiable and well nigh intolerable public gossip it is, surely, hard to blame the public for it? A leader of such influence as he had cannot abdicate abruptly; above all a leader from whom so many tender, troubled souls, whom he had first wakened, reasonably expected further guidance. If he was encompassed by perplexity, as he said twenty years after in bitter memory, and if that perplexity credited him for the next three years with mysteriousness and a disengenuous reserve, what more natural, seeing that he would not speak out one way or the other? Yet how could he speak out, torn as he was by unacknowledged doubts and secret desires? He could not make the whole world his confidant. He could hardly explain to the newspapers that he had doubts about the Anglican system which, for all he knew, might vanish if the newspapers would only be so good as to give him time and leave him to wrestle with his thoughts in peace. They persisted, "What *is* Newman doing at Littlemore?"

"Doing there?" he cried. "Have I not retreated from you? Have I not given up my position and my place? Am I alone of Englishmen not to have the privilege to go where I will, no questions asked? Am I alone to be followed about by jealous prying eyes, which take note whether I go in by a back-door or at the front, and who the men are who happen to call on me in the afternoon? Cowards! If I advanced one step you would run

away; it is not you that I fear: *Di me terrent et Jupiter hostis.*
(The Gods and hostile Jove alone frighten me.)   It is because
the Bishops still go on charging against me though I have given
up.   It is that secret misgiving of heart which tells me that they
do well, for I have neither lot nor part with them.   This it is
which weighs me down.   I cannot walk into or out of my house
but curious eyes are upon me.   Why will you not let me die in
peace?   Wounded brutes creep into some hole to die in, and no
one grudges it to them.   Let me alone, I shall not trouble you
long."

If he could, twenty years after, in the *Apologia,* thus still
recall his torments so passionately, what must he not have
felt on that humiliating day when, on entering his cottages,
he found a flight of undergraduates inside, and Heads of
Houses, as mounted patrols, walking their horses round those
poor cottages, and Doctors of Divinity diving into the
recesses of his private tenement!   It was an intolerable impertinence; but, once more, he was not, as he claimed to be,
a private individual.   His Englishman's home, his Englishman's heart, was not an inviolable castle.   "From the end of
1841," he recorded, "I was on my death-bed."   He added
that a death-bed was scarcely a history.   His was a lingering
expiry, during which the ghouls and the friends alike tor-
tured him, whether they spoke it or not, with the one question which he simply could not answer: "Tell us! Tell us,
Newman!   Do you intend to become a Roman Catholic?"

2

The trouble in the minds of others gradually became a
torture to his own.   "The one predominant distress upon me
has been this unsettlement of mind I am causing.   It is a
thing that has haunted me day by day."   He could see from
the way his sisters, especially Jemima, watched his slightest
acts and words, how every incident surrounding him was

being observed by thousands of his former followers and ad-
mirers scattered throughout the country, thirsty for his help.
So, when in Easter, '43, his curate's sister became a Roman
Catholic, and he told Jemima, and Jemima told her sister-in-
law Anne Mozley, we find in pencil on the letter: "Anne
wishes it to be known it was done by *him* and not herself."
He had another similar painful experience when one of his
own inmates, Lockhart, went over to Rome that summer.
It forced him to resign the living of Saint Mary's, including
Littlemore, and produced painful letters from Jemima, en-
closing another from Anne Mozley, telling him plainly that
he had formed the minds of others, and "not accidentally—
he has *sought* to do so," and that having succeeded he could
not now shake off their charge.

"There is," she wrote, "something sad enough and discouraging enough in being shunned and eyed with distrust by neigh-
bours, friends and clergy, but while we have had someone to
confide in, to receive instruction from, this has been borne easily.
A sound from Littlemore and St. Mary's seems to reach us even
here, and has given comfort on many a dreary day; but when that
voice ceases. . . ."

In that Autumn of '43 this unhappiness that he was causing all over England came closer still. Harriett had been ill,
and Tom Mozley, with £50 borrowed in advance on account
of tithes, had taken her to Normandy for a holiday. There
Tom saw Catholicism in practice for the first time in his
life—mass being said, people crowding into the church, the
Sacrament being carried through the streets. Leaving
Harriett with friends at Caen, he came home in September
to his lonely rectory on Salisbury Plain and wrote to John
that he wished to become a Roman Catholic at once. When
John heard this news he realized that Harriett would blame
him, and that Tom, who had given no such signs before,
was acting on a purely emotional impulse. He hurried off

down to Cholderton—a day and a half going, and the same coming—for the sake of half a day with Tom, managed to restrain him by telling him that no man should act on an impulse in such matters, revealed his own unsettlement, and did his best to persuade him to wait at least two years before deciding. Tom agreed—one feels from his own account a little grumpily—and lived to write it all down, again, one feels rather sadly, as a slightly incoherent but unrepentant Rural Dean in Devon some forty years after. Harriett was naturally furious to be met by a half-Papist husband on her return from Caen and, as John foresaw, at once rounded on him as being *particeps criminis*. It was then, October 2nd, that he revealed to her how he had seen as early as the Summer of '39 that "Rome is the centre of unity and the judge of controversies."

She was still sparring with him in November, and John had nobody to look to for sympathy but Jemima; and even to her he could not send all Harriett's letters because the distracted woman was also saying unpleasant things about her sister:—

"You didn't see the point of Harriett's two letters," he tells Jemima. "I cut off half the first because it was so queer. Your bad looks was one of the queernesses. Poor Harriett is full of perversions and cannot really help it. The point is she quarrelled with me on a matter of fact—and then when she found she was wrong in what she *thought* I said, and that I *agreed* with her, still she would not let me off but attacked the spirit and tone of this opposite statement. You see this was not about old matters —she is determined to begin, and to keep up, something new and present."

Poor John! And much more so, poor Tom Mozley; defenseless on that wintry plain, in that mud-built rectory, being cross-examined day and night as to how long he had been nourishing these awful secret inclinations!

"But why didn't you *confide* in me?"

"I did! I did! I hinted *many* times to you!"

"I never took your hints. Hints indeed! Oh! How could you be so lacking in candour? And, besides, how can you not see? Is it not all as plain as a pikestaff. . . ."

One might also say, "Poor Jemima!" married into the Mozleys, feeling responsible to them for everything John did, taking a deep breath before opening every letter he wrote her—as, so she told him, she did before reading Tract 90—always trying to read his intentions between the lines of his evasive letters, always keeping a sheltering secrecy about the head of old Aunt Betsy, who was now living with her, and to whom any rumor of John's defection would be a cruel blow. At the time of Tom's affair she wrote sadly: "I see what we all need is *patience* with the course of events and with each other." She gave of it loyally to the end.

Harriett seems to have cut John after that. She died in Cholderton. A memorial tablet in the chancel of Cholderton Church gives the date 17th July, 1852.

3

He was now over forty, a bad age for any man to have to begin again; and he was more alone than he had ever been before, a bad thing for any man in an hour of trial. Even when he walked into Oxford he found himself out of place. "Everything seems to say to me: 'This is not your home.' The colleges seem strange to me and even the college serv-ants seem to look as if I were getting strange to them." And it must have cut him deeply to see quondam friends creep-ing away from him in his fall.

One of the most notable of these was the Archdeacon of

Chichester, Henry Manning who, in July, '41—so soon after Tract 90—had chosen to deliver a pointed and eloquent Charge in defense of the Reformation.[1] In charity we may say that it is possible that the moment itself was not chosen, though Gladstone once said shrewdly of him: "You know the difference between a rising and a falling market? Manning was always on a rising market." Also, there were plausible reasons why Manning should not rush to the defense of New-man. At a time when the anti-Tractarian war-cry all over the country was "Newman the Traitor," both in the secular and religious press, in leaders and in letters, it would have gravely disabled an Archdeacon of growing influence, and with leanings towards the moderate High Church Party, to have been ticketed as a Newmanite. He may reasonably have argued, too, that he was not compelled to denounce the Reformation because Newman did, or to refrain from assail-ing Rome because Newman was saying such things about Rome as "She alone, amid all the errors and evils of her prac-tical system, has given scope to the feelings of awe, mystery, tenderness, reverence, devotedness, and other feelings which may be specially called Catholic." Moreover, Manning was a man of peace who wished to remain on good terms with all parties; and, for all his caution, he *was*, most aggravatingly, being ticketed as a Tractarian. Even as late as October, '43, he was described in the ever-watchful *Record* as "one of the most noted and determined of the Tractarians"; an over-statement which alone should show us how relentless the witch-hunt became in the years after Tract 90.

Newman did not, at first, take Manning's neutrality hard: not even when, towards the end of '41, the Tractarians put up Isaac Williams for the Chair of Poetry, and Manning re-fused to vote; and, in his desire for total non-intervention, even refused to give his signature to a petition for the with-drawal of *both* candidates in the interests of peace within the university. It was not until the winter of '43 that Newman felt the Judas kiss. All this happened, we may note, while he was struggling with Tom Mozley.

From a series of most friendly and intimate letters, between October 14th and the 31st, written, as Newman said in one of them, from an aching and sighing heart, Manning elicited a message from Littlemore betokening such evident distress and unsettlement of soul that he at once ran off and showed it to Gladstone and Pusey as positive proof that Newman intended to secede to Rome. The news knocked Gladstone over. He wrote: "I stagger to and fro like a drunken man and am at my wit's end." It made him declare that Newman was like "some Faust gambling for his soul." Manning's cool, clear-headed, and immediate reaction was very different. He saw that if Newman fell all hope of Catholic progress was gone. All his and Gladstone's hopes for the High Church Party would be finished for ever if they were all to be tarred with the same brush. He decided that something practical must be done. Saying nothing to Newman he at once went down to Oxford and delivered a fiercely anti-Roman, Fifth of November, Guy Fawkes sermon from the pulpit so recently abandoned by his friend. He delivered this "fierce attack"—Gladstone's description of it —on the Sunday. That night he apparently began to have qualms. Those letters, those confidences he had shared, had been written by a friend giving and asking sympathy in, as Newman clearly thought, days that were equally hard on both of them. He decided to go down to Littlemore in the morning to defend himself. He did not get beyond the door. Newman sent out young James Anthony Froude to say that he was "Not at Home."

What he would have said we gather from his Diary, in which he wrote down his reason for preaching, as, where and when he did: "As Fellow of Merton I had to preach before the University on 5th November." He added seven other subsidiary reasons:—

1. Because such plainness is necessary.
2. Because others who ought cannot or will not.
3. Because my silence is misinterpreted.
4. Because unsettlement is spreading.
5. Because I did not choose the occasion or the subject.
6. Because there could be no personality.
7. Because it seemed a call of God's providence.

It was as well that Newman refused to meet Manning that day. He was not the man to use soft words on such an occasion, and Manning's explanation could only have produced the blunt answer that it was a lie. Manning was not obliged as Fellow of Merton to preach that day. He had not been a Fellow of Merton since his marriage ten years before. He went solely on invitation. He could have preached in any tone he chose. It is true that he was nevertheless fully entitled to give any sermon he thought proper, at whatever cost he was prepared to pay. His error was in hoping to have it both ways. In trying to have Newman as his friend, and as his victim, he exposed himself—to put it mildly—as a cold fish.

Two months later he wrote to Newman a letter of warm sympathy and affection. Newman, always glad to make up a quarrel, replied as warmly from his hermitage, beginning "My dear Manning," and ending, "I am, my dear Manning, ever yours affectionately John H. Newman."

4

It was somewhere around this time—the end of '42 and throughout '43—that he decided to give his whole mind to the principle of the development of doctrine in the Christian Church—that principle of which he had never lost sight since he first absorbed its rudiments from Hawkins twenty-five years before. His purpose now was more distant and final

than in '39–'40, when he first conjoined reason and the religious search. Then he had wished only to dissolve the coldly rationalizing Protestant state of mind which Faussett and his like interposed between him and the primal eras of the Church. Now, with all that had happened since working on all that had lain latent in him before, he desired not so much arguments as persuasions to justify his instinct that no amount of Catholic fancy-dress could change the nature of what Augustine had called "ravening wolves" into the sheep of the true Shepherd. He drove ahead on the great and broad principle that a cumulative, transcendent probability had the right to outweigh all his separate doubts, and carry him onwards—Romewards if it should so prove—to that final state of certitude which rises higher than the logical force of any of our individual conclusions.

This does not mean he launched himself blindly on a tide. He could and did do this with any sound general idea; but he would also take with him every precautionary instrument necessary to chart his course among its particular currents. In fact nothing shows his intellectual stubbornness, or call it prudence, so clearly as this slow and careful—one might surely, after what we have seen, say lifelong—development of the idea of development. Doubtless he was thought in Oxford an impetuous man, or had been so thought until they read Froude and knew what real impetuosity means. He knew himself better when he wrote down, years before, in drawing out a comparison between Hawkins and himself: "Newman is cautious for fear of being proved wrong." Indeed, a simpler mind would have arrived at the same destination far more easily and just as securely, if not by so interesting and tortuous a route. One is even puzzled by some of the distinctions he makes when he describes this crucial study; as when, in a single paragraph of the *Apologia* he says, "I gave my mind" to the idea of Development[2] at the end of '42; and, a few lines down, "In 1843 I began to

consider it attentively," and, in the next paragraph, outlines "the general view" to which he had come by July, '44; and at the end of '44—sick of irresolution, thirsty for that certitude in which one finally knows that one knows—says that he "came to the resolution of writing" his *Essay;* and, even then, he did not actually take up his pen until the beginning of '45!

5

How much of all this long delay between '39 and '45 was due to an objective resistance of mind, and how much of it was due to a purely subjective inhibition? Surely, the delay was almost wholly subjective and inhibitory? His admissions of earlier intellectual conviction are too numerous and too clear. Those of '39 to Rogers and Henry Wilberforce; of '42 to Robert Wilberforce; of '43 to Harriett; and in the same year to James Mozley, are all of a kind. "Last summer four years—'39—it came strongly upon me . . . that we were external to the Catholic Church. I have never got over this." Or there is the clear admission of November, '44, to Jemima: "A clear conviction of the substantial identity of Christianity and the Roman system has now been on my mind for a full three years. It is more than five years (this takes us back to '39) since the conviction first came on me, though I struggled against it and overcame it." But he goes on, switching to his subjective repugnances: "I believe all my feelings and wishes are against change. I have nothing to draw me elsewhere. I hardly ever was at a Roman service; even abroad I knew no Roman Catholics. I have no sympathies with them as a party."

What held him back, one feels, was a distaste for Romanism born of his upbringing, his social conditions, his English prejudices, his early Calvinistic training. As Jemima truly said to him towards the end, in defense of herself: "We have one-sided views from birth and education." He as much as

said so himself. We may remember that cold "mathemati-
cal" letter he wrote from school to his aunt, when he was
fifteen, chiding Harriett for being sorry to have to exchange
the rural Norwood cot for the High Street of Alton? In it
he had said, "Did you ever read Bishop Newton on The
Prophecies?" It was one of those early influences which, he
has told us in the *Apologia,* had convinced him of the "bigotry and cruelty of Rome," made him certain that the Pope
was Anti-Christ, told him about the evils that revolted
Luther, described for him vividly the horrors of the religious
wars, and in all—he confesses—so stained his imagination
that he did not cleanse it of a repugnance to Rome until the
year 1843. We may feel that he could not put pen to paper,
now, to trace the story of how Catholicism developed until
he had cleansed his imagination of this stain; or else it may
be that he dared not because he knew that once the pen began to move all would be over. And yet, even then, in January, '45, writing to Maria Rosina Giberne, he still evaded.
It was, he told her, a personal question. "Can I—not another, but can I—can *I* be saved in the English Church?"
The truth, it would seem, had by then become superfine.

6

As he wrote his book, and the combination of reason, instinct and desire melted the obstacles one by one he gave his
last public warning: his decision to resign his Oriel Fellowship the following October. At this, Jemima abandoned all
hope. Their letters of that Spring are still painful to read:—

"What," she moans, "can be worse than this? It is like hearing
that some dear friend must die. I cannot shut my eyes to this
overpowering event that threatens any longer. What the consequences may be I know not. O dear John, can you have
thought long enough before deciding on a step which, with its

probable effects, must plunge so many into confusion and dismay? . . . Our poor distracted Church seems to me in pieces and there is no one to help her. . . ."

And she thinks how sad it is that, even as she says this, he is thinking that she is lost in schism and error. He will soon —how soon?—be praying in the church that he had so often reviled for her who is praying for him in a church that he must henceforth deplore.

"How life is going!" he writes back. "I see men dying who were boys, almost children, when I was born. Pass a few years and I am an old man. What means of judging can I have more than I have? What maturity of mind am I to expect? . . . What in the world am I doing this for except that I think I am called to do so? . . . I have a good name with many; I am deliberately sacrificing it. I have a bad name with more; I am fulfilling all their worst wishes, and giving them their most coveted triumph. I am distressing all I love, unsettling all I have instructed or aided. I am going to those whom I do not know, and of whom I expect very little. I am making myself an outcast, and that at my age! Oh, what can it be but stern necessity which causes this? Pity me, my dear Jemima. . . ."

Tenderly she answers:—

". . . Indeed I do pity you, for I know you are just the person to feel the force of the sacrifices you are making more than most, without the excitement which carries most persons through such changes. And it needs no assurance from you for me to be sure that you do it simply because you think it right, when interest or love of ease would naturally draw you another way. This is my hope and my consolation. But I cannot fancy it otherwise with you, nor could I bear to think it possible. O, may you be rewarded now and hereafter in the way God thinks best. . . . I trust dear John you will attain that peace of mind without which life is a burden. Who should have it if you fail, who have been the means of comforting so many?"

A little postscript about Aunt Betsy's alarms would touch him almost as deeply as her own kindness. Jem visited him in the summer. She stayed at a Littlemore cottage. John dined or walked with her almost every day, attended church with her for the last time, and paid calls with her in the village where she and Harry and her mother and he had all so often worked together in the happy years. What would they have talked about in those rural walks? We can only guess. Cousin Eliza Fourdrinier has been for holidays to Herne Bay. That was pleasant: she would be near Mary at Canterbury. Does she write much? Yes, I sent her a jar of my own marmalade in May—and mittens and a pretty pair of slippers. Do you remember St. Leonards, Jemima? I haven't been there since I was nine and I went back there in January. And I went to Fulham last Summer. But you don't remember Fulham . . . and Grandmother taking me on her knee to look at the Bible. It is a chemist's shop now. Oh, John! they've built over that field! What a pity! It used to be full of cowslips. . . . Has Charles come down to Oxford since he came back from Germany? Charles! I have not laid eyes on him for nine years. They would talk a lot about Charles, back in London, full of indignation about Bonn University. His landlord on the Brüdergasse sold his clothes because he refused to pay his rent. He says he is astonished at the Germans' extraordinary illiberality of mind. Ah! John! but what about his own mind? He professes himself mad. However, as Frank says, to be able to discern one's own partial madness is a great proof that one is not mad. His address is 28, Frederick Street, Regent's Park. Do write to him. . . . Harriett is willing to have him. Poor Harriett! By the way, Jemima, he says your brother-in-law Charles owes him thirty dollars. I repaid those long ago— don't let him be upset about them. They could laugh about the farmer who called his bull "Dr. Pusey." They could chat happily about her children—Herbert and John and Henry and the baby Jane.　They would have lots and lots to gossip about.　They had all their lives to talk about during those last two weeks together.　Possibly he might talk of his book a little.　When she went back to Derby he said, happily, "A sweet, gentle person," and drew towards him the scarred palimpsest of his fateful book on Development.

7

This is, one feels again and again, a great essay that he wrote at such speed and in such emotional intensity; great as a prolonged, stubborn, persistent, varied exposition of one single idea that illuminates the processes not only of Christian and of all religious history, but of many purely secular institutions that obey similar laws of development and respond to like genealogical tests of purity.　There is, too, as it were, a subjective greatness about it, inherent in the circumstances and the man.　Related to Littlemore and Newman and the drama of his life, it is a great personal work of art; and like all confessions, or confidences shared with the world, this work of art has to be interpreted in relation to the man and to the moment of its writing.　When we read it in that context it is the subjective element which fascinates us the most, troubles us the most; as when we feel that an argument for this point or this is not so much a rational conclusion as the personal choice, or desire, or urgent need of a mystic longing to surmount the barriers that reason sets up between him and her goal.

So, when he develops the argument for the cult of the Virgin from the fourth century onward, and finds its seed in the Arians' puzzlement over texts which they could not employ to subordinate the Son to the Father, yet which, without altogether ceasing to belong to Him, seemed also to apply to a creature rather than a Creator, he says:—

"Thus there was left in their minds an unexplained wonder in heaven; a throne was seen, far above all created powers, mediatorial, intercessory; a title archetypal; a crown bright as the morning star; a glory issuing from the Eternal Throne; robes pure as the heavens; and a sceptre over all; and who was the predestined Heir of that Majesty? Since it was not high enough for the Highest, who was that Wisdom, and what was her name? 'The Mother of fair love and fear and holy hope,' 'exalted like a palmtree in Engaddi, and a rose-plant in Jericho,' 'created from the beginning before the world' in God's everlasting counsels, and 'in Jerusalem her power.' The vision is found in the Apocalypse, a Woman clothed with the sun, and the moon under her feet, and upon her head a crown of twelve stars. The votaries of Mary do not exceed the true faith, unless the blasphemers of her Son came up to it. The Church of Rome is not idolatrous unless Arianism is orthodoxy."

Surely one must feel, without denying his point of arrival, that this is not entirely the language of objective reason? Surely, rather, this is the mystic or the artist melting into the historical commentator and soaring out of every objective realm? After all, when we pass beyond the date of this book, and read what he has said of himself after his conversion, it must be a jolt to us to find him confessing that he never did understand such matters as, say, Transubstantiation, on which over a number of years he spent, as we have seen, a considerable amount of time and argument, until he actually had become a Roman Catholic. What, then, had all the previous argument been about? Or should we ask on what different level had it been conducted?

It would seem that to pass from Protestantism, or any of its aspects, to Catholicism one has to develop a new kind of mind. It would seem that Protestantism, splendidly common-sensical, with a fine emphasis on right behavior, stands in some entirely different intellectual world from Catholicism, so magnificently non-sensical or super-sensical, and with a glorious emphasis on mystical communion? To go from one to the other one has, like Norman Douglas's Flying Monk, to levitate a little. And as we follow Newman's thought from beginning to end it does, we must admit, become occasionally both a most exhilarating and a slightly disconcerting sensation to find ourselves slowly taking leave of the ground, as in those childhood dreams when we floated softly upstairs with our night-shirts billowing behind our pink heels, luxuriating in the liberty but fearful for the event. To say so is, perhaps, to expose oneself as something of a Philistine, even as something of a Rationalist, even as something of a Protestant, though one must take the risk to mark the flight of an angelic mind, and the work of art concealed behind the work of history, and the point, at the end of a long life of dialectic, where the poet vanishes beyond Hesper in his retreat from this darkening world and the reasons of this world, in his chase after the undying Sun.

Still he gave no outward sign. Indeed, for a while it seemed as if the one-time leader was being left behind. In the summer of '45, says Dean Church,

"the first drops of the storm began to fall. Then, through the autumn and the next year, friends whose names and forms were familiar in Oxford one by one disappeared and were lost to it. Fellowships, livings, curacies, intended careers were given up. Mr. Ward went. Mr. Capes, who had long followed Mr. Ward's line and had spent his private means to build a church near Bridgewater, went also. Mr. Oakeley resigned Margaret Chapel and went. Mr. Ambrose St. John, Mr. Coffin, Mr. Dalgairns, Mr. Faber, Mr. T. Meyrick, Mr. Albany Christie, Mr. R. Simpson of Oriel, were received in various places and various ways; and in the next year Mr. J. S. Northcote, Mr. J. B. Morris, Mr. G. Ryder, Mr. David Lewis. . . . We sat glumly at our breakfasts every morning and then someone came in with news of something disagreeable—someone gone, someone sure to go."

By October their lost leader could hold out no longer. Two of his inmates at Littlemore, Dalgairns and St. John, had already been received but were still living with him.   On October 8th Father Dominic, the Passionist, who had earlier admitted Dalgairns, was coming to visit his convert.   By then Newman had made up his mind, for on October 5th his Diary notes: "I kept indoors all day preparing for general confession."   Yet, even at this last moment he told nobody. On the 8th—a day of pouring rain—he wrote a similar letter to Jemima and to a number of his friends: "I am this night expecting Father Dominic, the Passionist. . . ."   That afternoon, as Dalgairns was taking his hat and stick to walk across the wet fields to meet the coach at The Angel, Newman said quietly: "When you see your friend will you tell him that I wish him to receive me into the Church of Christ?"

That fateful, wild and dismal day has been evoked for us by one of these converts, Frederick Oakeley: the Autumn leaves torn from their branches and pasted to the ground by the equinoctial winds; the eaves at Littlemore spitting and spluttering; the men waiting in rooms darkened by the downpour.   It was as if the very elements were Anglican in their lamentation at the approaching loss.   The priest arrived soaked.   After supper he went into the little oratory and Newman followed, to kneel and confess.   He was so overcome with emotion after it that Ambrose St. John and Stanton had to help him out of the room.   Dominic went his way.   The little group stayed on in Littlemore, going into Saint Clement's Oxford, on Sundays, for mass, following otherwise their simple rule, at a loss to know what to do next.

Amid the falling leaves and shortening days, Oxford men came back after the Long Vacation to find an Oxford without a Movement.   The great bell had gone still.   Keble said that the Spring had been taken out of the year.   "We felt betrayed," says Dean Burgon, "and we resented the wrong done to us."   The Winter nights closed in.   They were still in Littlemore. Christmas passed. Still they were there. Then in January Bishop Wiseman arranged that the Oxford converts should remove to old Oscott, which they rechristened Maryvale, and from which presently they would go to the College of Propaganda at Rome to prepare for Holy Orders. From there, finally, John Newman would return to England to spend the remainder of his life in Birmingham as an Oratorian priest.

That January Newman wrote to his friend Ambrose St. John, after the decision to remove from Littlemore had been confirmed: " 'Oblivescere populum tuum et domum patris tui' has been in my ears for the last twelve hours. I realise more that we are leaving Littlemore and it is like going on an open sea." On Sunday night, February 22nd, he at last tore himself away. He said: "I could not help kissing my bed, and the mantelpiece, and other parts of the house." He slept with his friend Johnson at the Observatory in Oxford. Some old friends came to dine, and others called to see the last of him: Copeland, Church, Mark Pattison, Pusey. He called on his old tutor at Trinity, Dr. Ogle; a farewell that reminded him of days when he used to be a freshman at Trinity where the snapdragons on the walls opposite his rooms used to glow in the sun, and he recalled how he had taken them as an emblem that he, too, would always be rooted in Oxford.

It has been felt by many that in describing Reding's farewell to Oxford in *Loss and Gain* he re-evoked the final parting:—

"The morning was frosty, and there was a mist; the leaves flitted about; all was in unison with the state of his feelings. He re-entered the monastic buildings, meeting with nothing but scouts with boxes of cinders, and old women carrying off the remains of the kitchen. He crossed to the Meadow and walked steadily down to the junction of the Cherwell with the Isis; he then turned back. What thoughts came upon him! for the last time! There was no one to see him; he threw his arms round the willows so dear to him, and kissed them; he tore off some of the black leaves and put them in his bosom. 'I am like Undine,' he said, 'killing with a kiss.'"

That was at about half-past eight on Monday morning, February 23rd, 1846. He did not see Oxford again—apart from such glimpses of its spires as one may have from a passing train—until he was an old man of seventy-seven, from whom, by then, the world had taken away almost every desire except the longing to leave it: an old Tithonus—a gray grasshopper, the evaporating mist of a forgotten morning.

EPILOGUE

1

THERE can have been few more lonely men in the world than the aging Newman. One feels that it was because he was so lonely that he kept on compiling those autographic remains, as he called them, sorting old letters, enquiring from Jemima about matters of pedigree, holding dearly to his memories of boyhood and youth long after his sisters and brothers had become foreign to him.

Jemima was his most faithful correspondent. She kept all his letters: from Genoa and Milan and Rome; she preserved the Italian sun, and the "snow over everything down to Ostend, and worse fog through Belgium" as he hastened home to say his first Mass on Christmas Day. She kept the quiet hours at Birmingham, their love and their quarrels, his birthday letters which he never forgot to write. In the very gaps of their letters she kept their silences. And yet, he told Maria Rosina Giberne that "My sisters are nothing to me, or rather foreign to me." For Jemima would not allow her children to see him, and she did not invite him to Derby for twenty years, and when at last she did ask him to come to Derby, he let out twenty years of suppressed bitterness on her graying head:—

"At the end of more years than I can count I have an invitation from you to Derby . . . never an invitation from your husband."

He pointed out coldly that when she had visited him at the Oratory, in '53,

"you said as plainly as possible, 'I come to see you because you are my brother, but I will have none of your belongings.' . . .

This sort of ignoring of what I am, and antagonism to me you continue down to this day. . . . None have so acted towards me as my near relations and connexions. Did I wish to revive the past I could say a great deal. . . . You cannot bring back past years. I am old now."

Eleven years later he visited her. And in the October of '79 she wrote, being then an old lady of seventy-one: "I knew you would not forget me. . . . We shall be glad to see you, dear John." But she died two months later, on Christmas Day. He told her children that he would say a Mass for her soul. They did not appreciate his solicitude.

2

Almost anybody else who had become a Catholic was now far more close to his heart: even somebody as foolish as poor Maria Rosina Giberne. How could those two ever forget that winter of '46, so long ago, when she—then still living with her *chère petite amie*, Selina Bacchus, at Cheltenham— wrote to him that she wished to become a Catholic. They had met at a Catholic Library in London and Newman had said, "Why, it is easy—I will call a cab and take you"; and she had cried, "Not yet! Not yet!" but he had already rung. Trembling with fear she had sat in with him, clutching his arm in her panic, and the two had bowled along to her fate, the handsome Juno who was almost a Lesbian, and the gentle ascetic who was almost a saint.

She has told us what happened when she at last relinquished his arm and he closed the door of the parlor behind her: "I found myself face to face with this terrible priest, as he seemed to my excited imagination, although I found him most gentle, almost shy. He pressed my hand gently in the English fashion, which reassured me. I said, quite simply, 'Sir, I wish to be a Catholic, but I am afraid of what it will mean to my family and my friends.' I forget what he said to me, but I agreed to meet again, and to come the next time before one o'clock. Oh! How miserable I felt! It was as if I had agreed to cut my throat and immolate myself." Three weeks later she is hurrying along the same streets, late for her appointment, muttering, "O God, if I am to be a Catholic make him be at the house, but if I ought not make him be gone out." We see her kneeling at the prie-dieu, while the priest sits concealed behind a folding screen, or *paravent*—"leaving nothing visible but a large and very red ear with the locks about it. I looked at the ear and wept silently."

"Shall I ask questions?" he asked.
"No, no!"
"At last, in spite of the efforts of the demon, I began, and soon all my life spread before the eyes of my soul and flowed effortlessly from my lips. . . . It finished in, I think, half an hour. I did not stir. I was filled with a peace until then unknown, and which I have felt only once since then. I cannot remember what my thoughts were. Of nothing? I remained tranquil at the feet of Jesus in a happiness beyond expression."

When she told Newman tears flooded his eyes and his voice trembled and he said—her story is written in French —"Maintenant je suis soulagé."
He would always feel infinitely tender towards that poor soul. Besides, it is, as he observed, one of the privileges and pains of Catholics to feel with Catholics all over the world.

3

When he was very old, so old as to be feeble, having endured many humiliations and disappointments, been frustrated almost wholly, yet now a cardinal, the sort of national figure, like Gladstone or Palmerston, whom one never thinks

of as having any domestic life at all, no more than a statue
or an immortal, he packed his carpet-bag one September
day in '82, and astonished them all at the Oratory by saying
that he was going down to Wales, to visit his brother Charles.
They had never known that he had a brother Charles. But,
then, had he not said to Maria Rosina: "My friends have not
known my world in which I live."

Charles had now been living for some thirty or forty years,
maybe more, in the little Welsh port of Tenby.[1] Why
Charles chose Tenby nobody can say. It is a pretty place,
on Carmarthen Bay, old, picturesque, quiet: the Gosse who
was the father of *Father and Son* loved it and wrote a most
happy unGosseian book about it. Perhaps Charles got his
last job there, and there lost it in his usual way, and there
abandoned all work, for good. He had lived during all
those years at his brothers' expense, but after a style so
modest as to be ascetic, in the garret-room of a double-bank
of twenty-two cottages on the edge of the town. The place
is called Saltern or Lower Saltern, sunk deep below a road
called Marsh Road that leads out of the town towards
Penally, Manoriber and Pembroke. Those massed cottages
of Saltern must have been, in his time, among the poorest
dwellings in Tenby, fronting a swamp through which ran a
sluggish stream, brown from oxide of iron. Nothing remains
of them now but a few stumps: they were demolished some
years ago as unhealthy. His landlady's name was Eliza
Griffiths, better known locally as Alma Griffiths because she
lived in Alma Cottage.

It is a strangely moving experience for anyone who knows
that he lived there and that his brother called on him there
to walk, as John would have walked that glorious September
day, in 1882, out of the town, far from the sands, the hotels,
the tea-shops, the crowds, the chatter of the beaches, the
quiet bustle of the tiny harbor, and the wonderful view over
Carmarthen Bay, down under the viaduct, behind the tarry

old railway sheds to this backwater on the edge of the salt-marshes. Behind the railway-sheds one turns to the right along a worn path beside the stream among the weeds and past the fallen walls. One can only guess where cottage Number 5 stood. There is the cry of seagulls. He could, lifting his garret window on its notch, peer over a wide expanse of marsh towards low, distant hills. He would hear the shunting of trains. When the wind blew from the east or south-east he would hear the sea. In the winter the marsh became a ruffled lake. In the winter the lower floors of these cottages were several feet under water. One comes on correspondence in the *Tenby Observer* complaining about these Marsh Floods. Perhaps C. R. N. was moved to "write to the papers"? He did, in '75, sign a Requisition to the Mayor to call a public meeting to discuss a scheme for dealing with this flooding that must have made his winters doubly dreary, and the antique sewage that must have tainted the summer air.

In the *Athenaeum* of March 29th, 1884, Thomas Purnell—in his day well-known as a journalist, essayist and novelist—wrote the following description of Charles in Tenby:—

"For four years I had the inestimable privilege of enjoying his close intimacy. This was from about 1857 to the middle of 1860, and never before or since have I met a man endowed with so rare an intellectual equipment. He was a recluse. He seldom left the house, and when he went out he did not often enter the town, but walked for his exercise along the road which led from his door into the country. This was generally in the evening or at night. . . . Dressed in a pea-jacket, with a shawl or a rug thrown across his shoulders, and with a sou-wester over his head, he marched along—rigid, erect, with staccato step, looking not to the right nor to the left. He wore shoes (sometimes slippers) and, as his trousers were short and wide in the legs, a considerable interval of his white socks was left exposed. Once, I recollect, when he came to me to tea, he was followed to the door by a crowd of gaping urchins, whom I had to disperse with the threat of a stick. He sought seclusion. His health and means and inclination made him averse from society. The rector called on him, but was not admitted; visitors to the town who had known his brothers would send in their cards, but they received no response; local medical men, when they heard he was ill, volunteered their services, but they were declined with courteous thanks, conveyed by letter.

"I was more fortunate. One afternoon, about to be caught in a shower of rain on the Marsh Road, I sought shelter in one of these cottages overlooking the lake created by the little stream which finds its way from the Vale of St. Florence to the sea through a series of sand dunes forming the shore of Tenby Bay. While waiting for the weather to clear, I casually took up a weekly newspaper strangely annotated in manuscript. Such marginalia had surely never before been contributed to a newspaper. I inquired as to the authorship, and then, for the first time, discovered that Charles Newman resided at Tenby and in this house.

"The landlady—whose attentive and persistent kindness to her distinguished lodger is worthy of every sort of praise—knew me, and, on my expressing a wish to meet the author of the marginalia, readily undertook that I should see him. Two days afterwards I called at the house in the Marsh Road, and was at once ushered into the presence of Newman. He stood at the top of the topmost stair. I cannot imagine a more distinguished head and face. There was a touch of Mephistopheles in him. There was also a touch of Jupiter Olympus. Although dressed in ill-fitting clothes, and with a sort of blanket over his shoulders, he appeared to me to be the ideal of courtly grace. He bowed me, without a word, into his apartment. This was in the roof of the building and the only light came from a window which opened with a notched iron bar. The room was as meagrely furnished as Goethe's study in Weimar. A bed, a chest of drawers, a table, and two or three chairs, with a few books, constituted the whole of his goods and chattels.

"The owner of the room having closed the door, moved a chair for me to the fire, took one for himself, and bowed again, leaving me to open conversation. I have now forgotten how we broke the ice; but in the result I got on admirably, and from that day for years I had the happiness of visiting my new friend two or three times a week."

Purnell does not tell us that Charles liked to be addressed as Dr. Newman, as we gather from three very old residents of Tenby who still remember him from their childhood, some twenty years after Purnell knew him and from about the time of John's visit. One says: "I was about six years of age when, as a child, I joined others in play and as we flocked together I remember that 'Dr. Newman' was a name to think about, for he was somewhat odd and seldom seen out of the house. . . ." Another remembers that they used to call out after the odd old man, "Old Daddy Newman!" A former resident of Tenby, who must be about ninety years old, records: "The old man was distinctly erratic. For instance, he never spoke of Queen Victoria, but always called her Mrs. Guelph." It is this resident who records that when John Henry came down to Tenby Charles refused to see him.

"Not at home!" What a lot of things, both sad and pleasant, absurd and aggravating, John had to recall as he returned slowly from the marshes, up the hill, to his hotel, The Royal Gatehouse, and stood in his window looking out over the beach and the sea. People would still have been bathing. ("Tatler" in the local paper speaks of the "glorious weather," and that day's issue gave the temperature as 68°.) Old Philip Gosse's book[2] describes the beach at low-tide, with the brawny bathing women, uncouth and uncorseted, carrying their delicate charges—slender figures in long sable robe and dishevelled hair—down into the waves. "We cannot hear the shrieks, but we see with horror the arms dashed up in despair as the helpless victim is ruthlessly plunged beneath the whelming wave. It is too dreadful," he says. "Let us turn from the Thalassine immolation." So may His Eminence have turned away with a sigh for his dying brother.

The long daylight fades. The long beaches become vacant. There is a slight movement in the tiny harbor where a dark-red sail is being shaken out. It flaps a little, until, with a faint creak of the gaff, the mainsail rises, and then the jib. . . . How Hurrell would have loved this sight! Was there, too, perhaps a dim stir of memory for Palermo and the orange-boat to Marseilles. . . . ? The trawler moves into the green sea. All of them together on holidays, when they were kids, at St. Leonards, or at Brighton. . . . Mother that day climbing the sheep-path with Charles and himself. Father bowling down to Hastings with him in the gig, sitting up straight, flicking the whip. The ponies at the cottage at Norwood. The journey to Alton, and how Grandmamma had to have a nip of brandy at Kingston, and Aunt Betsy telling him that Harriett had cried for Vine Cottage and the heath. Charles had been good in Alton. He used to keep the books in the brewery. . . . The tavern in North London. The bankruptcy. . . . The lodgings near Covent Garden. Charles at the Bank. Charles out of work. Charles at work. Charles at Boulogne. Charles at Bristol. Charles at Bonn. . . . A light in a window heralds the September dusk. Along the lone sands the sea flickers with a splendid luminosity. The sky is indigo. Slowly the sea grows dark and cold.

Charles lingered on for eighteen months. John paid for the funeral and the tomb: a gray slab, called the Forest Tomb, in the Anglican cemetery, overlooking the hill-up, hill-down of Tenby, and the bay, and the open sea. It was John who chose the inscription, "Domine Misericordia Tua in Saeculum Opera Manum Tuarum ne Dispicias." ("O Lord, of Thy eternal mercy, despise not this the work of Thy Hands.")

That ought to have ended Charles. But Charles had always had the art of turning everything, even Death, into farce touched by squalor. Two months later a Mr. Whit-

aker[3] wrote from the office of *Whitaker's Almanack,* in
Paternoster Row, to His Eminence that a needy acquaint-
ance—who turns out to be the Mr. Purnell who had known
Charles in Tenby—has temporarily "parted" with a bundle
of seventy letters written by Charles, some of which are
"very questionable indeed," for the sum of £5. It may be
that His Eminence may not object to their publication, or
he may prefer "to have them suppressed, or to use a less
unsavoury word unpublished?" Mr. Whitaker thinks they
could be got for £15 or £20. John sighed and paid up;
though not without asking whether, if he did buy, another
batch might not appear "from (say) a new quarter." He
was surprised to find that they were much less offensive than
he had feared; even if Charles did once speak of him as an
old cat, and of Frank as a prig, and rudely of the whole family. The letters do not now exist. One by one he must have
watched their little acrid flames dissolving Charles into dust
and ashes in his study fire.

4

Frank frequently visited him in Birmingham, and went on
making these kindly visits when into his eighties. They
talked always of neutral subjects. This could hardly have
given much trouble to Frank, whose hates and enthusiasms
over the years had come to include such things as Vege-
tarianism, Woman's Suffrage, Mixed Bathing, Flogging for
Criminals, Cruelty to Animals, Teetotalism, Land Reform,
Kossuth, Mazzini. . . . He believed that plants feel pain.
He had a high opinion of the intelligence of bugs. Once at
a breakfast party he met the Hungarian Minister for Justice
and started off full-cock: "Herr Vukovich, I have never been
able to understand how it is that you have not introduced the
Bactrian camel into Hungary." It was just as well that he
had this rag-bag mind, for he was by now a caricature of that

type of kind-hearted, ineffectual, agnostic, Liberal English-man whom John least admired. Their talk would have had to be a kind of amiable figure-skating around one another.

They must have looked odd side by side in the gas-lit par-lor: the cardinal in his black soutane and scarlet skull-cap, and Frank suited only his comfort in his dress—six inches of leather at his trousers' ends in muddy weather, three over-coats, the top one green, and if he felt a trifle chilly he would cape himself in a rug with a hole cut in it for his head, on which he perched a very wide, white or light-gray felt hat, all above a goatee beard, high, Indian cheek-bones, long, lank hair, and a scimitar nose, the remains of a facial beauty that in his youth had been like a Greek gem.

He wrote a bitter memoir of his dead brother. He did it in the cause—so he averred—of Protestants and Protestant-ism. He died in 1897, seven years after John, aged ninety-two, and that is the end of the Newmans.

APPENDIX AND NOTES

He was a very poor man. Will of Wm. Newman, from Ely Consistory Court. Proved May 5th, 1742. (Administration, March 28th, 1749, to Richard Rolph, brother of Elizabeth Rolph during minorities of her children.) The pedigree is as follows:—

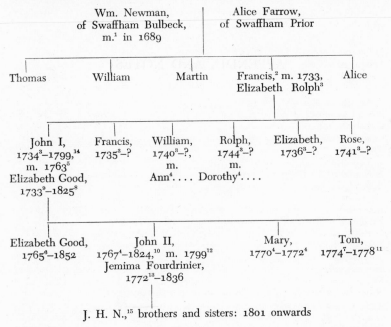

| Wm. Newman, of Swaffham Bulbeck, m.[1] in 1689 | Alice Farrow, of Swaffham Prior |

Thomas   William   Martin   Francis,[2] m. 1733, Elizabeth Rolph[3]   Alice

John I, 1734[3]–1799,[14] m. 1763[5] Elizabeth Good, 1733[9]–1825[8]

Francis, 1735[3]–?

William, 1740[3]–?, m. Ann[4]. . . .

Rolph, 1744[3]–? m. Dorothy[4]. . . .

Elizabeth, 1736[3]–?

Rose, 1741[3]–?

Elizabeth Good, 1765[6]–1852

John II, 1767[4]–1824,[10] m. 1799[12] Jemima Fourdrinier, 1772[13]–1836

Mary, 1770[4]–1772[4]

Tom, 1774[7]–1778[11]

J. H. N.,[15] brothers and sisters: 1801 onwards

[1] Swaffham Priors registers. [2] Freedom of City grant. [3] Swaffham Bulbeck Registers. [4] St. George's, Hanover Square registers. [5] St. Andrew's, Holborn, registers. [6] St. Katherine Cree registers. [7] St. Ethelburga's registers. [8] Chiswick Parish Church registers. [9] Ditto and entries on family Bible in possession of Mr. John Mozley. [10] St. Paul's, Covenant Garden, registers. [11] St. Leonard's, Shoreditch, registers. [12] St. Mary's, Lambeth, registers. [13] Fourdrinier pedigree. [14] Letter from the Vicar, Camberwell, September, 1949, testifying that John I was buried there on July 5th, 1799. [15] St. Benet Fink's registers.

Additional details will be found in an extended pedigree printed in two articles in *Notes and Queries*, 1951. It gives Thomas, above (1690–1759), as a tailor, and it also agrees that his grandfather was a tailor. Somebody in the intermediate generation is also almost certain to have kept the trade in the family.

CHAPTER 1

[1] See Appendix.
[2] Administration granted to his mother, 1749. See above.
[3] See above, reference No. 5.
[4] The records of the Worshipful Company of Musicians, now deposited at the Guildhall Library, contain the following entries. A search of the complete list of admissions in the 18th century reveals only two Newmans:

When made free.	Name and abode.
1764. May 24th.	Jn. Newman, Grocer, Leadenhall St.
1793. Aug. 12th.	Jn. Newman, Oilman, 25 Fore St., Cripplegate.

An examination of the wills of these two John Newmans eliminates the second because his wife is named Mary, and his daughters and sons are Elizabeth, Charles, Samuel and Robert. Our John Newman's wife, as we have seen, was Elizabeth, and his children were John, Elizabeth, Mary and Thomas.

The other John Newman, the Grocer, is evidently identical with the John Newman of a document preserved in the Mozley family, grant· ɡ the Freedom of the City of London to John Newman, June 28th, 1764. (The discrepancy between this date, June 28th, and May 24th in the above entry is not relevant, as the process of joining a Company and of being made a Freeman are distinct processes.)

Furthermore, in 1822 John II was admitted to the Freedom of the City of London (here I quote from a letter of the Clerk of the Chamberlain's Court, July, 1949) "by Patrimony in the Company of Musicians on 25th June, 1822. He was born on 25th October, 1767, in the Parish of Saint George's, Hanover Square, *and was the son of the John Newman who had been admitted to the Freedom of the City by redemption in the Company of Musicians in June 1764.* This latter John Newman is noted in the Freedom records as having been a coffee-man. There is no information about him other than that." The facts tally.

A minor point of agreement is that the first child of John I, Elizabeth (Aunt Eliza), was baptized in *Leadenhall Street,* at St. Katherine Cree's.

Wilfrid Ward gave John II as the *only* son of John Newman of *Lombard Street;* both statements are incorrect. There *was* a John Newman in Lombard Street, a goldsmith; but his will shows that he had no connection with our family. Wilfrid Meynell says J. H. N. was born in Birchin Lane. The pedigree compiled by Mr. John Mozley, *Notes and Queries,* November 3rd, 1945, must be corrected in one respect, i.e., the identity of John I.

Note: As to John Newman's choice of the *Musicians'* Company, in those days nobody was permitted to trade in the City unless belonging to one of the Livery Companies and the prospective trader entered indifferently into any Company which had vacancies. Thus Henry Fourdrinier, father of John II's wife Jemima, is called Citizen and Draper, though by profession a stationer.

[5] John II was baptized at St. George's, Hanover Square.
[6] The Rate Books of Saint George's, at Westminster Library, give, under

1768, a John Newman at this address. By 1772 he has left, and in the London Directory for 1772 there is a John Newman, grocer and tea-dealer, at 37 King Street, Cheapside. King Street is near St. Lawrence Jewry. He is there until 1779. This may be our man, but biographers have before now too readily accepted *a* John Newman as *the* John Newman.

My only reason for equating the Brick Lane John with our John is that there is no other John Newman listed, and he *was* in the district, as the baptism of his children at St. George's shows.

[7] This brother Rolph, or Roff, had his child Roff John also baptized at Hanover Square, in 1770, soon after Mary Newman had been. There are no other Newmans but John listed as residents hereabouts, so Roff may well have resided with his brother John.

[8] Letter from the Rev. H. F. Bishop, St. Giles' Vicarage, Camberwell, 20th September, 1949.

[9] AM. I, 26.

[10] TM. I, II.

[11] Will of William Newman, tailor, made 11th November, 1704, and proved 30th August, 1718. He left three acres of land to his son William and three to his son Francis. This son William, who since he evidently married while landless may have also been a tailor, handed on his three acres to the later Francis who was father of John I. But he had added to them since he had eleven acres to bequeath in all. See Pedigree in Appendix.

[12] Ambrose Heal's *Signboards of Old London Shops.* Will of Henry Fourdrinier.

[13] Fourdrinier pedigree.

[14] Will. Dated 6th December, 1796.

[15] *Ibid.*

[16] Marriage registers, St. Mary's, Lambeth.

[17] *Post office London Directory,* 1802.

[18] Information taken from Hilton Price's *London Bankers;* contemporary Directories; G. E. C.'s Baronetage; and information kindly supplied by Mr. Frank Prickett.

[19] Sewer Rate Book, 1801. Holden's *Triennial London Directory,* 1802.

[20] Will of Henry Fourdrinier.

[21] Baptisms, St. Benet Fink. He was baptized April 9th, 1801. The births of the other children are fully attested by various Newman letters, diaries, etc.

[22] J. H. N. to Aunt, St. James's Day, 1844. JMC.

[23] AM. I, 394. "My father had a house at Ham, near Richmond from 1804 to 1807." AM. I, 17. "I had never seen the house since September 1807." He is not correct as to 1807: v. WW. II. 339. He sent (MW. 2) flowers from there in 1808 to his mother, and again saw it in 1813. A curious lapse of memory.

[24] It appears on John Rocque's map "Ten Miles Around London," 1747.

[25] AM. I, 318.

[26] AM. I, 393 ff.

[27] J. H. N. to Aunt, St. James's Day, 1844. JMC. "I think you left (i.e., Fulham) in 1804." J. H. N. to Aunt, October 30th, 1816.:—"The place in which she (i.e., Harriett) has delighted these last *eight* years." They were there, then, from *c.* 1806–1808 onward.

[28] See Harriett's *Family Adventures;* 22, 69, 76, 86, 140.

CHAPTER 2

[1] The following material comes from *Annals of Ealing*, by Edith Jackson, London, 1898.

[2] Frank Newman says that in his time there were 190 pupils. Jackson (*supra*) gives "considerably over 300" in one place and "365" in another. J. H. N. (in AM. I, 26) says "200 boys, increasing to 300."

[3] *George Alexander Macfarren*, by Henry Banister.

[4] AM. I, 17.

[5] AM. I, 16.

[6] AM. I, 16.

[7] AM. I, 26, 27.

[8] J. H. N. to Jemima, January 23rd, 1845 (JMC.); and J. H. N.'s diary. He may have gone back to Ealing *during* the summer, for there is an entry, "School, August 8."

[9] *Family Adventures*. By the Author of *The Fairy Bower*, etc. (London, 1852), p. 65 ff. In these tales Harriett used the second names of her brothers and sisters: e.g., Charles becomes Robert, and John becomes Henry. In my excerpts I have, for convenience sake, used the correct names.

[10] *Ibid*, p. 1 ff.

[11] *The Life and Death of the Sublime Society of the Beefsteaks*. (London, n.d.)

[12] This material down to "not a christian at all" is based on *The Early History of Cardinal Newman*, by Francis Newman. (London, 1891.)

[13] *The British Magazine*, May, 1836, quoted in *The Evangelical Revival* by S. Baring-Gould, London, 1920, p. 317.

[14] *A Practical Exposition of the Epistle of S. Paul to the Romans*, 1843, Preface: quoted in S. Baring-Gould, above.

[15] AM. I, 123 ff.

CHAPTER 3

[1] *Pigot's Directory*, 1822. The *Victoria History of Berkshire* says that Ramsbottom and Leigh had breweries in Thames St., Windsor, in the early 19th century. A famous "Queen's Ale" was brewed there. In 1835 the business was sold to Nevil Reid & Co., who sold it to Meux, who now have a brewery in Thames St.

[2] *History of Alton*, Winchester and London, 1896. This history says Mr. Hawkins' Manager was James Newman Frost (*sic*) who was related to Cardinal Newman and whose family were said to have been brewers at Alton.

[3] Local tradition; author's visits to Alton; *History, op. cit.;* information kindly supplied by W. Hugh Curtis, F.S.A., Honorary Curator the Curtis Museum, Alton, and the Secretary, Courage & Co., Ltd., London, who now own the Brewery.

[4] These quotations from AM. *passim.*

[5] Entry Books of Orders made in Bankruptcy: 1710–1832; B. 1–160. Orders, 1821. See also *London Gazette*, November 1st, 1821; May 21st, 1822;

September 3rd, 1822; all concerning the bankruptcy and his debts. Also *London Directory*, 1820.

[6] *Robson's Directory*, 1819. *Pigot's Directory* for 1822–1823 gives the address without any number. The Poor Rate Books give it as No. 16.
[7] Poor Rate Books.
[8] AM. I, 44.
[9] MW. 54.
[10] AM. I, 52.
[11] AM. I, 42.
[12] AM. I, 43.
[13] AM. I, 47 and 56.
[14] F. 11.
[15] The Memoranda of J. H. N. preserved at the Oratory, Birmingham, supply the information of this section to end of chapter.
[16] DNB, *sub* John Pritt Harley.

CHAPTER 4

[1] Ch. Newman to Aunt: February 27th, 1827. (JMC.) The words are in pencil on the letter.
[2] *Chiswick*, by Warwick Draper, London, 1923. *Old Kew, Chiswick and South Kensington*, by Lloyd Saunders, London, 1910.
[3] JMC.
[4] JMC., August 29th.
[5] AM. I, 55.
[6] MW. 60–61. I suggest "a little later" because they moved to Kentish Town at the end of 1821, or in January, 1822.
[7] *London Gazette*, May 21st, 1822.
[8] Letter of J. H. N., July 2nd, 1871: MW. 57.
[9] Freedom Admission Book, 1776–1881, of Worshipful Company of Musicians, June 25th, 1822. "John Newman of No. 13 East St., Red Lion Square."
[10] The only letter I have seen which gave the number of the York Street house is H. to Jem., April 15th, 1824—but the number is rubbed out!
[11] Parish Registers of Saint Paul's, Covent Garden.

CHAPTER 5

[1] *Bygones Worth Remembering*, by G. J. Holyoake. London, 1905.
[2] In B.M. Library.
[3] Addresses compiled from various letters.
[4] Information kindly supplied by the Bank of England.

CHAPTER 6

[1] AM. I, 104. Bashfulness and awkwardness, AM. I, 107. Evangelical, AM. I, 111, 115. Calvinistic beliefs, AM. I, 104. Rawness, AM. I, 105.

[2] Later cut down to allow Merton College to extend southward.
[3] AM. I, 175.
[4] *Vide. Lives of Twelve Good Men,* by John William Burgon, London, 1888. *Reminiscences of Oxford,* by W. Tuckwell, London, 1900.
[5] AM. I, 130.

CHAPTER 7

[1] "Newman's Brother in Ireland," *The Irish Monthly,* May, 1947, by John Hennig.
[2] TM. Addenda p. 430. "Newman as a rule—indeed I cannot remember an exception—would have nothing to say to physical science. He abstained from it much as he did from material undertakings and worldly affairs generally. He would be impatient of it, as something in the way, not worth precious time."
[3] From Tuckwell and others.
[4] AM. I, 133: TM. I, 382, 395; Dean Burgon, *op. cit.,* 201: and Oxford tradition.

CHAPTER 8

[1] All this reconstruction of the girls' interest in the Wilberforces is based chiefly on their letters, mostly in JMC., which are far from explicit, and sometimes farther still from being legible. Like all such letters they teem with vague references and doubtful initials of the type of: "H. actually acknowledged to me and lamented the falsity of her idea last year about R. C. (?) W."; which takes much deciphering, consideration, collating, and guessing before one decides, regretfully, that it must refer to Richard Coke Wilmot and not to Robert Isaac Wilberforce. One spends hours, in vain, over: "Oh! The Absurdity about George. There is no secret made about the matter now. Everyone speaks out . . ." (One wishes the writer of the letter would!) Again, "W. W." could be a William Wilberforce, a Woollett Wilmot, or a William Wilson. "R." could be a Rickards, a Robert or a Richard. R. A. could be an Anderson. It is only by collating many jigsaw bits of letters, dates and contexts that I have elicited the main lines of the story and I may well have misinterpreted one or two details. I have shirked the laborious task of giving all my proofs point by point, and in doing so devoutly wished, not for the first time, that there existed a Newman Studies group to document such problems as this. (It is an interest surely of as much value as the elucidation of obscure literary references in *Finnegans Wake.*)
[2] J. H. N. to Jem, July 11th, 1836.
[3] Mary to Jem, August 9th, 1827.
[4] Mary to Jem, October 16th, 1827. JMC.
[5] J. H. N. to Harriett, October 5th, 1827.
[6] Addition by H. to Mary's letter to Jem, October 16th, 1827. JMC.
[7] Mary to Jem, October 16th, 1827.

[8] Autobiographical MSS. in English and French at the Oratory, Birmingham; TM.; AM.; Letters of J. H. N.

[9] I have not been able to identify this Nuneham cottage beyond the reference to "the adjoining inn." Nuneham village is a street of cottages, mostly built by the Harcourts for their workmen.

[10] The Newman houses around Oxford have been established with the help of Father Henry Tristram; addresses and dates on letters; the knowledge of Mr. Edward Cordrey of Oxford; and by personal exploration around Oxford.

[11] H. to Aunt. November 28th, 1829. JMC.

[12] GMC.

CHAPTER 9

[1] JMC.: JHMC.

[2] Addresses taken from various correspondence.

[3] Bank of England records: JHC.: JHMC.

[4] For Froude I have used only published works.

[5] *Parochial and Plain Sermons:* 8 vols. The sermons are dated at the end of "Sermons on Subjects of the Day," pp. 413–420.

[6] Newman on the arts is almost always deplorable. See "Newman's Essay on Poetry," by Geoffrey Tillotson. Harvard Studies in Comparative Literature, Vol. XX.

[7] From I. G. Sieveking's *Memoir* of F. W. N. London, 1909; M. R. G.'s MS.

[8] Information kindly supplied from the records of the Bank of England.

[9] Ellis politely speaks of her as his wife. I have so far failed to find a record of the marriage in any contemporary register.

CHAPTER 10

[1] Published letters mainly, in AM.; *Verses on Various Occasions;* for the visit to Segesta see especially AM. I, 350; 344—to Harriett. Personal visits to Enna and Segesta.

[2] AM. I, *passim.*

[3] AM. I, 473; 475; 479; 480; 485.

CHAPTER 11

[1] Personal and Family Letters, 1827–1845, at Birmingham; February 12th, 1834.

[2] June 26th, 1836.

[3] He saw Frank only twice in the twenty-two years between 1833 and 1855. See Letter to Isy Froude, July 9th, 1855, in WW.

CHAPTER 12

[1] Essay on Development of Christian Doctrine: 1890, p. 53; O. U. Sermons, XV, 20, 23.
[2] *Via Media*, 1877, I, 220.
[3] In Burgon, *op. cit.*

CHAPTER 13

[1] 1839. In two articles "reviewing" the Tracts.

CHAPTER 14

[1] From Purcell's *Life*.
[2] See F. D. Maurice on this in *Lectures on Hebrews;* and *Frederick Denison Maurice*, Cambridge, 1951; by H. G. Wood.

EPILOGUE

[1] Chiefly from considerable personal investigation by Major Gerald Fox, Town Clerk of Tenby, his friends, and a personal visit. Also two letters, March 23rd and 26th, 1884, from Geo. Huntington, Rector of Tenby, to Cardinal Newman, describing Charles' end.
[2] *Tenby: A Seaside Holiday*, London, 1856: by Philip Henry Gosse.
[3] Letters to J. H. N., May 14th, June 6th and 24th, and the Cardinal's replies: at the Oratory, Birmingham.